MARIE CONNER
A Leading Lady

*Her Life and Civic Leadership
in a Bygone Era*

ELLE MOTT

Marie Conner, A Leading Lady: Her Life and Civic Leadership in a Bygone Era

Printed in the United States of America

Luminare Press
442 Charnelton St.
Eugene, OR 97401
www.luminarepress.com

LCCN: 2025916211
ISBN: 979-8-88679-972-9

Publisher's Cataloging-in-Publication
(Provided by Cassidy Cataloguing Services, Inc.)

Names: Mott, Elle, author.
Title: Marie Conner, a leading lady : her life and civil leadership in a bygone era / Elle Mott.
Description: First edition. | Eugene, OR : Luminare Press, [2026] | Includes bibliographical references.
Identifiers: LCCN: 2025916211 | ISBN: 9798886799729 (paperback) | 9798886799736 (eBook)
Subjects: LCSH: Conner, Marie, 1904-1987. | Women political activists--Oregon. | Social action--Oregon. | Activism--Oregon. | Women civic leaders--Oregon. | Community leadership--Oregon. | Oregon--Social conditions--20th century. | LCGFT: Biographies. | BISAC: BIOGRAPHY & AUTOBIOGRAPHY / Women. | BIOGRAPHY & AUTOBIOGRAPHY / Social Activists. | HISTORY / Social History
Classification: LCC: F881.35.C6 M68 2026 | DDC: 979.5/043--dc23

Table of Contents

PREFACE

Marie's quoted words are garnered in part from oral conversations with me, as I remember them, and in part from her letters found in her column "Needs of the Needy," published during the 1950s in *The Lebanon Express* newspaper in Lebanon, Oregon. At times, her prose has been edited for space or clarity. Otherwise, I tried to keep her words intact as much as possible. Likewise, I treated the words of other notable people in the same way. My intention behind minimal editing of other people's words is to allow their own voices to impart their meaning to you. Other sources, which are included in the bibliography, were also referenced to convey their words.

This is my third book, and the inspiration for it came from my first book, a memoir titled *Out of Chaos*. I wrote my memoir to show that no matter what mistakes we make or what problems befall us, we can, through our own actions, overcome them. Marie is at the heart of my memoir. She was not shy in voicing her thoughts and opinions. I recall all too well her eyes piercing my own—at least the one good eye I can see with—as she imparted her words of wisdom when I was younger. My memories of her motivated me to create a better way of life for myself, which I described and shared in *Out of Chaos*. Following the release of my memoir, I set about finding out why my strength came from her.

Thus began my journey to re-create Marie's life. I started gathering the pieces, then set the project aside when life got busy. When I came back to it, I was startled by the intensity of the documents which lay in front of me. At first, the pieces of my research appeared as a sort of puzzle, with stories out of order, and I felt confusion amid my awe. I continued in my quest for more than two years, sifting through and expanding on my research. Throughout it all,

Marie served as a great muse for me.

Many archived newspapers, too numerous to individually name as they number well over one thousand, were scoured in my research. Some newspaper clippings were used solely to gain a surmised understanding of the era, culture, weather, or other useful insight, whereas others were referenced for more in-depth details. These archived clippings served as a secondary source of information and were obtained from digitized repositories, which are listed in the bibliography.

In writing Marie's story—and in so doing, exploring how our American culture and society evolved through the twentieth century—I remained true to the historical context of those years. There are words in this book, many of which can be found in the opening pages, that may evoke uneasiness regarding the nature in which people spoke during that time. Although our country is currently rife with political discord, my hope is that you do not get ensnarled by language that could be deemed offensive today (for example, "the mailman" instead of "the postal carrier") and instead keep your focus on Marie's message.

Although her story takes place in bygone days, it seems particularly relevant today given the upsetting and unsettling stories we read and hear about in our daily news. It is from diverse acts of courage and belief that human history is shaped. Each time we stand up for an ideal, or act in a way that will improve our life and the lives of others, or strike out against injustice, we are shaping our world and the views of those who live in our society. Will we sit idly by to see how our world turns out? I hope not. I hope you will take the message inherent in Marie's legacy to make a positive difference wherever you can.

PS: I would love to hear your feedback! When you're finished reading this book, I encourage you to leave an honest review wherever you shop or hang out, whether online or in person. Even just one or two sentences is fine. Reviews help small-press publishers and also guide other readers in choosing their next book.

Part 1

Jennings, Oklahoma, circa 1910.

Chapter 1

— ❀ —

In a Burst of Thunder,
Marie Comes into this World!
1904–1912

Drifting dirt and sand swirled into clustery dust devils on Main Street. Mr. Gosney's pace kicked sandy soil aside. He had put a hop and a skip into his steps. Voice pitched high, he announced, "I have a new son at the house and it's a boy!" He stopped to share more of his news with businessmen lingering outside their establishments. "He weighs twenty-two pounds!"

The Locals section of the *Jennings News* on August 30, 1906, tells us that a fellow proprietor responded, "Harry, I think you have another guess coming."

Jennings, a family-friendly town in Pawnee County of Oklahoma Territory, stood as a proud township for successful businessmen. Main Street boasted a quiet and orderly saloon, two liveries, two broom factories, a blacksmith, a machine shop, several mercantiles, and, since 1901, the Bank of Jennings. Three churches also served the townsfolk. The two broom factories alone revealed Jennings to be a town that kept pace with the rest of the territory. Housewives found immense value in a durable broom to sweep away the ever-present red dirt. The wild weed of broomcorn was, unlike elsewhere, abundant in the territory, and the flatlands that encased Jennings were blanketed with buffalo grass and tall stalks of yellow prairie grass.

It was a fine day with a warm August breeze and a clear summer sky that seemed to smile down on Harry for all he was proud of. For over two years he had done well as an agent for Mr. Guthrie's steam laundry, but that was only a side job. His real passion lay in his barber skills. As proprietor of Harry's Tonsorial Parlor, he was one of few men who did business from a stone building, an expense that scarce men could afford. Most businesses existed out of either wooden or sod structures, prone to fire and storm damage. Harry's parlor had a bathtub, and men reveled in paying ten cents for a bath when they stopped in for a shave. Next door in another stone building was a confectionary, a business that Harry co-owned with Mr. Pearson. And now he had a new son at home.

Born that morning, Frank wasn't Harry's first child, or even his first son. Yet Harry could never have too many sons, he reasoned. He'd see to it that his boys grew up to be fine young men. Harry had one daughter, and he certainly didn't need any more girls.

The beautiful weather made this day especially good, unlike the evening his daughter was born. That night, an unrelenting rainstorm, which had broken days of a cold drought, had clamored at their house walls. His wife, Laura, had birthed their daughter in their bed with a midwife in attendance. No doctor would have wanted to travel in the middle of a wet night just for another girl to be born, Harry had concluded.

In a burst of thunder, Violet Marie Gosney came into this world on that dark, stormy night of January 20, 1904, in Jennings. Unbeknownst to Harry then, his daughter would grow up to become a headstrong woman, one who would break free of the boundaries he placed on her. In Harry's eyes, any daughter of his was to grow up to become a helpmate for her husband, not to fuss with matters outside the home. That was how it was in that era: Men made decisions, and their wives obeyed them. With no apparent need to change how things were, Harry trusted his daughter would learn everything she needed to know from her mother. He was wrong.

Violet Marie Gosney would make herself known. As an audacious woman and a trailblazer driven to help others, she would be loved by people—so much so that they would name her their leading lady. She would also have children, grandchildren, and great-grandchildren, all of whom would respect her as their family matriarch. Her first great-grandchild, as an older adult, would be drawn to peel back the layers of a woman whom today's era would be privileged to meet, if only so that we too can understand that boundaries can be broken and barriers overcome. If she could change the world, so can we.

Marie, as they called her, was little more than eighteen months old when Harry's new son, Frank, arrived. She already had two other brothers: Glen had turned ten years old earlier that month on August 11, and Harry, her father's namesake, was six.

It was not that Harry had ignored the birth of his daughter. On the contrary, when the chilly January weather cleared, he had treated the Ladies of the Maccabees to a fruit basket with oranges, bananas, and other delicacies. He grew many fruits on his land and would have included cherries in the basket had they been in season. It was on a Tuesday, February 2, that he handed those ladies their fruit basket, and in exchange, they showed their respect with words of congratulations. The Ladies of the Maccabees, a fraternal organization, was renowned for its well-chosen membership among local prominent women. Many organizations and civic groups existed in that age for townsfolk to choose from, and belonging to one or more was the customary societal outlet. It was also a key way to stay informed of the latest happenings, participate in the passing of city ordinances, and, for men, make important business decisions. Harry's wife, Laura, was active in the Eastern Star fraternal organization alongside Mrs. Foil and Mrs. Bishop, whose husbands had strongly influenced the formation of Jennings, with Mr. Bishop as the Bank of Jennings's proprietor.

MANY SETTLERS AND their families poured in for the 1889 land rush, which led to the creation of Oklahoma Territory. Prior to that, the area was Indian Territory. Other land rushes followed, the largest in American history being in 1893, depleting land belonging to the Cherokee tribe. Harry had been little more than a lad during this time, still living with his parents and siblings in Kansas.

Before those land rushes, the Homestead Act of 1862 had opened Western lands, including the Indian Territory of both Kansas and Oklahoma, to qualified citizens. With it, a new philosophy of assimilation emerged, which favored bringing Indians into the United States as individual citizens rather than allowing them to have lands with tribal sovereignty. That philosophy conveniently left many acres of land open for settlement, absolving the need for Indian resettlement as other states had chosen to do.

Until its statehood achievement, which came in late 1907, Oklahoma was a land divided into three geographical areas: Oklahoma Territory spanned centrally north; Indian Territory lay in the eastern portion and was home to the Cherokee, Osage, Pawnee, and other Indian tribes; and Oklahoma's western panhandle was its neutral zone, an untamed wilderness. More than three dozen Indian tribes called it home. It was a land rich with soil for farming and opportunities for businessmen, a place demanding cohabitation between white American men and Indians. It wasn't a place for foreigners or "Negroes." Mr. Gosney, as stereotypically American as one could be at that time, fit right in.

Those with the Gosney name usually weren't ones to stay put. Rather, they were more apt to move westward to seek even greater fortunes and opportunities. If it weren't for his friendly neighbors and good fortune, Harry might have later questioned what kept him and his family there. He had married Laura in Conway Springs, Kansas, in 1894, where they soon had their first child, Glen. By 1900, Harry had moved his family to Oklahoma Territory through the acquisition of a mortgage for land, where his second son was born. Other than Main Street, street names weren't commonly used in Jennings. Rather, and according to the 1910 Federal Census, their house was on Block 16. Back in Conway Springs, Harry had learned his trade as a barber. Later, in Jennings, his tonsorial parlor stood among the first of many business ventures he undertook.

In 1904, when Marie was born, the Gosney name went back more than two hundred years in America. A historical publication, *Gosney Family Records, 1740–1940, and Related Families*, authored by Georgia Gosney Wisda, gives an account by Alex D. Gosney ascertaining that Gosneys first arrived here in 1492 on the Spanish caravel *La Pinta*. There is no doubt that in the mid-1600s, Gosneys helped settle this new country. Come the early 1700s, Gosneys began leaving England, Scotland, and Germany in droves, settling primarily in the townships of Culpeper and Orange Counties in Virginia Colony. A few Gosneys also came asea to the Province of New York, an English colony, to stay as farmers.

Harry's father and other Gosney relatives settled in northern Kentucky, which shared the state border with Ohio and Indiana along the Ohio River, not far removed from Virginia. Thus, some Gosneys moved to Indiana. Interestingly, Kentucky was a slave state, while Indiana and Ohio quickly enacted laws to abolish slavery. This could have implied a division in political beliefs among the Gosneys, as many Gosneys in Kentucky owned slaves.

From there, many Gosneys continued west, into Kansas and Missouri and other points westward. When the wagon trains discovered the Oregon Trail, the Gosneys were among the first to join up. Mr. Luther Gosney homesteaded in Oregon in 1853, where he and his wife had many children. By 1904, the year Marie was born, Gosneys were well known all across America, from Virginia to Kentucky and Indiana, to Missouri and Kansas, and from New Mexico Territory to Idaho and into Oregon and

Washington State, not forgetting those who stayed in New York. Wherever one lived, there was bound to be a Gosney.

Perhaps supporting Harry's decision to remain in the area, the Jennings population was ever steady, not waning from about 350 people year after year—a respectable number in the territory, even if less than that of Oklahoma City. This population was enough for telephone lines to be installed, which served forty-six customers in 1905. The telephone company's biggest customers were local businesses. Harry was one of few men who also answered calls from a house phone and could be reached through an operator connection at phone number 215.

The weather could at times be cumbersome. Prairie winds blew continuously. Red dirt and sand always seemed to seep into sidewalk crevices in an unstoppable way. While this territory was rich with oak, cottonwood, and pecan trees, it was also ladened with cows and their dung. And sometimes an oil well ran wild, covering anyone even miles away with a coating of black grease, which then had to be scraped and sandpapered off their clothes. It had been that way ever since oil was discovered nearby in 1904.

Wild buffalo once dotted the prairie, giving its land a dense blackness as far as the eye could see. By the time the Gosney family arrived in Oklahoma Territory, however, the buffalo were few and far between. Earnest slaughtering for their hides to send east on the trains, along with aggressive trading between white settlers and Indians, had nearly wiped them out. But life was good there, so Harry pushed thoughts of moving westward aside.

HARRY'S WIFE, LAURA, along with their children, often traveled from Jennings to Kansas to visit for a few days. There, Marie and her brothers came to know her maternal grandparents, Mr. and Mrs. Charles Fowler, who lived in Conway Springs, Kansas, as well as her paternal grandfather, Mr. John Gosney, who lived in

Cleveland, Kansas. Marie's paternal grandmother, Mrs. Elizabeth Gosney, had died in August 1901, before Marie's birth.

A horse-drawn buggy took them on their travels from Jennings to Kansas. It was a full day's journey for the 134 miles north to Conway Springs, and about 40 miles further northeast lay Cleveland. Until 1907, wagons and buggies had to follow the trails blazed by those who had gone before. In 1907, though, Harry contributed a sizeable two dollars to help fund a road construction project and then supervised the men who built the roads.

The train was an option for their family trips, yet documentation hasn't been found to support that they traveled by train for their visits. It was in 1903 that the Arkansas Valley and Western Railway constructed a line from West Tulsa, Oklahoma, to Steen, northeast of Enid, Oklahoma. Its passenger line passed through the outskirts of Jennings. Toward that year's end, the Missouri, Kansas, and Oklahoma Railroad laid tracks from Agra to Osage, both in Oklahoma, which connected Jennings to outside markets. By 1909, outbound shipments from Jennings included cattle, hogs, sheep, and cotton.

Marie lived much of her early childhood in Oklahoma—first when it was a territory, then in its statehood—but not exclusively. Rather, she became accustomed to frequent relocations in Oklahoma and Kansas, as Harry often moved the family depending on where his business ventures were thriving. One town was Coffeeville, Kansas; another was Cleveland, Oklahoma, not to be confused with Cleveland, Kansas. From Jennings to Cleveland, her father was known as a steady booster and pusher. In today's words, we would say he was a shrewd businessman, well respected by some and feared by others.

Aside from Harry's business ventures, including a grain and feed store that he owned, he also dabbled in politics. In mid-1907, Harry was elected to serve as Jennings's city clerk. However, the outgoing city government body didn't step down for Harry and other incoming officers. Thus, several newly elected officials, Harry included, filed a mandamus in court at Guthrie, Oklahoma, in June to force Jennings's government to let them take office. Later that same year, in November, Oklahoma Territory and Indian Territory, along with its neutral zone, collectively became the forty-sixth state in America: Oklahoma.

In early 1910, Harry was sold a tract of land in Cleveland, Kansas, by Mr. J. M. Frantz. Harry had the intention of making it one of the most valuable lots adjacent to the city. His plans included a crescent-shaped driveway on the east side of the tract to bring the driveway nearer to the house, which would be an eight-room two-story modern structure on a knoll high above the city. It is documented that Harry stated that, with the prospect of the interurban railway being built from Hutchinson to Arkansas City via Wellington, Caldwell, Medford, Enid, and Guthrie, it would be possible for him to sit on his east porch and see the electric trolley cars as far as twenty miles away. Wellington to the southeast was plainly seen from this tract of land. It is doubtful that his plans came to fruition, however, as there are no found records attesting to this—and besides, Harry soon relocated his family again.

MARIE BEGAN SCHOOL when she was only five and a half years old in Jennings in September 1909. It was but a primary year for her. Come 1910, she was enrolled as a first grader at the school in Conway Springs, Kansas, and did well in her attendance record. In 1911, Harry moved the family back to Jennings, where, in September, she proceeded into the second grade. Miss Lola White was that school's music instructor. Marie's favorite lessons were singing and learning to play the piano. It was noted and documented that Marie had perfect school attendance that November, which was likely commonplace for her, as there was no place for a girl according to her father.

Games with marbles were a favorite pastime for schoolchildren during their recess hour. Marie's classmates included two girls: Irene Cain and Georgie Tompkins. Also listed on the school roster, but a year behind Marie, were Bernice Jackson and Orpha Conner. Marie stayed close to the girls, not liking to play with boys as a result of the sour note her brothers had instilled in her. They had always sided with her father against her. Being children themselves, her brothers—usually Harry Junior and red-headed Frank, who was the closest to Marie in age—acted out by pushing the schoolyard outhouse over while she was inside. Or so she attested as an older adult looking back to when she was a young girl with blue eyes and, yes, also with red hair.

When they lived in Jennings, and when the weather wasn't too hot in the summer months, musical concerts were held in the local park, each time with a live band. The music was likely acoustic or classical with violins, unlike the jazzy blues performed in the Deep South. Jennings was too far removed in terms of both location and culture to welcome sounds of cacophony. Furthermore, her father, who was conservative in nature, served in their local Commercial Club, and it was that group that ensured summer concerts, as well as the annual Fourth of July celebration, went on in Jennings.

Come August 1912, Marie began her third grade in school, this time in Cleveland, Oklahoma. However, she would do no more than show her face that school year, as her father relocated them yet again, this time much farther away, far from her friends and grandparents. It's unknown whether Harry divulged any word of his plans to his wife. He certainly didn't forewarn his fellow businessmen. Rather, townsfolk were astonished as news spread like wildfire, and newspapers picked up the story all too quickly in Cleveland, nearby towns in Kansas, and beyond.

The publication in the *Jennings News* on September 12, 1912, read as follows:

People of this section were breathless Monday when the news came from Cleveland that H. A. Gosney, an old resident of Jennings, but late of Cleveland, had left for parts unknown.

On the early train Saturday morning, his wife and three youngest children left for northern points, and he and his eldest son, Glen left on the early train Sunday morning to the south. This was the last word heard from any of them. Their departure was not noticed by anyone at Cleveland until Monday morning when their feed store failed to open as usual. This caused an alarm, and officers of the First National Bank at that place phoned to this city to see if his whereabouts could be learned.

After investigating it was learned that he had left the country with something over $2,000 to the good, with a number of friends holding the sack.

Chapter 2

— ✿ —

In a World of Adversity and Opportunity, Marie Grows Up
1912–1922

In the decade between 1912 and 1922, Marie faced self-discovery as the world exploded with changes. At eight years old in 1912, she was old enough to recognize that a sudden interruption from the only life she'd ever known now faced her. She would have to be brave and steadfast, not wanting to hide behind her father's lead as he wished the best for only his sons. Rather, she would push onward, if only to strive to be a positive changemaker among her newfound friends. As their only daughter, she had no sisters to look to in the way of a role model, but through her community involvement, Marie would find women to show her how to achieve great things.

Following her family's unprecedented departure from Oklahoma in 1912, her father, Harry, and her eldest brother, Glen, stayed briefly with her father's sister, Lucy, who lived in New Mexico Territory. The family then reunited in Idaho, where they stayed for a short while. One state to the west lay Oregon. The Snake River and forests abutted their border. Soon after reuniting, they settled in Bend, Oregon.

It is unknown what connections, if any, Harry had in Bend. The city is situated in central Oregon, a large, geographically diverse state with the Pacific coastline as its western border. Oregon's leading metropolis was and remains Portland, a city in its far northwest corner, inland a short way, not far south from the state of Washington, with only the Columbia River between them. Many hamlets, towns, and cities sprung up from Portland, stretching down to the state's southern border, California. Much of this stretch is called the Willamette Valley. The barren and cold Cascade Range is 260 miles long in mountains and lies between this stretch of cities and central Oregon, where Bend remains the prominent city.

In 1911, railroad service began for Bend residents, and that was likely how the Gosney family arrived. Prior to that service, the nearest railroad station was one hundred miles away, in Shaniko, now a ghost town, and from there, people traveled in any way they could to reach Bend, often on foot or by horse. While carriages and buggies were available for that last leg of the journey, they were more of a last-resort option. Roads from Shaniko to Bend were nothing more than rutted dirt and dangerous curves, perilous in nature, which caused carriages to overturn.

At the turn of the century into the early 1900s, central Oregon was the largest territory in the United States without a railroad. When abundant ponderosa pine was discovered in the barren region known as the Deschutes Valley, commercial interests paid attention, first by building the Oregon Trunk railroad line. Then, in 1916, two lumber companies moved into Bend—Shevlin-Hixon Mill and Brooks-Scanlon Lumber Company—which provided millwork for many residents, both men and women.

In 1912, Bend was still a young city, incorporated in 1904, with a history that went back but a few years before that. Its youth seemed invisible as year after year the population soared along with businesses, families, and social events. It grew rapidly with a tenfold increase in population in just a decade, from less than five hundred residents in 1910 to more than five thousand in 1920.

In 1902, irrigation service began for farmers, and in 1905, water service for all. In 1906, telephone service began, and in 1910, electricity replaced kerosene and gas lights. Bend's first fire department started in 1905 with thirty-one volunteer firemen and a team of horses.

Being that Bend was in the middle of wide-open high desert, its city streets easily became dusty from the traffic of horses and buggies. Occasionally, a motorcar made its way across the desert and onto Bend streets. Those motorists wore dusters, or face coverings, along with goggles to breathe through the dust clouds that kicked up. In 1910, the residents invested in a sprinkler system. Daily, a dray team of horses hauled a six-hundred-gallon water tank through the downtown streets to spray down and calm dust clouds. It was an ideal solution, but in the hottest months of the year, its spray of water quickly got lost in the volcanic soil as it penetrated the dust.

A 1909 brochure published by the Great Northern Railway described the Deschutes Valley as being fertile for farming, fruit growing, stock raising, and lumbering. The brochure included the promise of "tens of thousands of farm homes for settlers." Perhaps that was what drew Harry to bring his family to Bend.

In 1913, Harry's land and business lots in Oklahoma were foreclosed on, absolving him of debts and ties to those business undertakings. Now in Bend, also in 1913, he acquired a forty-acre cattle ranch through a mortgage. Three acres of the ranch were managed by his older sons, Glen and Harry, who harvested alfalfa and tended to a dairy cow and chickens. Those two boys also shined shoes at ten cents a pair downtown on weekends.

Although successful at ranch farming, Harry continued in his fervor as a barber with two successful shops, the Log Cabin and, later, the Union Barber Shop. Aside from his estate and barbershops, Harry did as he had before. He acquired even more land, some in Benham Falls near Bend, for which he was the highest bidder in a 1917 land drawing. He also continued in political work, serving on committees in support of governing officials. Furthermore, he held a church secretarial position for several years, was an active member of the Masons, a fraternal organization for men, and from 1918 represented the local barbers' union at the State Federation of Labor. Marie's mother, Laura, was active in their local chapter of the Order of the Eastern Star.

Harry's business reputation, for better or worse, followed him. Bend's local newspaper, *The Bulletin*, ran a story in July 1917 stating that some of his cattle were shot over a grudge. The boys, moreover, had occasional mishaps or outright troublesome behavior. One challenge that befell them occurred in 1917, when Marie's younger brother, eleven-year-old Frank, suffered a broken leg when toying with iron rods on a railroad track. Marie's three brothers excelled in school, though, and were members in a newly formed organization: the Boy Scouts.

The family's stately home on the ranch was in the heart of the city, not far from the river. When the mills began operation, Harry rented out as many as four rooms at a time for millworkers. The house was a modern home with electric lights and water service. Their telephone number was 2171.

<hr>

MEANWHILE, ANOTHER FAMILY, the Millers, also relocated from Oklahoma to central Oregon. Mr. Edwin Miller had married and then started his family in Yukon, Oklahoma, farther south from the area the Gosneys had come from. From there, the Miller family, large with four girls and two boys, first moved to Vancouver, Washington, near Portland, Oregon, on the northern side of the Columbia River. Then, in October 1916, they moved onto Mr. Newton's farm in Corvallis, west of Bend. Here, Edwin's children attended school, with his second-oldest daughter, Doris, completing eighth grade in May 1918. She began high school that fall.

A year later, in the fall of 1919, Mr. Miller moved his family to Bend, where he purchased an eight-thousand-acre farm with a mortgage. A few months beforehand, in August, Edwin and his second-oldest son, Randall, had arrived before the rest of the family to work in the mills. Randall was seventeen years old. Doris was fifteen, the same age as Marie, although a year ahead of Marie in school.

Marie and Doris became friends. Maybe they met in school or in town, or maybe through their piano playing—like Marie, Doris was also a skilled piano player. What is known is that Doris proceeded through high school, whereas school records for Marie become obsolete after October 1919, when she was listed as a freshman but absent from school due to illness. In this era, some children didn't finish high school. It wasn't at all scrutinized or looked down upon when a student left school once done with the eighth grade. However, future census records attest that Marie did, in fact, complete twelfth grade.

When the Gosneys had first arrived in Bend, Marie attended school in a three-story wood-frame building built in 1904 to serve all students, from grade school through high school. It had replaced the first schoolhouse built in Bend in 1887, a one-room log cabin. Her school was located at the north end of downtown, close to where they lived. Then, in 1913, a school bond was issued that allowed for the construction of the Reid School to replace it. The Reid School was a modern schoolhouse and large enough for their swelling student population of 241 children. Ruth Reid remained their principal. The new school was also three stories high but was built on a concrete foundation. It boasted indoor plumbing, water fountains included, and had a central heating and boiler system, built-in electric clocks, and an external fire escape system. The building was crafted from locally quarried pink volcanic tuff.

Thus, Marie spent two years as a student in one schoolhouse; then, in September 1914, she started fifth grade at age ten in the new Reid School. Surrounded by a lawn with ponderosa pine trees and a paved walkway, the school featured double-leaf doors under a vestibule to the entryway through which students entered to find their respective classrooms. The building was spacious with high ceilings and steep stairways along with high bay windows to give natural light to all the classrooms.

With Bend's population ever increasing, the city soon outgrew this new school too. Within a few years, it couldn't accommodate everyone. Temporary classrooms were then opened in various buildings and businesses throughout downtown. That solution served students until 1924 when a new school was built, long after Marie's school days. If the census records were incorrect and Marie did in fact leave school before twelfth-grade graduation, perhaps overcrowding contributed to that decision.

If anything gained favoritism for the Reid School, it was its encouragement of extracurricular activities and competitions. The boys dominated in sports and the girls in clerical office skills. Marie's friend Doris earned recognition through typing competitions and her help with the school's newspaper and yearbooks.

Doris could be seen as a go-getter, not letting anything stop her in what she set out to do or where she planned to go. At not quite sixteen years old in February 1920, she unfortunately broke her forearm when attempting to crank-start the Ford motorcar she was using. As she healed from that injury, she persevered.

Marie and Doris were alike in their perseverance. They had much to give to their community and were not ones to let the world go by without their input. Yet while Doris showed that tenacity in school to her teachers and peers, Marie's passions and efforts moved her beyond the confines of the overcrowded classroom environment.

In the city of Bend, businesses grew, millworkers were never short on work, and city folk found entertainment in an array of respectable establishments, even with the 1914 Oregon enactment of prohibition. It was also a time in which changes, some nationwide and some worldwide, inevitably affected Bend residents. In this decade, war and a pandemic happened, the women's suffrage movement gained great strides, and fashions changed with the times. Whether one engaged in a fraternal organization, participated in community gatherings, read the local newspaper, or talked among family and friends, there was always the undercurrent of how one should act or feel and what issues should or should not be supported.

The local newspaper was inundated with those issues. On Marie's thirteenth birthday, in 1917, a syndicated news story had a picture of women on the lawn of the White House demanding rights for women to vote. They assembled with picket signs and, according to the article, wore suffragists' colors of purple, yellow, and white. President Wilson saw them yet ignored their pleas as if they didn't exist.

Women had been granted voting rights in some places but not yet at the national level. Those rights, where they existed, were varied and oftentimes first took effect in local municipalities, sometimes on a limited basis. Oklahoma hadn't yet allowed women to vote when the Gosneys left in 1912. However, Kansas had granted partial voting rights to women in 1887, limited to municipal elections. Then, in November 1912, it granted full women's suffrage.

Oregon had already granted voting rights to women in 1912, in part due to pressure from its neighboring states of Washington, Idaho, and California, all of which had passed women's suffrage laws between 1896 and 1911. Oregon's law would be amended in 1916 to state, "No negro, Chinaman, or mulatto shall have the right of suffrage," and would remain as such for several decades.

It would be in August 1920, when Marie was sixteen years old, that the national passing of the Nineteenth Amendment under the presidency of Woodrow Wilson occurred. During that ensuing time, Marie sidestepped her father to advocate through her event participation that women mattered.

For one, when Marie was fourteen years old, she shared her talent for the piano in front of an attentive audience. She was a piano student under Mrs. Genevieve McLaurin, and on the evening of Thursday, March 28, 1918, she performed in a recital along with twenty-two other piano students at the Liberty Theater. Although not the only theater in town, it was well attended, known for its performing arts collaborative. It had opened the summer before, in July 1917, and offered photo plays, feature films, vaudeville, and orchestras. Its feature films didn't lack in the popular stars of the day, including Charles Ray, Vivian Martin, and Mary Pickford. A popular choice for moviegoers was feature star and comedian Charlie Chaplin, and on the weekend following Marie's Thursday night performance, the theater's matinees were his films.

When Bend residents attended events, whether at the Liberty Theater or elsewhere, they dressed in their finest. As Marie blossomed into a young woman during that decade, fashion and clothing also changed. With material rationing during the war, girls' dresses became simplified. Gone were the smocks and pinafores, and in their place were plain dresses fitted at the waistline that stopped at knee length. Knickers, or long socks, were worn with their dresses.

The corsets and other undergarments donned by Marie's mother and other women, which contorted their bodies, gave way to relaxed alternatives. Women who worked in the Bend mills often opted for men's trousers, overalls, or other utilitarian clothing. Young men, hoping to impress the ladies, continued to wear three-piece suits but with pant legs no longer than ankle length and sporting turned-up cuffs.

For society women, such as the women Marie looked up to, dresses prevailed. Dresses had softened, though, into a more natural silhouette while not forgetting to emphasize the bust. Bright colors and softer materials replaced the drab harshness worn the decade prior. Shoes with a distinct but low heel complemented their dresses, which were tapered right above the ankles.

Aside from the theaters, Bend residents also found entertainment at the Hippodrome. Due to its large ballroom space, orchestras often played there. It also hosted meetings for well-established community and fraternal organizations, offering a large seating capacity. It was the preferred place for out-of-town guest speakers.

One such visiting speaker was Mrs. Emma Neidig of Los Angeles, recent past Supreme President of the Fraternal Brotherhood, a mutual aid organization. In 1918, it had members from fourteen states and accepted men and women as members and officers, all on an equal footing, unlike most fraternal societies. Mrs. Neidig spoke at the Hippodrome on the evening of Wednesday, June 12, 1918. A musical performance was included in the event, in which Marie performed a piano solo.

Marie also hosted the initial Willing Workers meeting in her home on the afternoon of Tuesday, June 11, the day before her performance at the Hippodrome. That recently organized club, which stemmed from the Christian Church Sunday School, was started to foster a spirit of helpfulness throughout the community. The local news in brief from their newspaper later that week gave Marie's response to her meeting: "It had a good attendance and everyone who attended enjoyed the program and refreshments."

Meanwhile, in that spring and summer of 1918, World War I was in its fourth year. News lines with updates carried over into the Bend newspaper and were constant reminders that many fellow students and family members were overseas in a series of major battles between nations. An armistice would finally be declared later in November of that year.

Marie's eldest brother, Glen, went to war as a serviceman with the army. He arrived in Camp Fremont, California, on May 1, 1918, and soon after was stationed in Siberia, Russia. There, he stayed with the army until nearly a year after the war ended when, in October 1919, he would return to Bend with his service completed and in good health.

In the midst of accepting the war and embracing simple manners of dress, another wave of challenges fell on Bend residents. Immediately following a scarlet fever outbreak, the world was hit with the Spanish Flu, which was labeled as a pandemic in February 1918 by the Centers for Disease Control and Prevention, a government agency. Bend was afflicted hard by those diseases. At first, downtown streets emptied and some businesses shut down. Yet—if only as a stress reliever from not only the pandemic but also the war and other issues—businesses didn't keep their doors shut for long. Rather, people simply stayed home if not feeling well, as that was the advice that doctors, business owners, and club officers gave. Thus, Marie continued as a piano student and showed up for her scheduled performances at the Liberty Theater and the Hippodrome. The pandemic came in three waves, and in its third wave, which happened later in the year of 1918, Bend was quarantined for two months.

For those ill with the Spanish Flu, Bend had one hospital. A preventive serum was also available through physician offices. The hospital had only seventeen beds, so many people afflicted stayed home, where they either recovered or died. A teacher, twenty-eight-year-old Kathryn Grace Vandevert, was among those who died. A local resident, Arthur Pringle, routinely and voluntarily drove doctors to wherever they were needed. Especially influential in helping those who were homebound and sick was Miss Kitty Rockwell, who was originally from Yukon, Canada, and had retired in Bend. She was also known as Klondike Kate, her stage name as a vaudeville singer and dancer. While she lacked nursing skills, her help was found in visits to deliver medicine, food, and other needed supplies. Although she was known for her racy past, people were grateful for her hospitality.

Holidays were greatly celebrated, surely out of an appreciation of what people were blessed with. As the pandemic ended and businesses were back in full swing, those celebrations became larger in ideas and in attendance. Christmas 1920 proved it so.

Marie was one month shy of turning seventeen years old when, on Friday, December 24, 1920, Bend held its fifth annual Christmas Tree Program for all residents of the greater area, some coming from other towns in Deschutes County. Held in the YMCA gymnasium, it was the largest one yet, much larger than in its prior years. Firemen were present and on duty to turn people away when the gym reached its full capacity at 1,400 people. It was a well-planned event overseen by a committee that included the YMCA, the Shevlin-Hixon Band, the two mills—the Shevlin-Hixon Mill and the Brooks-Scanlon Lumber Company—and the Women's Civic Improvement League. While religious, it was an all-inclusive program open to everyone, shown as such by the inclusion of committee members who represented five churches varying in denominations. Under the direction of three schoolteachers, the event was catered to families and prepared to treat one thousand children with gift bags from Santa. The Red Cross would later distribute gifts to any children who couldn't attend. The mills provided the giant decorated Christmas tree. Randall Miller, the brother of Doris, Marie's friend, still worked as a laborer in the mills. So too did Doris's boyfriend, James Schnur. They were likely in attendance, as it was a grand affair not to be missed.

The evening program began at six thirty as the audience was led in the song "Hark, the Herald Angels Sing." An invocation was then given by three reverends, each in their own turn. Music, recitals, and tableaux, which were scenes performed by silent actors in costumes, were in the entertainment's lineup. The gym's lights were dimmed for the show. Illuminated lighting on the Christmas tree showed the smiles on children's faces. More than nine hundred children were present and likely wiggling in their seats in awe of the engaging spectacle.

At one point, stage lights focused on a shiny black piano in anticipation of the next presentation. Marie emerged from backstage and took her seat at the piano. She gave the only piano solo, playing "Angel Voices." Her performance was under the direction of Miss Marie Brosterhous, who also directed the Shevlin-Hixon Band. That band played several numbers and concluded the event with the song "America."

On the evening of her seventeenth birthday, in 1921, Marie performed a piano solo in the entertainment section of a program held at the Hippodrome. The program was presented by the Women's Card and Label League of Bend, a committee under the Central Labor Council. Mrs. G. H. Baker was hostess, and the guest speaker was Mrs. L. Gee from Portland. Their message to the attendees, who were primarily members of local unions, was that "only by purchasing commodities bearing the union label could buyers be sure that they were using articles made under proper conditions." Dancing followed the meeting adjournment.

Later that same month, another committee under the Central Labor Council—the Bend Laundry Workers' Union—held a dinner for its members and friends at the Seattle Kitchen in Bend. Two speakers gave information pertaining to organized labor. One speaker was Mr. G. H. Baker, whose wife had hosted the program with the Women's Card and Label League earlier in January. About twenty people attended the dinner, Marie included.

The Women's Card and Label League also held a social event with buck-and-wing dancing at the Hippodrome on the night of Tuesday, March 14. Aside from the band, which performed orchestra music, two piano solos were given. Marie performed one of those two solos for the guests, who numbered more than three hundred.

Easter soon followed, with all Bend churches having something planned. The Christian Church held a special evening service on Easter Sunday, March 27. Marie gave a piano solo for the prelude to that program.

Marie was a member of the Girls Club with the Christian Church. In August of that summer, the reverend and his wife and daughter hosted a camping trip in Tumalo. While it had failed as a town, Tumalo had become a recreational area for outdoor enthusiasts, surrounded by forestland and a trickle of a creek alongside the Deschutes River, which flowed north from Bend. Marie and eight other girls went.

As 1922 DREW nigh with 1921 ending, so too did Marie's girlhood days end. She would be eighteen in January. The Girls Club with the Christian Church continued to meet, and the Bend Laundry Workers' Union as well as the Women's Card and Label League remained forthright in their activism. The Liberty Theater, the Hippodrome, and other places continued to bring people in for committee programs and for dancing and music. World War I and the pandemic were gone, and the Nineteenth Amendment, which had passed the year before, had given women a voting voice. Many occasions arose for Marie to make a meaningful contribution to her community.

Through the challenges that Bend had overcome, Marie and her friend Doris were cognizant of how women had prevailed. There was the school principal, Ruth Reid, and there was Klondike Kate. There were women millworkers, union advocates, keynote women speakers, those in the suffrage movement, and other women who were front and center. Marie had denied the lowly place her father assumed for her. Out of that explosion of changes, Marie had, during a tumultuous decade, grown up to be a headstrong young woman.

As opportunities continued for Marie, Doris prepared to graduate from Bend High School. During the school day on Thursday, May 31, the high school's senior class held a special program. Several students spoke, with one expressing regret over leaving school life behind and at the same time eagerness at taking their place in this world. Comedic acts were also performed, and a piano duet was played by Doris and another classmate. The class colors they had chosen, crimson and white, were explained to represent the virtues of bravery and purity.

Graduation commencement was held on the evening of Friday, June 2, with an alumni reception the next day, Saturday. Doris received her diploma. Following the busy commencement season, which had been full of parties and outings, the advent of summer motoring and vacation season began on Sunday, causing a lull in social events that week. Doris and Marie, though, were anything but lulled. Rather, at the end of that week, Doris, her brother Randall, Randall's friend and coworker James Schnur, and Marie made their appearance at the Baptist parsonage. It is unknown when Marie's relationship with Randall became something more than friendship. What is clear is that they did have a close relationship.

Marie's father was not with her when the foursome arrived at 406 Wall Street at the corner of Georgia Avenue. Nor were any other Gosney or Miller family members with them. Reverend F. H. Beard welcomed the four of them into his home. On that Saturday morning of June 10, 1922, Doris and her boyfriend, James, were married. So too were Randall and Marie.

Chapter 3

Out of Downfalls and Hardships,
Marie Rises to Meet Her Newfound Community
1922–1937

In the summer of 1922, Marie was young at eighteen years old, and the man she married also young at twenty. Marie's reasoning behind marrying Randall may have been something other than it was the next step in their relationship: It may have been her way of being free from living day to day under her father's regime. While we have to rely on speculation to understand why she got married, we can also come to understand how her newfound life caused her to persevere toward her womanly self-worth.

Randall rented a house at 77 McKay Street for them. It was a small, one-story house riverfront to the Deschutes River and near the mills where he worked. Their life wasn't limited to Bend, though. He kept strong ties to his friends in the Corvallis area, whom he knew from when he'd lived there with his parents from 1916 to 1919. Occasionally, they attended his friends' social gatherings, each time staying overnight before their drive back to Bend.

Corvallis is situated 120 miles northwest of Bend and was similar in size and population to Bend at that time. Five miles farther west of Corvallis is Philomath. Plymouth, now a ghost town, was also on the outskirts of Corvallis. Today, a drive from Bend to Corvallis can be done in three hours. However, the cars then weren't made to drive as fast. On average, a speed of twenty or twenty-five miles per hour was normal.

In the early 1920s, when Marie traveled with her husband to the Corvallis area, their drive consumed a half day. To leave Bend in their motorcar meant leaving the thick forests of ponderosa pines behind. Their travel stretched into several hours while they saw the Cascade Range ahead. Finally, the barren land, save for blowing tumbleweed, gave way to traverse the mountain range through the McKenzie Pass. A January 1924 newspaper article out of Corvallis described a road trip that Randall and his brother took from Bend, stating that they made the trip in good time at six hours.

When Marie and Randall attended socials in Bend, there were more of her friends than his. A month after they were married, they were guests at a birthday party for Miss Ethel Lewis. At that event, lawn games were played and dancing was enjoyed.

In December 1922, Randall secured an elected position with a fraternal organization, the Modern Woodmen of America, which served as a union to represent millworkers. James Schnur, who had married Randall's sister Doris during their double wedding, was also elected to serve. Randall's responsibilities in that union didn't seem to take precedence for him. Rather, he chased after the profits to be found in the connections he made through his friends.

With prohibition already in effect for several years, some people, such as Marie, were at ease at social events without alcohol. There were also many people who ridiculed the prohibition act, and Randall, along with his friends, was no exception. He took many trips to Corvallis, leaving Marie home alone.

Federal prohibition had begun in 1919, and Oregon residents were already savvy as to how to evade those laws. In 1914, Oregon had enacted a law to prohibit the manufacture and sale of intoxicating liquors except for medical, scientific, sacramental, or mechanical purposes. Prior to 1914, prohibition laws were limited to the level of municipalities, and thus, some Oregon cities already had laws in place limiting alcohol. In 1916, that state law was amended to permit the manufacture and sale of malt liquor, provided it contained only 4 percent or less alcohol. At the same time, that amendment was strengthened in that it forbade the importation of intoxicating liquors for beverage purposes.

Bootlegging became the successful consequence of prohibition for Oregonians and profitable to those who dared defy the law. It involved a network of manufacturers, distributors, and buyers who spanned the West Coast states, up to Canada. It also involved moonshine, which, in central Oregon, earned the name of "white lightning." If anything was different between the onset of Oregon prohibition and when federal prohibition followed, it was that prior to 1919, bootleggers in Oregon met penalties of short jail time and simple fines, whereas with federal prohibition, bootleggers, if caught, could potentially face prison time in the state penitentiary.

Central Oregon encompasses almost eight thousand square miles at three counties wide, with Bend at its heart. Its many towns and cities were spread out, leaving vast open land dotted with caves and abandoned homestead shacks. The high desert region was the perfect hiding ground for distillery operations and rum-running. Unlike in Portland and other congested northwest cities, lawmen had an ever-difficult time finding or capturing those in the illicit business. Out of that great capacity to hide, central Oregon became the moonshine capital of the Pacific Northwest.

The region's arid climate made it difficult for farmers and live-stock herders to be successful, but making moonshine, or white lightning, proved easy. A man already had all he needed: his choice of barley, wheat, or cornmeal, along with some sugar. With those ingredients and a copper boiler with coils, his profits could be made, saving him from losing his inhospitable land.

Opposition to illegal undertakings with alcohol was spear-headed primarily in the Woman's Christian Temperance Union, which was forceful in many places, including central Oregon.

Powered by women volunteers, its movement targeted men's alcohol abuse and how it harmed women, children, families, and society as a whole. With women's suffrage already in full swing leading up to 1920 and beyond, its presence added to the mood that fueled communities in their daily activities. That undoubtedly influenced Marie as she faced opposing views. She had grown up to dislike alcohol for the problems it caused, only to accompany Randall to social gatherings where she found that the business of alcohol was a normality. Faced with that double-edged sword, she had to determine which course to follow in her journey to be an honorable young woman.

As 1922 passed and 1923 unfolded, Marie's housewife duties prevailed. Randall worked his mill job in Bend but also made frequent trips in his bootlegging runs. Their first child—a son, Richard Lyle—was born on Monday, December 31, at St. Charles Hospital in Bend.

As sweetly as 1923 ended, their Bend roots fell to the wayside in 1924. Randall, now full throttle into his bootlegging, moved the family west. After a short-term rental in the summer of 1924 at Mr. and Mrs. Bert Taylor's home in Corvallis, they next rented from Mr. and Mrs. Walter Newton and their large family on their farm in Plymouth.

In less than a year, they moved back and forth between Corvallis, Plymouth, and Philomath. It was hauntingly reminiscent for Marie of when her father had often relocated their family between Oklahoma and Kansas in her early childhood. Unlike her father, though, it wasn't any business undertakings that caused her husband to move, other than his bootlegging. Randall was adrift, lacking in any real focus or pursuits. Their Bend life had provided a respectable income from the mills. Now, he was a general laborer wherever work was needed and dependent on the men from whom he rented.

Aside from the friends they had through the Taylor and Newton families, they were also well acquainted with the Goben family in Plymouth, whose son, Ken, had been Randall's class-mate. That November, Marie, Randall, and their son, whom they called Dick, were guests at the Goben home for Thanksgiving dinner. Any promise of hope in a new year was not shown to Marie as 1925 dawned.

Less than two months after that holiday dinner, Randall was arrested. On Friday night, January 2, 1925, Sheriff S. N. Warfield and three accompanying men formed a posse and lay in wait at a home in Philomath for Randall and an accomplice, Clifford Hood. Randall and Mr. Hood never showed up. The posse returned Saturday night and successfully apprehended them. Sheriff Warfield took them to Corvallis for a midnight trial under Judge Penson, who had recently retired but was called in. The men were charged with unlawful possession of intoxicating liquor. With liquor in their hands when arrested, they pled guilty and were convicted. They immediately paid their fine of one hundred dollars each, or nearly two thousand dollars in today's money, and then were released from custody.

In February, the family moved again, this time to Philomath. Marie was six months pregnant and had her hands full with Dick, who was now a toddler. Randall continued his frequent traveling and bootlegging while working odd jobs. When they were together, they were often guests at the Goben home for dinner or in attendance at social events with them.

On Sunday, May 31, Randall was not around when Marie was admitted to the hospital in Corvallis for the birth of their second child, a daughter, Betty Jean. As Marie told her story, looking back as an older adult, she said, "He never came to the hospital, nor did he return home." Meanwhile, the Gobens took baby Dick into their home to care for him while Marie was giving birth.

Marie and her daughter stayed with a friend in Corvallis following her abandonment. Their Corvallis stay was but temporary and gave way to Marie returning to Bend with two babies in tow. Dick was now a year and a half, with red hair and blue eyes. Betty was still a newborn. Marie's married life was gone, and yet out of that downfall, she persevered.

MARIE RESUMED HER activities in Bend with the Christian Church, where she had been active before marrying. For one, she participated in an event on Monday afternoon, February 22, 1926. It was a silver tea program presented by the ladies of the church and opened with the group singing "America the Beautiful." For that patriotic event, many states were represented, each by one or more of the ladies according to where they were originally from. Some sang a song, some spoke about their home state, and some performed a musical piece. Marie represented Oklahoma with a piano solo of the song "Dixie's Land."

Life in Bend at twenty-two years old as a single mother in 1926 did not suit her well. Should anyone question where her husband was, she was as forthright and honest as she could be. While divorces weren't unheard of, Marie was surely met with frowns by the ladies in town for that social taboo. If anything did not sit well for Marie, it was that her father's frown was unmistakable. As his only daughter, she had disappointed him. No one in Marie's family that she knew of had ever been divorced. Today, tracing Marie's lineage back no less than five generations proves her right.

She remembered growing up with only three grandparents. Her grandmother on her father's side had died young, yet her grandfather had never remarried. To be married only once was how it had always been done in Marie's family. Aside from finding strength from her innermost self to fend off those frowns, she also had to be strong as she cared for two young children without their father.

As if with an instinctive response to their remarks, Marie relied on her ingenuity to overcome the hardships that faced her. What she would find in doing so would inevitably take her far from Bend, farther than the reaches of Corvallis. She met Clarence through a brother of his who lived in Bend, whereas he lived in Portland, same as his parents and several of his many brothers and sisters. Marie described Clarence as mild-mannered and kind, and even later, in her older years, she never wavered from her feelings, saying, "He was very giving."

Clarence Leroy Conner had served in World War I in the Philippines as a cook from May 1917 until September 1919. He had returned from his military service to live in Des Moines, Iowa, before returning to Portland. In Iowa he had worked as a farmhand, but now he was pursuing a career as a printer, which only began to open opportunities for him.

Although Clarence was born in Damascus, Oregon, his family had lived in Iowa for a few years when he was young—his parents were originally from Iowa, and they still had relatives there. After several years, his father, Christian Dale Conner, moved the family back to Oregon, settling in Portland. Clarence's father, like Marie's, was also a barber and owned his shop. Clarence attended high school in Portland and then was drafted into the army.

In September 1926, Marie and Clarence traveled to Stevenson, Washington. Situated on the banks of the Columbia River, the city lies within a gorge loved by outdoor enthusiasts for its scenic beauty. It was about a five-hour drive for them from Bend, or if they traveled from Portland, about a two-hour drive. On Tuesday, September 21, the day before Clarence's thirtieth birthday, he and Marie were married.

Clarence accepted Dick, who would be three years old in December, and Betty, now a year and a half, as his children. They lived in Portland for a few years, where Clarence worked as a foreman for *The Montavilla Times*, a neighborhood publication. On November 21, 1927, they had a son. They named him Clarence Dale but right away called him Billy. He looked much like Clarence, with brown hair too. In September 1929, they had been married three years, had three children, and had another baby on the way.

For Americans, the 1920s had been fruitful with career possibilities for men, economic growth, and easy buying power. As Americans felt they had a comfortable life, their overly confident perspective next pushed New York stockbrokers to make a dreadful mistake. It was brought on by a chain of events from investors who borrowed money to buy more stocks, which caused weakened real estate values and then, ultimately, panic selling. Thus, in late October of 1929, the stock market crashed, and many Americans immediately went broke. Then, on November 17, Clarence and Marie had their fourth baby, a daughter, who they named Peggy Marie.

Spawned by the stock market crash, America entered the Great Depression. Oregonians could feel their hardship in their agricultural and lumber industries through depressed prices for those commodities. Closer to home for Clarence and Marie, the construction activity in the Portland metropolitan area came to a near halt. As more people became destitute, the Salvation Army and the Red Cross were among the philanthropic agencies who tried to help.

In 1932, Joseph Carson was elected Portland's mayor, and through his nine-year tenure, he relied less on federal aid and more on putting men and older boys to work. Roads and bridges were built, and dock work resumed at the shipyards. He furthermore fought a city housing authority and, by doing so, prevented home values from collapsing.

While Mayor Carson in Portland was as initiative-taking as he could be, Washington, one state north of Oregon, was reactive with a new Democratic Party that set up a powerful labor movement. Their new priorities, political in nature, built cultural institutions, an aerospace station, and parks. Like Oregon, they built roads, bridges, and dams. They also constructed an interconnected electrical grid system to provide electricity delivery between businesses and consumers. The United States would come out of the Depression in the late 1930s, when investments in the war effort of World War II would inevitably advance the economy.

Meanwhile, Marie's father, Harry, had sold his land in Bend in 1927 to also relocate to Portland. When the Great Depression fell on them, Marie's parents had already secured a new home, and Harry was able to continue his career as a barber. Marie's brother Harry also moved his family to Portland, and her younger brother, Frank, soon followed. Frank got married and settled there in 1929. Her eldest brother, Glen, stayed in Bend as a farmer.

IN THE EARLY 1930s, Clarence and Marie lived in Washington—first in Vancouver, then, come 1934, in Ritzville. Their fifth and last child, a daughter, Patsy Lea, was born on April 30, 1934. Their family was now complete. Their oldest child, Dick, had turned ten years old at the end of 1933. Betty, at almost nine years old, took after Marie in looks but only had a tinge of red in her otherwise blonde hair. She was tall for her age and had a healthy physique and a distinct smile. In November, Billy would be seven years old, and Peggy five. Wherever they lived, they easily built friendships. A favorite pastime for Clarence and Marie was to play cards with other couples, oftentimes their neighbors.

Family time at home involved Marie at her piano or their family tuning in to a radio program. The radio station out of Portland was the first in Oregon to affiliate with a national broadcasting company. This Portland station had the first variety show in the nation and was the first to have quiz programs, library programs, and debates, among other firsts. *Covered Wagon Days* was a popular variety show, with its cast of characters performing live for their broadcasted program. Their radio gave the family many listening choices, from music, sometimes live, to stories to Marie's favorite: soap operas.

Shortly after Patsy was born, Clarence's career sent them back to Oregon, first to Salem, then Lebanon. In Salem, he worked for *The Oregon Statesman* newspaper. He next gained career advancement as a printer when, in 1936, he accepted a position with *The Lebanon*

Express. This newspaper had undergone many changes and now, as of 1936, was under new ownership. It needed new men to run it, and Clarence was entrusted with the challenge.

Each relocation was a necessity for the advancement of Clarence's career, all while jobs were few and far between for many people. While the Great Depression persisted, newspapers still had to be printed. Clarence's chosen career path in this industry was a godsend. It kept his family from being among the growing number unable to meet their basic needs. Clarence and Marie proved that when times get tough, the tough get going.

Their Lebanon relocation put them thirty miles due east of Corvallis and eighty miles south of their parents and other family members in Portland. Although they weren't as far from her parents as they had been in some relocations, Marie likely felt the distance gave her the needed freedom to build her life without the overshadowing presence of her father, Harry. It was an opportunity to look forward to her future while not letting go of her love for her parents.

At first, they rented a house on Rose Street. When his career advancement appeared to be one that would outlast America's troubled economy, Clarence purchased an older house that, if documentation is correct, was constructed in the year 1890. In August 1937, they moved into it, at 471 Park Street. That house would be their family's forever home.

This Park Street home was placed on the National Register of Historic Sites in 1994. In a list compiled by the city of Lebanon, it was described as an L-shaped Greek Revival house with a gable roof. Although this entry was riddled with errors, we can conclude from that documentation that it was a two-story, 1,608-square-foot home on a lot sized at almost seven thousand square feet. Unfortunately, the house was the subject of a fire in the year 2023 and then was demolished.

More recent documentation detailed the layout of the house. Its front-facing square window had a view of Park Street that caught the evening sun as it set in the western sky. Inside the house, this window appeared tall, stretching almost to the ceiling from the baseboard. Two smaller windows faced north, with a fireplace in between. Baseboard heating was another source they used for warmth. Marie's piano would have been situated in the northwest corner, catty-corner to the fireplace. It was their main room for family time and to be with guests. On the south end of the room and opposite her piano was a parlor. It was partitioned off by a sliding wooden door and was the best possible space for overnight visitors. The parlor's window had a standard window height on a street-side wall. Only when inside would one notice that there were two rooms that faced the street, and not what appeared to be just one.

Deeper into the house, access to a spacious kitchen and its dining area would have been found. A standard bathroom at full size was nearby. Another full-sized bathroom was upstairs with three bedrooms. Their girls ideally shared a room, and their boys shared another room. An attached garage was on the back side of the house, with an alleyway that, in 1937, was used by four residences and was accessible by Rose Street to the north and Vine Street to the south.

Nestled in a good neighborhood, Clarence and Marie's spacious home accommodated their five children: Dick, who would be four-teen that December; Betty, twelve; Billy, almost ten; Peggy, almost eight; and Patsy, who had turned three years old a few months earlier. Their older children excelled in school activities. Dick entered seventh grade in the fall of 1937 as the elected class president. Betty was a competent swimmer, earning recognition at an event earlier that summer. Billy participated in sports, with football on the horizon for him. Their little girls, Peggy and Patsy, rounded out the family, sporting the red curly hair from Marie's genes, and often in pigtails.

At the close of 1937, many Oregonians questioned whether there would ever be an end to their difficult times. Yet a rising optimism was in the air for Clarence and Marie. They had a comfortable home and healthy children. He had a rewarding career, and in their fortitude, Marie would embrace opportunities to be a worthy part of their newfound community.

Part 2

In observance of Business Women's Week by the Business and Professional Women's Club, Lebanon, Oregon, Marie Conner (at left) receives an orchid corsage from Peggy Hatfield (at right).

Image Credit: *The Lebanon Express*, October 20, 1950.
(Eggen Photo)

Chapter 4

Homelife

June 1937–April 1943

Their Park Street home was like home to many out-of-town family guests, from its early days in the summer of 1937 onward. It was as if Marie had to show her parents and other relatives that her blemished past was behind her, as if it had never even existed. She didn't talk about that past. Rather, her focus was one of intention, to show that her life was flawless. In doing so, she had to ignore the strife that had been in their family relations ever since she was but a girl trying to find her way in this world. Her father held tight to his misgiven attitude of her worth as a woman. She would prove him wrong.

She was a well-received neighbor and community member in their city of Lebanon, Oregon. Clarence had a respectable job with their local newspaper, *The Lebanon Express*. And they had a beautiful home for their children, whom they were rearing to become fine, upstanding young adults. Yet there was more to do, Marie knew. It would happen. She would see to that.

Even before they moved to the Park Street house, Marie's mother would occasionally stay with them for several days at a time. In June 1937, Marie's brother Frank, who also lived in Portland, came with his wife and son for a few days as well. In July, friends from Ritzville, Washington, where Clarence and Marie had lived in 1934, stopped in for an afternoon visit on their way to a summer vacation on the Oregon coast. In September, Frank and his family returned for another visit. Frank and his wife stayed for the day, whereas their little boy, Jack, stayed for two weeks.

Although their home was lively with visitors, Marie and Clarence also felt the sting of loss. Clarence's mother had died in June 1937. In February 1938, his father and one of his sisters traveled from their Portland homes for an afternoon visit with them. That summer, in June, their nephew Jack returned for another lengthy visit.

The other homes in their neighborhood were much like theirs. They were family houses, each just large enough to accommodate those who lived in them. Their home was as spacious as it was cozy. Off the large front room, they had a smaller room, their parlor, to offer to overnight guests, along with one of two bathrooms close by. Two bathrooms were both sufficient and necessary for Marie and her family. Marie's dressing area and bathroom were essential for her. She took great care and pride in her morning routine with hygiene and choosing the perfect outfit for the day.

It was commonplace for the front room or living room in one's house to be furnished with plenty of seating space and a full-sized table used for dining, sewing, crafts, or playing games. Most homes kept at least one card table and sometimes more. These were portable, sturdy tables used for playing cards and then folded up and put away when not in use. Living rooms also commonly had a standing ashtray near the couch and chairs, even if no one in the family smoked. A console radio—that is, a radio built into an aesthetically pleasing cabinet that stood on the floor—was a must-have. To have a piano in the home, as Marie did, was also commonplace for families who had a piano player.

Marie ensured that her family's home was kept clean and furnished with modern furniture and appliances. Some mothers in the neighborhood appeared to be comfortable with an unkempt home. Not Marie. She had no tolerance for toys, schoolbooks, or children's games scattered about, whether in her home or another's. Those items belonged in children's bedrooms.

Park Street was a family-friendly street with clean sidewalks, well-manicured lawns, and many flowering trees. Mrs. Bert Connet, whom Marie came to know as Madge, and her husband and children lived one block down at 387 Park Street. Mr. and Mrs. Paul McCracken also lived nearby, and Marie knew Mrs. McCracken by her first name of Hazel. The children in these two families were close in age to Marie's children.

Peggy, Marie's middle daughter, would grow up in her dad's footsteps. Marie had expected her to be in Girl Scouts. Peggy would be in that and other girl groups when young, but as soon as she was old enough to join her dad at his newspaper job, she didn't hesitate to do so. While a little girl, she tagged along with him, and then when old enough, she would work beside him.

Peggy's younger sister, Patsy, was more than happy to please Marie in her choices of activities. She was also a girl who liked to have fun and was often a guest at children's parties. While Clarence and Marie's other children grew up fast, Patsy seemed to relish evermore in her youth, whereas Peggy's older sister, Betty, quickly outgrew her girlhood days. She liked the friendships found when joining groups for young women and attending their events.

Billy, their middle child, was headstrong and independent. He excelled in school and in his boyhood hobbies. His interests would lead him to great things. On the other hand, their oldest son, Dick, was a drifter, indecisive, and uninterested in family affairs. He was the wayward child for Marie. At times, he tried to please her, such as when he was elected class president when they first arrived in Lebanon. However, accomplishments from his endeavors would be a seldom occurrence.

Lebanon was a safe place for resident children to grow up. They played and studied together. Children respected their parents and their friends' parents. It was a carefree time despite the ever-present war that took their older brothers to faraway, unseen places.

This was a small city that was founded by early pioneers and continued to thrive in its businesses, farms, and people. Two industries led the economy. One was the wood products industry, with a paper mill that began in 1891 and then doubled in size by 1936. Many other mills also assumed residency in Lebanon during the 1930s, causing its population to swell and averting any pain from the Great Depression.

The other prosperous industry, and the one that Lebanon residents took the most pride in, was their strawberry fields. Farming and food processing were abundant in the Willamette Valley, in which Lebanon was nestled at its southernmost tip. Farmers grew a rich variety of berries, nuts, and vegetables. Strawberries were by far Lebanon's leading crop. An annual summer celebration began in 1909 to promote this fact. In 1931, this celebration was officially named the Strawberry Festival. It attracted strawberry farmers from all over the Willamette Valley, and out of tradition, Lebanon always hosted it, and always in June.

Portland has always been Oregon's largest city. From here, the Willamette Valley stretches southward for 150 miles. Oregon's capital, Salem, is located a little more than the halfway point from Portland south to Albany. Corvallis is southwest of Albany, while Lebanon lies southeast. Many small cities and towns are sprinkled throughout. The Willamette River flows the entire length of this valley, flowing north out of the Calapooya Mountains where that range abuts Corvallis and Lebanon. Another range of mountains called the Oregon Coast Range is to the west with the Oregon coastline west of that, whereas the Cascade Mountain Range is to the east. That range is the one Marie had crossed as a young woman traveling between Bend and Corvallis.

Lebanon is in Linn County, and Albany is its county seat. Albany has always been the larger of the two, leaving Lebanon with that hometown feeling with its mere three thousand residents in

1940. Lebanon's population would double to nearly six thousand residents in 1950, partly due to the country's demand for its plywood during the World War II years. Albany would also nearly double in size during that decade to ten thousand residents in 1950.

Both Lebanon and Albany offered a wide array of entertainment, social functions, and group gatherings. Residents in this part of the Willamette Valley often traveled to one of these two cities or to one of a number of other nearby places for events. Later, Marie recalled her opportunity to travel during that time period. She said she loved the freedom found in getting in the car and going anywhere she wanted.

Aside from out-of-town events, Marie also liked to host social gatherings in her home. When Clarence wasn't at work, he helped with entertainment duties, but Marie was fine when left on her own. She was a woman with self-worth who wasn't afraid to speak her mind and always had the ability to smile wide. People were drawn to her radiant temperament.

On Sunday evening, September 18, 1938, Clarence and Marie hosted a dinner party in their home. They had been in their Park Street house just over a year, having moved in during August of the year before. It could have been a housewarming party. It was also the weekend before Clarence's forty-second birthday and their twelfth wedding anniversary. Marie might have confided in Madge, Hazel, and other close friends that Clarence wasn't her first husband. After all, if one did the math, it didn't add up. Their two oldest children were past twelve years in age. Dick would be fourteen years old that December, and Betty was thirteen.

However, in her elder years, Marie shared that it was when Betty needed identification to drive that she discovered from her birth certificate that Clarence was not her biological father. Since that secret was kept from their children for many years, it could easily have been kept hush among their friends as well. When confronted in an amiable way by a friend, Marie could have smiled, twirled her right forefinger in a voluminous curl atop her head, and then looked straight into her friend's eyes to say something like, "It's been many wonderful years."

At that Sunday evening party, six couples joined them for dinner. An informal discussion about new civic groups in town was an enjoyable way to relax around their formal dining table. Surely, they also played cards. With eight people present, two card games, and each card table having two couples, it would have been Marie's chosen way to celebrate Clarence's birthday and their wedding anniversary.

Of the many get-togethers they had with friends for a card game, one was on Friday evening, August 4, 1939. They played pinochle with Mr. and Mrs. Leonard Simons. In one hand, Clarence presented a double run in trump, worth 1,500 points, making them the winners. While possible, it is rare to achieve a double run. It was a triumphant game for them. Yet Marie preferred bridge over pinochle. Like pinochle, bridge is a partnership game with two pairs of partners. It is a trick-taking game with rules that progress in complexity. As the play ensues, points and penalties are tallied and recorded on a score sheet. Those who are excellent bridge players often play in tournaments, or duplicate bridge.

Pinochle, bridge, and other card games were popular in the 1930s and '40s. There were countless card clubs in Lebanon during that era. Dedication and achievement were driving forces in that rave. Partnership loyalty was also prevalent. Prizes given at card parties kept the games fun. The logic required for the skill to play bridge caused it to be an intrinsically attractive game. Marie's ardent passion to play card games would stay with her for a lifetime. She and Clarence often played with the Cardette Pinochle Club. Later, in 1940, Marie would join the newly formed Bid-Away Bridge Club. It was in these card clubs that Marie met new people. Here, she befriended ladies who then introduced her to civic opportunities.

Aside from her friendships, Marie also tended to her children and their activities, giving approval where it was due. She expected her children to choose wisely in their interests. Her oldest daughter, Betty, joined a fine and respectable youth group in the Baptist Church, known by its acronym—the JWWG—rather than by its full name. While their family didn't regularly attend any church, Betty was old enough now, at fourteen, to choose her own church calling. On Friday evening, March 17, 1939, Betty hosted a JWWG party in her home, complete with shamrock decorations. Their guild leader and several girls attended. Betty served refreshments that she had prepared herself. It was but a social affair with Chinese checkers and other games. Their formal meetings were held monthly at the Baptist Church with a potluck dinner.

Later that year, Marie and her family acknowledged Thanksgiving during the last week of November with a family trip. In 1939, it wasn't yet a federal holiday, but it was an American tradition for families to come together in celebration. Each year, Lebanon folks followed their mayor's guidance, who depended on their state governor to decide which Thursday to observe it on. Sometimes they opted for the third Thursday, and sometimes the last Thursday. Even so, some families departed from any recommendation as to when.

On the last Saturday of that month, Marie went to her parents' home with five-year-old Patsy. On Sunday, Clarence and the other children joined them. Billy and Peggy had recently had birthdays: Billy's twelfth birthday was earlier in the week before they had left for their trip, and Peggy had turned ten years old a few days before that. The weekend visit with Marie's parents was their time for a Thanksgiving meal, forgoing any big meal preparation at home. Cooking wasn't among Marie's strengths or interests. It was also an opportune time for Marie to show her father that she was a good mother with well-behaved children.

The new year, 1940, was a busy one for daughter Betty. In February, she attended the JWWG State Convention in Salem with several other girls. Two girls in the Salem group were from the

Hatfield family who had relatives in Lebanon. Afterward, at their regular meeting on Monday, February 26, Betty gave a report of the convention and also again led devotionals.

Springtime sprung forth Girl Scout activities. In early March, Betty's Girl Scout troop had its annual cookie sale, supervised by Mrs. Elmer Whetstone and two other women. Like the other girls, Betty wore her crisp brown Girl Scout dress, knocked on doors, and canvassed her neighborhood to sell cookies. It was later reported that they had set an all-time-high record for their 621 boxes of cookies sold. Betty sold the most cookies, at 93 boxes. The girl who sold the second-greatest number of boxes—70—couldn't compare to Betty. Betty's achievement was something for Marie to be proud of.

A rainy season was in front of them, which brought a fierce windstorm on March 28 and 29. On these two days, inside the armory and under protective shelter from the nasty weather, a garden show with exhibits was held. Many residents had entered their prized flowers, homemade birdhouses, and other arts-and-crafts items to display and be judged. The Boy Scouts and the Girl Scouts each had a strong presence in the show. Through the Girl Scouts, Betty entered a terrarium she'd made. It won a third-place ribbon. Again, Marie was proud of her oldest daughter.

On Friday evening, April 12, the Girl Scouts had a formal dinner at their troop leader's home. Betty then wrote a short article and gave it to her dad, who ensured it was published in their local newspaper. She described her leader's home as being decorated lavishly with candles and flowers. Their dinner was buffet style. Games were played. But the main event of the evening, as Betty wrote, was dancing to the Virginia Reel, a traditional folk dance with precision steps for couples that was commonly taught in American schools.

Betty also occasionally helped her dad at his newspaper job. So did Billy, and sometimes, although less often, Dick helped too. They were young but old enough, according to Clarence, to learn how the newspaper business worked and to understand the important role it held for residents. Clarence was the shop superintendent, and there were many tasks the children could do to help the people that he managed on the production floor. They helped him out of a desire to please him. Peggy looked forward to when she could help him with the newspaper, not out of an expectation placed on her but as a way to be even closer to her dad.

That summer, Betty went camping. Her Girl Scout troop had a camping trip every summer. That time it was different in that they went to Camp Firlinn, located on the banks of Crabtree Creek, which not only was in its opening season but also in its first week to welcome campers. They stayed a full week. Peggy also went but as a Brownie and for only a three-day trip. The Brownies were an organization for girls too young to be in Girl Scouts.

Billy was also involved with activities. He was growing up fast and would be thirteen years old on his next birthday, in November. No longer a little boy, Billy preferred to be called Bill. In August of that summer, he entered a model airplane construction contest. The contest was sponsored by the Lebanon Variety Store and had one rule: the construction supplies used should cost no more than ten cents. Bill built a biplane, painted its wings and tail yellow, and gave it a blue fuselage. Lebanon's only privately licensed pilot, Mr. Ralph Scroggin, judged the entries. Out of twenty entrants, two first-place awards were given. Bill earned first place in the junior division.

Marie was also an award winner, even if in mere fun. On Wednesday, October 16, she won a score award in her pinochle game with the Cardette Club. On Monday, October 28, she cohosted the Bid-Away Bridge Club meeting with Mrs. Floyd Connet, who was known by her first name of Florence to those close to her and was Mrs. Madge Connet's sister-in-law, Marie's neighbor and friend. Their husbands were brothers, and they also had a third brother, whose wife Marie would also come to know. They met in Mrs. Florence Connet's home, and Marie helped her serve refreshments.

Card clubs in Lebanon usually met weekly, taking turns with hosting duties. Only women were members in the Cardette Club and Bid-Away Bridge Club. When husbands attended, they were considered to be guests and not members.

Shortly into the new year of 1941, Marie attended the Bid-Away Bridge Club meeting, again in Mrs. Florence Connet's home. They met for a luncheon on Monday, January 6. Aside from cards and lunch, they also held officer elections for 1941. Marie was chosen to be their reporter. A week later, the Bid-Away Bridge Club met for an evening get-together in Marie's home with Mrs. Florence Connet as cohost. Four new members were welcomed into their club: Mr. and Mrs. Ed Miller and Mr. and Mrs. Simons. Although the Millers were a namesake to Marie's first husband's father, there was no relation. When the club met in the first week of February, Marie and Mrs. Florence Connet won prizes for their play. In March, Marie again hosted one of their meetings. In the first week of April, Clarence joined them. Both Marie and Clarence won prizes in their game.

Meanwhile, Bill received a letter in the mail in late March from the Guam postmaster. Back in November, Bill had sent a letter to the post office in this territory asking for a three-cent Guam stamp to add to his stamp collection. Considering six months had passed, Bill was surprised to get a reply. The postmaster explained in his letter that a typhoon had struck the island in November, which caused damage to their post office. Bill's letter was found in the wreckage as one of few surviving pieces of mail. The postmaster included an old Guam Guard Mail stamp with his letter, stating that Guam now used United States postage stamps. Bill's new stamp was valued at eighty cents, and in proud ownership, he treasured it. Bill set his sights on one day visiting Guam. For now, though, he was a thirteen-year-old boy under his mom's wing.

On Thursday evening, May 22, Betty's Girl Scout troop presented a style show and musical. It had taken them several weeks to prepare for it, with them earning credit toward their personal health badges. At the show, each girl modeled age-appropriate attire, with some in dresses and some in slack suits. Betty sported a yellow wool suit for street wear. Girl Scout council members and mothers were well entertained. Before the month's end, Betty had her sixteenth birthday.

That summer, Marie's brother Frank and his family, who had moved to San Francisco, California, visited them in July. Their mother, Laura, visited at the same time. Laura returned in August for another visit. During that summer, Marie's eldest son, Dick, began working odd jobs. He was seventeen years old and wasn't achieving high marks in school like Marie's other children.

In October, Marie cohosted another card game with the Bid-Away Bridge Club at Mrs. Florence Connet's home. In November, it was Marie's turn for them to meet at her house. Mrs. Florence Connet assisted Marie in serving refreshments.

Also, that autumn, there was talk about starting an auxiliary group for the wives of Lebanon firemen. Clarence had just begun his training to become a volunteer fireman. It was the first organized and trained team of volunteers to assist the fire department. While the department had always used volunteers, it had previously been dependent on who was nearby to show up and help during their fire calls. However, it would be much later when an auxiliary was formally created.

As 1941 closed out, Marie's four youngest children were doing well. Betty had transferred from Lebanon High School to attend business school in Portland and was staying with Marie's parents during that time. She would come home for Christmas. The two younger girls, Peggy and Patsy, were proceeding well through their Scout activities.

Bill was also a Scout. On Saturday morning, February 28, Bill was one of a few select boys in their Boy Scout troop who earned an overnight camping trip. Winter weather could be perilous for Lebanon residents, and the year 1942 proved no different. The boys arrived at Trout Creek Forest Camp to find two inches of newly fallen wet snow. It snowed more as Bill and the other boys used what they had learned in their scouting methods. They built a forest shelter out of dead fallen timber and maintained a campfire to keep warm and to cook their meals. On Sunday morning, they trekked through deep snow to the lookout station atop Rooster Rock. Two more hours of hiking put them at a ranger station. Here, they measured the snow and found it had accumulated to nine inches deep. That afternoon, having completed many tasks and earning more badges, they returned home. Marie was proud of this son. If only her other son was more like him.

When the winter weather subsided, Marie and Clarence had another succession of out-of-town family guests in their home. In May, one of Clarence's sisters and her husband and son made an afternoon Sunday visit. In early July, Marie's brother Glen, who had moved to Bremerton, Washington, made the rounds to visit Oregon family members. Marie's home for a brief visit was one of his stops. At the same time, Marie's nephew Jack arrived. He would spend the summer with them. Ending the summer, Marie's parents spent Labor Day weekend with them.

Meanwhile, Dick dabbled in a new venture. Back at the onset of summer, he started a group, the Victory Club, in response to the ongoing war. He had already done his civic duty by registering for the draft, as was compulsory, but thus far he hadn't been called for military service. His Victory Club was open to all boys and girls, but most members were of his family: Bill, Peggy, Patsy, and his cousin Jack. They held rubber, scrap iron, and paper drives. They then turned in these items to earn money, which they spent on war bonds and stamps. Dick's Victory Club was short-lived. Although it disbanded, it did make children aware of how to help during these war years.

The autumn brought fun for the children, leaving Dick's futile and depressing ideas in the dust. On Saturday, October 3, Mrs. Madge Connet hosted a birthday party for her daughter, Janet, who was turning eight years old. Mrs. Hazel McCracken helped Mrs.

Connet with party arrangements. Eighteen neighborhood children of varying ages attended, including Peggy and Patsy. They played games, ate birthday cake, and gave Janet gifts. Another neighborhood party for children was held on Halloween night, a Saturday, at the McCracken home. They wore costumes, played, and had refreshments. Children had a hard time guessing who Peggy was in her costume, and for that, she won a prize.

In December, Marie took honors with her Bid-Away Bridge Club. In the first of two meetings, she won first prize for her score, and then later that month, second prize. Both parties were held close to her home, with the second one hosted by Mrs. Roy Weeks, who lived only a few houses down from her. Aside from a friendly competition at cards, it was a lively time with refreshments and socializing. More so, it was a time for Marie to hear about the different groups that one could belong to in Lebanon. For one, many of her fellow bridge players were also members of the Order of the Eastern Star.

Early in the new year of 1943, on Monday evening, January 4, Clarence and Marie attended an Eastern Star meeting. It was one of several fraternal organizations in Lebanon and open to membership for both men and women. These groups gave people a place for fellowship in an organized setting. When Marie was a little girl, her mother, Laura, was active in the Eastern Star as a charter member of the chapter in Jennings, Oklahoma. When the family moved to Oregon, Laura transferred her chapter membership.

Likewise, Marie must have been a member even before they lived in Lebanon. In 1943, Marie was an officer. Members are usually well known in their Eastern Star chapter before appointment or election to be an officer or even to serve on a committee. Mrs. Hazel McCracken was a member, as was Mrs. Elmer Whetstone. Marie knew Mrs. Whetstone, or Vada, as people close to her called her, as a council member of Betty's Girl Scout troop. Dr. Joel Booth was another member, well known both in the Eastern Star and in their community.

The Marguerite chapter of the Eastern Star met at the Masonic Hall in Lebanon on the first Monday of each month, except during the summer. Philanthropic work was important to them, and they showed so in their support for members who volunteered through other groups. Giving monetary gifts from the chapter to worthy organizations was their common practice.

Like many other fraternal organizations, the Order of the Eastern Star is based on Christian principles. However, members can be of any religion, not limited to Christianity. Membership qualifications relate to membership in the Fraternal Order of the Masons. Only past Master Masons and women related to Masons can be Eastern Star members.

The emblem for the Eastern Star is a five-point star. Each point represents a biblical heroine: Adah, Ruth, Esther, Martha, and Electa. Each heroine has certain qualities and is symbolized with a specific flower, jewel, and color. Oftentimes, a woman who is in one of these five officer positions wears a customized dress to portray the heroine she represents. Members attend their meetings wearing their finest clothes, with women adorned in long floral or colorful gowns. These star points are five of the nineteen officer positions. In their hierarchy, the worthy matron, a woman, and the worthy patron, a man, lead their chapter.

On that early January evening in 1943, the Marguerite chapter had a public installation for incoming officers. Marie was installed as Ruth. As one of the five points in their star, her color was sunshine yellow, characterized by a strong yet sweet personality. Topaz was her gem, and her flower was a yellow jasmine. The International Order of the Rainbow for Girls, a related fraternal organization for girls that was established in 1940, assisted in the ceremony. After the installation, their meeting was closed to members only. One of the reports given was about the Red Cross work that some members were involved with. Following their short business session, they joined their guests for refreshments. Mrs. Vada Whetstone was the committee chairman in charge of that.

One week later, Marie attended their firemen's auxiliary group. It had started in 1942 and met monthly in support of their firemen-husbands. Clarence, as a volunteer fireman, attended weekly fire drills and was often called to duty. Their meeting was hosted by Mrs. Jack Stolsig on Monday evening, January 11. They had officer elections, and Marie was voted in to serve as reporter for 1943. In February, they had their annual banquet for the volunteer firemen.

They were but a small, close-knit group of women, and yet the State Fire Marshal's Office rated them as the best in the state. They were the only firemen's auxiliary in Oregon that had bylaws. Later, the State Fire Marshal's worthy announcement was reported in the early-April 1943 meeting for the state Civilian Defense headquarters and then printed in *The Lebanon Express.*

As opportunities opened up for Marie to be a part of her community, she began to relax in her motherhood role. Her children, for the most part, were making fine choices in their paths to adulthood. In the many family visits Marie had with her parents and other relatives, she was able to show them that her life was good. It was a foundation for Marie, and she looked forward to social functions and community involvement. She was intent on showing her father that she, as a woman, would—through her due diligence and then some—make her hometown the best it could be. She was his only daughter, and although he often voiced that she should not be concerned with matters outside of the home, she was intent on proving him wrong.

Chapter 5

Life and Death
April 1943–April 1945

Marie's youngest child, little Patsy, would be nine years old in this year of 1943. Her birthday was on April 30. Marie honored her with a party almost two weeks early, on Monday afternoon, April 19. Their home was lively with several school friends and neighborhood girls. Janet McCracken, whose eighth birthday party was back in October, attended along with her brother.

Patsy's friends gave her gifts, and Marie made sure that each guest received a party favor. Her birthday cake was elaborately frosted in pink icing and served with ice cream and punch. Their home overflowed with pink balloons. As the party ended, Marie handed out balloons so each child could take some home with them.

MARIE WAS A regular attendee with her card clubs, as well as with the Eastern Star and the firemen's auxiliary. In the Bid-Away Bridge Club, she had earned a score prize back in February and again in May. Also back in February, the Marguerite chapter of the Eastern Star had held a benefit card party with money raised to fund a refrigeration unit at the Masonic Lodge, where they had their meetings. On a Sunday afternoon in July, the Masonic and Eastern Star picnic was held at Bates Park. This event had a large turnout for swimming, games, and a picnic basket dinner.

On Tuesday afternoon, August 24, Marie attended a bridal shower given by her good friend Mrs. Madge Connet. It was a surprise party for two sisters in the Speasl family, both engaged to be married. Guests, all of whom were women relatives or friends of the Speasls, arrived early to surprise the two young ladies. Marie sat ready at the piano. When the two sisters arrived, Mrs. Connet welcomed them into her home, and Marie played the wedding march as they walked through the doorway. She played more piano selections while refreshments were served. That afternoon, they made a bridal book and offered gifts.

To prepare for social times, Marie did her utmost to look her finest. Her personality alone could carry her far, but for her, to be well dressed no matter the occasion was just as important. She had a mantra that she'd often tell herself and others, and this outspoken thought would always be with her, even as an older woman: "Remember, blue and white always go together."

She had many white blouses and often paired one with a skirt. For social times, like bridal showers or card parties, a dress with a full-swing skirt was one of her choices. For business meetings, pictures show that pencil dresses, sometimes with a suit jacket, were her go-to choice.

In her morning routine, Marie used cosmetics to complement her chosen outfit. Her skin tone was pale in comparison to her red hair, but that didn't stop her from applying bold lipstick. A dash of lipstick showed that a 1940s woman was lively, ardent, and feeling free from her country's recent hardships. Fuchsia and light red-orange were common lipstick colors for ladies at that time. For those who dared to flaunt their look, cherry-red lipstick was an option. With a taste for sophistication, Marie's choices were hues of brick red, mahogany, and crimson. Lipstick was more than a fashion choice. It was also a skin protectant. In that part of Oregon, women considered lipstick to be a lifesaver in that it protected their lips from the damaging impact of wind and cold weather.

Marie used lipstick to define her lips and enhance her natural beauty, perhaps in an attempt to draw attention away from her red hair. She also used foundation and blush ever so lightly to give her face a porcelain look. She groomed her eyebrows and used a pencil to color in the perfect arch. Only after giving attention to her hygiene, opting for the right outfit, and then applying her makeup and styling her hair was she ready to meet the world with her smile.

As summertime melted into the fall, Marie's three younger children began a new school year. Bill and Peggy were both in high school. The oldest McCracken boy was also in high school as a junior and on the football team, same as Bill. Their athletics coach was Mr. Bud Page, a young man who was new to school teaching. His wife, Dorothy, was closer in age to Marie's daughter Betty. Like Marie, Mrs. Dorothy Page also played piano. Betty was a young woman now, at eighteen years old. She had finished school and lived at home.

On Wednesday, October 20, Betty hosted a going-away party for a friend. A Halloween motif was used in the decorations. Marie was pleased her oldest daughter had grown up to be a well-liked woman who did good for others.

As winter fell upon them, Marie could look back on nearly a full year of meetings and social gatherings with the Eastern Star. It was time for new officers to be elected and appointed. This was done at their meeting on Monday evening, December 6. It was also their annual Turkey Dinner. Members and their families numbered over one hundred in attendance. Marie had served on a twelve-member committee to set up their dining hall. In sync with the holiday season, holly and red candles adorned the tables. Mrs. Ray Gleason was elected to be worthy matron, and her husband to be worthy patron. Marie was chosen to be Martha, another heroine and point in their star. As Martha, Marie's color was green, characterized by renewed life. Emerald was her gem, and a fern was her flower. Their installation would be on January 3.

On Monday evening, March 13, 1944, Marie and several other officers from the Marguerite chapter attended the Eastern Star's district meeting, held in nearby Brownsville. Several prominent visitors also attended, including the grand chapter representatives for both Mississippi and New Mexico Territory, as well as for Oregon. The decorations were an effective combination of yellow forsythia and red camellias.

The last half of March brought another score award for Marie in her Bid-Away Bridge Club, with her earning the high score. March also brought Marie's mother, Laura, for a week's stay with her family.

In early April, Clarence was promoted to team captain as a volunteer fireman. The volunteers had grown to four teams. In the little more than two years since the fire department had started its organized teams of volunteers, a vast improvement was seen in their work. Oftentimes, a fire call meant that someone's house wiring had faltered or a pan with grease on the kitchen stove had gotten out of control. Those fires weren't too difficult to extinguish, unlike the occasional times they had to battle a much more consuming fire. While Marie's family celebrated his promotion, a bigger family celebration was underway.

On Saturday, April 29, their daughter Betty, who would be nineteen years old at the end of May, was married to Mr. Andrew Peckham. Ten years her senior, Andrew was originally from Iowa, and his parents and much of his family still lived there. He had been a Lebanon resident but now resided in The Dalles, a city a little over an hour's drive east of Portland. When Andrew lived in Lebanon, he worked with a company on the construction of a housing project. His work as a carpenter took him to The Dalles to help another building company. Betty and Andrew planned to live in the Commodore Apartments there.

Clarence and Marie drove to The Dalles for the wedding, which was in the parsonage of the Methodist church. Andrew's parents, Mr. and Mrs. Randall Peckham, who lived in Iowa, also came. Betty's maid of honor was one of Andrew's sisters, who lived in Portland. It was an eight o'clock evening service and officiated by the reverend. Betty wore an orchid dress and matching hat with black-and-white accessories for this formal affair. Her corsage and the flowers she carried were gardenias, rosebuds, and lilies of the valley. Clarence gave her away in marriage. Marie wore a blue dressmaker suit with a corsage of pink carnations and rosebuds pinned to it. After the ceremony, they had their wedding dinner at a fine nearby restaurant, The Olympic.

Returning home from the wedding of her oldest daughter, Marie turned her attention to her youngest daughter, Patsy, who turned ten years old that Sunday, April 30. Marie gifted her with an extension in her piano lessons, which were being taught by an accredited piano teacher, Mr. Charles Hargrave. He was a graduate of the Chicago Conservatory College, the first music conservatory in the United States. Marie thought highly of the piano as an instrument and wished that all her children could play it. No event was complete without the mood and balance that only a piano could offer, or so Marie would always believe. Childhood toys were replaceable. Musical talent wasn't. It was a gift to both of them, for Patsy to learn and for Marie to have a piano player among her children.

In celebration of National Music Week, a piano recital was given on Monday evening, May 8. Patsy was one of several young students who performed under the direction of her piano instructor. It must have taken Marie back in memory to when she was young, playing the piano for large crowds. She knew what it was like to have a talent and for people to appreciate it. With a sense of honor, she couldn't be more pleased with her little girl.

In June, Lebanon received a visitor, whom Marie knew from her younger years. Kitty Rockwell Matson was staying with the

Washburn family enroute from a Portland visit to her home in Bend. Marie knew her as Klondike Kate and as the woman who had helped many people during the terrible Spanish Flu pandemic in 1918. Marie had fond memories of Klondike Kate for her strong presence as a woman who changed life for others in a positive way. It is unknown whether Marie saw her during this June 1944 visit.

On Saturday morning, June 24, Marie drove to The Dalles with Patsy to visit Betty and Andrew. Early the next day, they all went to Portland to visit Marie's parents. Clarence drove to her parents' home with Bill and Peggy later that day. Dick wasn't with them. He was almost twenty years old and seemed to always be doing his own thing. Sometimes he lived at home with Clarence and Marie, and at other times he rented an apartment in town.

Marie's parents were celebrating their golden wedding anniversary. The day centered around them and not Marie and her family. Thus, this was the needed distraction to keep away any questions regarding the whereabouts of Dick. He was the blemish in Marie's idyllic family and something that Marie would rather not face.

On Monday morning, Clarence returned home with Bill and Peggy. *The Lebanon Express* was expecting him in to work that day. And Bill was expected at Gates Camp, where he had a summer job assisting forest park rangers. He would drive there from home, about an hour northeast, to the foothills of the Cascade Mountain Range. Marie stayed until Tuesday, when she returned home with Patsy.

That fall, in the new school year, Marie's daughter Peggy, who was almost fifteen years old, was among a few select students accepted into the Future Craftsmen Club. This was a trades and industrial program, created the year before, for students to learn a vocation. Peggy would learn the newspaper trade as she worked alongside her dad, Clarence. Students in this program were required to work no less than fourteen hours a week, with their school day split between work and school. They earned credit for their work that counted toward the credits needed for high school graduation.

The apprenticeships varied in length depending on the trade. The printing trade that Peggy was accepted for was a six-year commitment, to extend two years beyond her high school graduation.

Aside from school and working at *The Lebanon Express*, Peggy, like her dad, enjoyed bowling. Clarence bowled more for fun. Peggy, though, showed a serious stance in the sport, which would earn her recognition and trophies in the years to come. In September, Clarence attended a meeting for those interested in forming a men's bowling league. They decided on an eight-team league, and it was determined that the teams would continue their schedule to bowl twice weekly, on Tuesday and Thursday evenings at Lebanon Alleys. They elected officers for this newly formed league. Clarence was selected to be first vice president, with Mr. Jack Stolsig as president. Mr. Stolsig was also a volunteer fireman, and his wife often hosted meetings for the auxiliary, of which Marie was a member.

Meanwhile, Betty and her newlywed husband, Andrew, returned to Lebanon to live in early August. The work he had been called to The Dalles to do hadn't panned out. Until he could secure a stable and promising career, they would stay with Marie and Clarence. However, only a few days after they arrived, they were called away to Iowa. Andrew's father had become gravely ill. While Betty and Andrew were in Iowa, he passed away at age ninety-one. In late August, Betty and Andrew returned home to Marie and Clarence.

At the end of the year, mid-December brought several events to the household. On Saturday evening, December 10, Clarence and Marie attended an Eastern Star housewarming party for Marguerite chapter's worthy matron and patron, Mr. and Mrs. Ray Gleason, and their daughter, Nancy. Guests showered them with food baskets, and the chapter gave them blue Tiffin glass bowls as a gift. It was a large gathering spent socializing.

Come the Friday evening of the next weekend, Marie attended an initiation meeting to see Patsy become a Tenderfoot Scout. In a year, she would be old enough to be a Brownie, and then later a Girl Scout. Several girls became Scouts. Janet Connet was one of them.

On Tuesday evening, December 19, Clarence and Marie attended the American Legion's annual Christmas dinner. It was potluck style with roasted turkey. Guests were asked to bring a pack of cigarettes for donation to the patients at the veteran's hospital in Portland. Back in 1921, their first national auxiliary president had started the network of hospitals to serve veterans, which today is part of the Veterans Administration.

The business meetings for the American Legion and its auxiliary were on the third Tuesday of each month and usually at the Masonic Lodge, normally with a potluck dinner and entertainment. Clarence, as a World War I veteran, was a member of Santiam Post 51. Marie was in its auxiliary, Santiam Unit 51.

The American Legion was a social support group for war veterans and for those on active military service and had started in 1919 as a national organization. Moreso, its members volunteered to help worthy causes. Their Lebanon unit was large, nearing one hundred members by 1945, and their post was likewise large in membership.

For the weekend of New Year's Eve, Marie's mother, Laura, came for a visit. Marie's nephew Jack, Laura's grandson, had been on an extended stay with Marie's parents. Laura brought Jack with her, and they stayed overnight.

Two days later, barely into the new year of 1945, the Marguerite chapter of the Eastern Star had their public installation ceremony on January 2. This year, Marie was installed as Esther, another point in the star. As Esther, Marie's color was white, characterized by humility. Diamond was her gem, and her flower was the white lily. Mrs. Clair Ford was installed as worthy matron and Mr. Frank Groves as worthy patron. Their chapter was large at over one hundred members. With guests and family members present, the ceremony room overflowed. Clarinet music and singing sweetened the formal affair's milieu. Dr. Booth's wife played the piano as each officer was installed. There was then a short business session for members only.

Afterward, members rejoined their guests and families waiting for them in the dining hall, which was decorated with New Year's figurines, greenery, and tiered candles in the five Eastern Star colors of red, blue, green, yellow, and white. Mrs. Ford received many gifts, including a lifetime membership from her husband. Marie and the other officers were given flowers.

Later that January, Marie won the prize for high score with her Bid-Away Bridge Club. Both Mrs. Floyd Connet and Mrs. Bert Connet were present, as were their newest members, Mrs. Weeks and Mrs. Simons. Mrs. Floyd Connet hosted this meeting.

On Tuesday evening, March 20, Marie attended Santiam Unit 51's meeting with the American Legion. They presented the post with a cake in honor of the birthday of its national organization. Clarence, though, wasn't at his post meeting. Nor was he with his bowling team, who met this same night. On this evening, Clarence escorted Peggy to a banquet dinner for the Future Craftsmen Club. Peggy and other club members, along with their employers and guests, totaled seventy people in attendance. The dinner was an annual event. Peggy had been a member since the start of the school year. At the end of the school year, she would be promoted from an apprentice helper with *The Lebanon Express* to an apprentice linotypist.

They heard from several speakers that evening, some from the school board and others from an apprentice council. The state director of vocational education was their keynote speaker. Music was included, with "America the Beautiful" as one song presented. Each apprentice student was named, and Peggy surely stood at her turn. They also observed a moment of silence in remembrance of three students who were absent due to military service. Following the closing remarks, someone sang "The Star-Spangled Banner."

ON APRIL 17, Clarence and Marie attended the American Legion. During their dinner hour, and before going into their post and unit meetings, a moment of silence was observed with bowed heads in memory of President Franklin Delano Roosevelt, who had passed away suddenly on April 12. Although the country was saddened by this loss, Marie found a moment of happiness.

Three days after President Roosevelt had died and two days before their American Legion meeting, Marie had become a grandmother. On Sunday, April 15, Betty and her husband, Andrew, had their first child, a boy. They called him Randy. Although Marie's first husband, Betty's biological father, was Randall, the namesake was only a coincidence. Betty and Andrew named their son after Andrew's late father, Randall James. Happiness was actually an understatement for Marie. She was ecstatic to be a grandmother. To her, it was a badge of honor.

Any plans for Marie to show her father that she was now a grandmother came at the most inopportune time. On April 19, only four days after her first grandchild was born, Marie went to Portland to visit her mother and see her father, who was in the hospital. He had been ill with complications from arterial blood clots and had just come out of an operation. A few days later, her father was sent home from the hospital, and Marie soon went home as well.

Only a few days later, Marie returned to Portland. If only she had given Patsy an early birthday party, as she had done two years before. This year, Clarence would be in charge of the birthday celebration for their youngest child. Her birthday fell on a Monday, but Marie must have figured that if her party was held a day or two early, Clarence would be home from work to tend to it. He would do fine on his own in hosting a party for her. Peggy surely wanted to help too, Marie reasoned. Anything that put her beside her dad, Peggy was happy to do.

Back at her parents' home, Marie kept close to her mother. Her father lay in bed, unable to find the energy to recover or to engage in any real conversation. There wasn't much she could say to her father. She wanted to let him know that her life was good and that he too had a good life, but words of this nature to him never came easy for Marie. She was one to show her father how her life was, not tell him. It had never been her place to tell her father anything. He had always expected her to respect his choices and opinions. Marie and her mother knew their place with him, and that was one of loyalty and reverence.

On Sunday, April 29, her father slipped out of consciousness. Harold Gosney was sixteen days shy of his seventy-sixth birthday. On the one-year wedding anniversary of Betty and Andrew and the day before Patsy's eleventh birthday, Marie's father died.

Chapter 6

— ❧ —

Going Places in Life
May 1945–June 1947

Marie had Clarence at her side for her father's funeral, held in Portland under the auspices of the Parkrose Masonic Lodge. His services were at Colonial Mortuary, and he was buried at the Lincoln Memorial Park cemetery on Tuesday, May 1, 1945. Harold Gosney's newspaper obituary gave a short account of his life and named those he'd left behind. His new great-grandson was not mentioned.

As Marie wrestled to make sense of her father's death, she focused on her commitments to the American Legion and the Eastern Star, not forgetting her meetings with the firemen's auxiliary and the card clubs. Marie likely attended Santiam Unit 51's first fall meeting on Tuesday evening, September 18, which followed their potluck dinner with the post. Mrs. Stanley Stewart, unit president, hosted this meeting in her home. They discussed committee work and their general goals for the coming year. For Christmas, the American Legion would send a fruitcake to each Lebanon family who still had a son in service overseas.

In October, Marie had an Eastern Star function. She went with several Marguerite chapter members to Portland for the

Grand Chapter Conference. They had an installation for incoming state officers in their two days of business sessions that began on October 1. This fifty-sixth annual event had been postponed by three and a half months due to wartime restrictions. More than seven hundred members from 146 Oregon chapters were in attendance.

In November, Marie's daughter Betty joined her as a guest at a Bid-Away Bridge Club meeting hosted by Mrs. Florence Connet. While Marie didn't earn a score prize, she nonetheless scored, taking home the floating prize.

During this last half of 1945, following her father's death and as she gave her attention to her memberships, World War II was also ending. Germany had surrendered in May, and the war officially ended in September. Servicemen, the sons and brothers and husbands of her friends, were finally coming home. For Marie, changes beset her. She could not stand by and watch. She also needed to step away, if only to pause and give serious thought to where her life was going.

In the first days of December, Marie did just that. Her mother, Laura, joined her for a two-week vacation. They went by car to California, where they visited Marie's younger brother, Frank, and his family. While Marie was gone, she trusted that her children were fine. Clarence was a good father.

However, the high school would lose their 1945–46 football quarterback when, in early December, Bill left school for the navy. He had turned eighteen years old in late November and enlisted soon after. While Marie and her mother were away, Bill went to Portland, from where, on December 4, the military sent him to the naval training base in San Diego, California.

When Marie came home, her mother returned home to Portland—but only to pack. They had decided that Laura would move into the cottage at Marie's home. It had been recently built, and Betty and her husband, Andrew, had lived in it while staying with them. They had since moved out and into an apartment with plans to build a house. The cottage sat empty. With Laura advancing in age and her husband, Marie's father, now gone, it was the right thing to do.

THE NEW YEAR OF 1946 dawned on Marie after her return home. With dedication, she was ready for the next step in her life, one without her father. She had events to attend and children to care for. Two of her children were still in school, with Peggy in high school.

In the grade schools, students had not only teachers to guide them but also the parent-teacher association. This organization, the PTA, had started in Lebanon in January of the year before. The group had been optimistic but saw a low turnout from parents in its first year. So, back in the fall of 1945, they laid plans to seek volunteers to serve as classroom mothers. Their duties could range widely, from fundraising for needed school supplies to hosting events. This aligned with the PTA's main focus of acquainting parents with teachers.

In January 1946, Marie was among the first to sign up to help with this goal set by the PTA. Patsy, her youngest, was in sixth grade at Queen Anne School, one of two grade schools in Lebanon. They accommodated grades one through eight, after which students proceeded into high school.

Two days after Marie's forty-second birthday, she was one of twenty-four mothers who attended the Lebanon PTA meeting, held at Queen Anne School. Room mothers were selected for both grade schools. Marie was elected as the Queen Anne room mothers president for a one-year term. Under Marie's leadership, the room mothers decided that Queen Anne's first fundraising project would be a bake sale so they could buy an outdoor drinking fountain.

The firemen's auxiliary and the Eastern Star also saw Marie in January. Mrs. Hazel McCracken played the piano for the Marguerite chapter's installation ceremony. Marie wasn't an officer this year, but she would be on several committees alongside Mrs. Vada Whetstone, Mrs. Kee Buchanon Groves, and Mrs. Ralph Scroggin, whom Marie now knew as Grace, along with other members. Mrs. Groves had retained her maiden name, Buchanon, when marrying Mr. Frank Groves, who had been their 1946 Eastern Star worthy patron.

A week before, Clarence and Marie had attended a fireman's banquet. It had been an annual event before the war, and now that wartime restrictions were lifted, they gathered together for the first time in several years. An invitation had been extended to the volunteer firemen and their wives, bringing the total in attendance to over two hundred people. One special guest was Mayor Peter Tweed, and their master of ceremonies was Mr. Jack Stolsig, whose wife often hosted meetings for the firemen's auxiliary. The banquet was held at the Church of Christ. Ladies from the church prepared their turkey dinner, and church girls served the meals. A high point of the banquet was the presentation of a huge home-baked cake in honor of Mayor Tweed's birthday. Brief speeches were then given, and a moving picture show followed.

The first of several PTA bake sales was on the first Saturday in February at Bob's Market. City folk still called it Ellis Meat Market, its prior name. As the room mothers sold their home-cooked casseroles and desserts, Marie explained, "Proceeds of the sale will be used to buy school equipment."

The PTA had their first anniversary in January and celebrated it on Tuesday evening, February 5—three days after their bake sale—which coincided with Founders' Day for the national PTA. The weather that day was fierce with rain and wind, yet they had an excellent turnout. As the Queen Anne room mothers president, Marie gave a business report with an account of their ongoing fundraisers and membership growth. The other room mothers president, that of Santiam School, also gave a report. In the entertainment portion, Marie played the piano.

As their bake sales continued, the proceeds purchased not only the drinking fountain but also a heating system for the school's gymnasium. Pleased with the enthusiasm from the room mothers, Marie thanked everyone involved, saying, "This active organization has been unusually good."

Meanwhile, playing cards with her Bid-Away Bridge Club wasn't something to miss. At a mid-February meeting, Marie was honored with a score prize. Their card tables were adorned with Valentines and red decorations.

On February 19, Marie and Clarence attended the American Legion meetings. Their post and unit welcomed members from out of town, honored past presidents, and installed newly elected officers. Marie was that year's finance chairman for Santiam Unit 51. As usual, dinner and entertainment were part of the evening. In commemoration of President's Day, each dining table was decorated with red, white, and blue candles. The place cards at each seat were paper hatchets to symbolize the story of President George Washington cutting down a cherry tree. Entertainment was given in part by the Junior Women's Club, who performed a skit. Group singing brought the meeting full circle.

Their next meeting with the American Legion was on March 17. This time, they were hosts to the Willamette Council of the American Legion, which comprised members from posts in Linn County and its neighboring counties. Lebanon Mayor Peter Tweed also attended. Their special guests were Gold Star Mothers—mothers of loved ones who died in action while serving in the war. This group, American Gold Star Mothers, continues to exist today, honoring anyone whose family member has died while in military service.

Oregon Governor Earl Snell was the keynote speaker for this American Legion meeting and informed attendees of the need for housing, education, and vocational opportunities for veterans. They also held an initiation ceremony for a record-breaking fifty-eight new members to their post. More than two hundred people in attendance were served during their dinner hour. After dinner, they enjoyed music performed by the Lebanon High School Band.

A few days later, also in March, Clarence and Peggy attended the annual banquet for the Future Craftsmen Club. There were currently twenty-four high school students in this trades and industry program. High expectations had been placed on these apprentices. Peggy wasn't one to let them down. She enjoyed her work with her dad and appreciated this opportunity.

On April 8, Marie represented her Queen Anne group with the Lebanon PTA at the Linn County PTA meeting held in Sweet Home. They held elections for county officers who would start their terms in September. For entertainment, the children in Sweet Home Grade School, also in Linn County, performed an orchestra piece.

The next day, Marie went with Mrs. Jack Stolsig, Mrs. Cal Edwards Jr., and her good friend Mrs. Grace Scroggin to a sewing class with the Singer Company in Salem. This was more of a good time with friends than any useful lesson. The homemaking duty of sewing wasn't in Marie's skillset to be honed, nor was it an enjoyable hobby for her. Marie most often turned to a store-bought suit rather than piecing together a dress with needle and thread.

After their Salem excursion, Marie attended her Bid-Away Bridge Club for an evening of cards and refreshments. Her oldest daughter, Betty, went with her as a guest, as she also liked to play bridge and often hosted informal card parties. Mrs. Florence Connet was their hostess.

In other news that week, Marie and Clarence received a letter from their son Bill. He had been home in February for a short furlough. In his letter, he said he was currently in Pearl Harbor of the Hawaiian Islands. The naval ship he was on would soon set sail for Shanghai, China. It was too soon to know when his next furlough would be, but he was doing well.

The Queen Anne room mothers had their last bake sale at the end of April. They had raised enough money to also buy a playground set for the younger children. Although already successful, Marie continued to encourage PTA participation. When she ran errands or visited people, she spoke up. The local newspaper reported her as saying, "All mothers of children who will be entering school for the first time next fall are especially invited to come and get acquainted with the mothers group."

Another fundraiser for the PTA was a series of card parties, sponsored by area businesses who awarded floating prizes. Their party on Friday evening, May 3, was their last event for the school year. It was held in the high school gymnasium, as that was the only place large enough to accommodate it. Seventeen tables of bridge and pinochle players enlivened this event. A trophy was given to the best player in the room. Some of the committee members that Marie had appointed for it were Mrs. Ed Thompson, Mrs. Don Childs, Mrs. Tom Gamblin, and Mrs. Norval Taylor. As Queen Anne room mothers president, Marie then chaired their last PTA meeting for the school year on Monday afternoon, May 13.

THE SUMMER MONTHS involved travel. In July, Betty's mother-in-law, Mrs. Jennie Peckham, came from Iowa to visit with her son's family. Jennie brought another grandson with her. Betty's son Randy, Marie's first grandchild, was now fifteen months old. In August, Marie went with Clarence to visit his brother Don, who still lived in Bend. It had been close to twenty years since Marie and Clarence had last been in Bend.

Come the new 1946–47 school year, meetings resumed for the Queen Anne room mothers. They held elections on October 3. New terms for elected officers would start in January. Overall, Marie's term as room mothers president for Queen Anne School was described by PTA members as an active and profitable season devoted to the cause of school improvement. Aside from elections, the upcoming November ballot was discussed, specifically a school fund measure that would be voted on. The room mothers asserted their active role to inform voters of its importance. They also decided to serve hot lunches to students on school days.

Although Marie's tenure as president would soon end, other opportunities with this organization would carry her forward. The Lebanon PTA, who oversaw the room mothers for both grade schools, had earlier elected her to be an officer. Unlike the room mothers, whose terms were from January to December, the Lebanon PTA officers served during the school year of September through May, same as the Linn County PTA officers. Marie was now the Lebanon PTA membership chairman, having taken office while serving the last few remaining months as Queen Anne room mothers president.

The American Legion met on October 15. Marie, as Santiam Unit 51 finance chairman, reported that 3,500 paper poppies were ordered from the Veterans Hospital in Portland and paid for. They would receive these in early May to commemorate Poppy Day. Their entertainment portion was provided in part by the high school's male quartet. Members also enjoyed moving pictures shown by the Mountain States Power Company.

While Marie had her social functions, her youngest daughter, Patsy, did as well. On Wednesday, the evening before Halloween, Patsy hosted a party with refreshments for eleven friends. All wore costumes, many as a witch or a ghost. Party favors and prizes were handed out.

In that same week, Marie's oldest daughter, Betty, became a member in the Wesleyan Service Guild of the Methodist church through a formal initiation ceremony. It was likened to when Betty was younger and in the girls' guild with the Baptist Church. She was also a member in the Junior Women's Club and helped in the leadership of a Girl Scout troop.

On Tuesday evening, November 19, the American Legion met for their monthly meeting and a holiday dinner. Thanksgiving would be on Thursday, November 28. Five years earlier, in 1941, it became a federally recognized holiday to be observed on the last Thursday in November each year. In her finance report, Marie stated that five dollars would be given to the community chest fund and ten dollars to the child welfare center in Roseburg for Christmas gifts. Marie also announced that they were still accepting donations for the Portland Veterans Hospital to help veterans buy Christmas gifts for their children. Another project was underway, an adopt-a-veteran program, for which Mrs. Opal Lyon would visit the Roseburg Veterans Hospital.

Marie's next function in November was with the Eastern Star. She went with several Marguerite chapter members to the Willamette Valley Matrons and Patrons Association meeting, composed of members in Willamette Valley to include Lebanon, Albany, and Corvallis. The Albany chapter hosted it.

On January 6, 1947, the Marguerite chapter held their installation ceremony, assisted by the Oregon grand chapter. Tapered candles and floral arrangements, all in shades of gold, lit up their ceremony. Piano music, a cornet solo, and songs by three high school girls filled the room. Marie was installed as organist. All the ladies who were installed wore matching peach gowns, trimmed with sequins. Their dresses were handmade by a member, Mrs. Lawrence Boots, who was a seamstress by trade. A group photograph was taken of all the officers and then later appeared in their local newspaper. Although it is a black-and-white picture, Marie's flaming red hair is unmistakable as she stands tall in the back row.

The love and care that Mrs. Boots had put into making their gowns is likewise unmistakable. Peach and other pale colors weren't typically in Marie's wardrobe. Left to her own choice in what to wear, Marie preferred dark colors so as to not clash with her red hair. Blue was Marie's favorite color. From cornflower blue to navy, all shades of blue pleased Marie. Yet Marie's wide smile in this picture shows her heartfelt appreciation for Mrs. Boots.

Marie would also serve on several committees in the social club with the Marguerite chapter. One was to oversee meeting arrangements. Their social club would meet each month on the third Friday with a potluck lunch. A series of benefit card parties was also scheduled, with a start date of January 20.

Monday, January 20, 1947, was Marie's forty-third birthday. She was the honored guest at a small card party and luncheon hosted by her daughter Betty. An arrangement of violets decorated two card tables for the party of eight. Marie's friends showered her with gifts as they whiled away the afternoon.

That evening, Marie forewent any family celebration. The first benefit card party, sponsored by the social club with her Eastern Star chapter, was about to begin. Mrs. Peggy Patchell, Mrs. Irene Ford, and Marie were event hostesses with Mrs. Gertrude Gleason, the event chairman. Some played pinochle, while Marie and others played bridge. If only out of the opportunity to play bridge, it could easily have been her favorite committee to be on.

Marie's daughter Betty soon hosted another card party, this time in late January and with the Junior Women's Club. Marie was one of two guests at this party. Their club also did philanthropic work, with recent donations going to the Children's Farm Home in Corvallis and to the Doernbecher Children's Hospital in Portland.

In the February PTA meeting, which was on the first Tuesday, discussion was introduced to send delegates to a seminar in Eugene in April. The state and national PTA were cooperatively offering a one-week course: "Problems in Family Life Education." Marie, as membership chairman, reported they had grown to 160 members, enough to send a few members to the seminar. In other business, Queen Anne room mothers announced that their first project was library book repairs. They finished their meeting with a musical program to celebrate the fiftieth anniversary of the national PTA. After a trombone piece was performed, Marie gave a piano solo in commemoration of Founders' Day.

On Friday, February 14, Santiam Unit 51 with the American Legion had a Valentine's Day game night. Their game nights were a monthly event, started the year before. Marie cohosted it in Mrs. Eva Stewart's home. Group singing added an extra dash of fun to their rounds of cards. World War I songs and barbershop harmonizing were their chosen tunes.

In the Eastern Star, the Marguerite chapter had a turkey dinner preceding their meeting on Monday, March 10. Special guests included a few grand chapter members who lived in Eugene and Albany. It was Religious Emphasis Week, a week set aside for spiritual growth that many groups, not just the Eastern Star, paid tribute to. Thus, they had a special speaker on this evening: Reverend Holly Jarvis. Mrs. Ruby Booth, Dr. Booth's wife, then sang two songs.

Toward the end of the week, on Thursday, March 13, the Willamette Valley Matrons and Patrons Association met. It was the Marguerite chapter's turn to host it. The Masonic Hall overflowed, with members from all over the Willamette Valley in attendance. After their business session, the Marguerite chapter presented a well-varied entertainment program, which began with two clarinet solos. Following a piano duet and then several songs by a quartet, Marie performed a humorous skit with Mrs. Ethan Hull and Mr. Ronald Gilson. The last portion of the entertainment was group games. They had outdone other chapters in their hosting duties.

Marie returned home from her Eastern Star meeting to greet an out-of-town guest. Her sister-in-law, Frank's wife, came to visit for a few days. It had been a year and a half since Marie and her mother, Laura, had traveled to California to see them. Also in March, Clarence and Peggy attended the annual banquet with the Future Craftsmen Club.

Marie's next Eastern Star event was only a week later, on Saturday, March 22. She went with Mrs. Hull, Mrs. Wilson, and Mrs. Vada Whetstone to Eugene for the Evangeline chapter's golden anniversary meeting. Four charter members from its inception fifty years earlier were the honored guests. A book of memoirs to detail their chapter's history was presented. It was an elaborate affair, complete with music.

Following this celebration, the Oregon PTA also had a golden jubilee. Inside the first week of May, Marie and six other Lebanon PTA members went to Portland to attend it. Their Lebanon group was one of only 26 out of 345 groups in Oregon awarded a superior rating certificate. Keynote speakers from across the country lectured on school education, health, world understanding, and parent-family life education.

On Saturday evening, May 10, the Santiam room mothers held a fundraiser at Lebanon High School. Marie was one of eight hostesses on a committee to oversee their buffet dinner. It was their last PTA social event for this school year and, for Marie, the last event with her serving as the PTA membership chairman, but other PTA events would resume in the fall.

In that same week, Marie also attended an Eastern Star function. Three members from the Marguerite chapter went with her to the Willamette Valley Matrons and Patrons Association meeting. The Woodburn chapter, located just north of Salem, hosted it.

Meanwhile, in early May, Clarence's bowling team scored honors in a tournament. The first-place winner had a high-scoring game. For second place, the competition was fierce. By just one pin and one point, Clarence came home grinning ear to ear, trophy in hand.

Marie's daughter Betty was also engaged in memberships. She was installed as historian with the Junior Women's Club during the following week. Marie and Mrs. Dorothy Page played the piano together as all the incoming officers were installed. Mrs. Page's husband had been Bill's high school football coach. Betty was quite active in this group and had recently hosted a musical tea program in which both high school and kindergarten students performed.

MERE DAYS LATER, the poppies arrived that Marie had reported on back in the October meeting with Santiam Unit 51. Mrs. Norman Ramsey of the Poppy Committee with the American Legion explained, "They are replicas of the wild poppies which grow in France and Belgium where so many of the battles of both wars were fought."

Disabled veterans had used crepe paper to make the delicate little red flowers. Each one symbolized the memory of someone who had died for America on land, at sea, or in the air. The Poppy Program started in 1924 and has continued to this day, with Poppy Day in May each year. Each poppy brings in a donation to help fund the many programs they give to. The group unpacked and counted the poppies to distribute them to wear on May 23 and 24.

Officer elections were held at their meeting on May 20. Mrs. Opal Lyon would be Santiam Unit 51 president. Marie and three other members—Mrs. Vada Whetstone, Mrs. Myrtle Cray, and Mrs. Willa Huston, who were also in the PTA—were delegated to attend their state convention with Mrs. Lyon in Portland that June. Mrs. Whetstone's husband, Mr. Elmer Whetstone, would be one of four men serving as delegates from Santiam Post 51. In all, nine would go.

June was a busy month with the American Legion, starting with Lebanon's annual Strawberry Festival. The American Legion and the Veterans of Foreign Wars jointly developed and administered all events for it. Then, their monthly meeting and dinner was on June 17. Lastly, their state convention was June 26 through 29.

The Strawberry Festival was a three-day event that began on Thursday, June 5. Clarence had arranged for the newspaper to go to print early, allowing him to accommodate his schedule around it. Marie was the chairman of the committee that had promoted its centennial tickets.

A historical pageant, "Lebanon's One Hundred Years," kicked off the festivities on Thursday evening. More than three hundred high school students were in its cast of characters. Mrs. Kee Buchanan Groves, a member of Santiam Unit 51 and the Eastern Star, wrote and directed this play. A large canvas mural served as the backdrop on the stage. The mural, created by high school art students, pictured the Cascades Range in the background, with the lower foothill country of Lebanon in the foreground and a miniature pioneer settlement at its base.

A coronation ceremony was held after the pageant in which Governor Earl Snell crowned their Strawberry Queen. She led their parade on Friday, after which the world's biggest shortcake, as the Lebanon folk claimed it to be, was cut and served. Undeniably, the shortcake was big, weighing in at five thousand pounds in the back of a flatbed truck. A carnival, a horse show, and an air show by local pilots added to the festival weekend. The tickets, which Marie had helped promote, were priced at fifty cents per child's ticket and up to a dollar and a half for an adult ticket. The proceeds helped Lebanon's community aid fund.

A recap of the Strawberry Festival was given at their meeting on June 17. The state commander, who was also in attendance, thanked the post for the committee work done by the unit. He said, "Marie worked very hard and long in putting over the sale."

Their three-day state convention was at the Portland Masonic Temple. On their first evening, they held elections but first determined who was eligible to serve. As their business proceeded through the weekend, topics were anything but light.

For one, a bitter floor fight broke out when delegates turned down a resolution that would have extended the deadline by which a man might have enlisted and still been eligible to be a legion member. In another heated subject, Reverend George Bailey was met with sharp criticism when he gave a speech purporting that communists were atheists and then threatened all godless people with the atomic bomb. In further explanation, he told of how fascism could be traced to its opposition: religion. He lastly warned against class and racial hatred. The national commander of the Military Order of the Purple Heart, who was present, sided with Reverend Bailey by urging the elimination of United States communism. Rounding out heavy talks, another speaker sparked discussion on how comic strips, moving pictures, and radio programs, all of which showed violence, contributed to juvenile delinquency.

Delegates brought forth some business to the state officers. They asked that member dues be waived for those on active duty with the armed forces, which was approved. In other matters, a scholarship fund for an Oregon veteran's orphan was considered, voted on, and passed. Consideration was also given to allotting money toward the Child Welfare Program and to sponsoring a member in their presidency candidacy for the American Legion's national level.

Their final session was on Saturday with an installation for incoming state officers. Mrs. Vada Whetstone was elected to be their national committeewoman. Mrs. Craig Coyner, who was from Bend where Marie grew up, was installed as state auxiliary president. Awards were also presented to those who had excelled in committee work with their post or unit. The drum corps from the Corvallis unit performed as their convention adjourned.

Convention-goers who had debated the heated discussions or who had received an earful from Reverend Bailey gained insight to bring back to their post or unit. Clarence supported Marie in all she did and in all that she was involved with. This convention, though, could have been a bit much for Marie, who wasn't the zealous type where religious matters were concerned.

Her belief in God was as simple as it could get: Same as the sky was blue and the sun would rise each day, so too would God always be God. In this simplicity, she wasn't one to proselytize or to question anyone's religious stance. Nor was she one to treat someone differently who was racially different. She recalled that as a little girl, Indians had lived in their Oklahoma and Kansas towns, whereas in these parts of Oregon, it was rare for her to see anyone who wasn't white. There was a Navajo community nearby, but they lived on a reservation and not in the city. She knew what it was like to be different in that she often received unwanted attention for her red hair, however kind the remarks were meant to be.

Arriving home from the convention, her family was a breath of fresh air for her. It was Sunday, and many people were at church. Marie's church preference was Lebanon's First Christian Church. However, Marie and her family didn't regularly attend, nor were they on any committees or actively involved with this or any church. While Marie and Clarence occasionally attended Sunday functions with the American Legion and other groups, Sunday was their family day. It was when they reconnected with each other in gratitude for their many blessings. Marie's youngest daughter, Patsy, had turned thirteen years old back in April, and this summer, in between school years, she was helping Clarence at his newspaper job alongside Peggy. Sundays were a day off from work for all of them.

Marie's son Bill was also home. He had arrived in early June on a forty-one-day furlough from the navy, with his tour in China over. She hadn't had much time with him. Now, she was free for a day to visit with him. Soon she would be in the midst of another full week, with another card party, a meeting with the firemen's auxiliary, and yes, time with her daughter Betty, who vied for her attention as she neared the due date for her second baby to be born. Marie would soon welcome her second grandchild into this world.

Chapter 7

— ❀ —

Faces and Places in Life
July 1947–August 1948

Katherine Marie Peckham was born on Wednesday, July 23, 1947. Her arrival was the perfect birthday gift for her great-grandmother, Laura, whose seventy-seventh birthday was on this same day. Katherine's older brother, Betty's first child, was two years old. Marie had been quite proud when her first grandchild, Randy, was born. There can only be one first grandchild. While Marie was happy to be a grandmother again, it was Clarence who strutted with glee over the dainty eight-pound confection, which was how he described her. Their daughter Betty took in all the gloating that she could as she introduced her new baby, bundled in pink, to family and friends.

Marie was in the midst of a busy month when her new grandchild arrived. She had attended the firemen's auxiliary July meeting and the Bid-Away Bridge Club twice already that month. Although the Eastern Star didn't meet during the summer, the American Legion still did, with their summer picnic at nearby Bates Park the weekend before, on Sunday, July 20. Their auxiliary's district president for the American Legion and her husband, the area vice commander, who lived in Springfield, came as guests to this picnic.

They had a short business meeting with a report given about their recent attendance at the state convention. Mrs. Opal Lyon, Santiam Unit 51 president, also announced her choices for incoming committee chairmen. Much of the day, though, was spent in recreational activities of swimming, horseshoe games, an ice cream social, and then a baseball game for the men.

Aside from Marie's new grandchild, another person would join their family. Marie's oldest son, Dick, got married in August. He had been living in an apartment in town and working odd jobs, currently as a laborer with the Silver Wheel Freight Company. He was twenty-three years old, going on twenty-four, and without much of a path in his life. He wasn't like Marie's other son. Marie could hope that by Dick taking on a wife, he would get his life right.

His bride, Lillian Folsom, lived in Lebanon with her mother and brother. She had grown up in Texarkana, Texas, where her father still lived. Before moving to Lebanon from Texas, she had finished high school and then attended business school. Most recently, she had been discharged after serving in the Women's Army Corps.

They had a small private wedding in Clarence and Marie's home with Lillian's mother and brother with them. It was Saturday afternoon, August 23, and a warm and sultry day at that. Their ceremony was in the living room, with Marie dressed in a green suit and at her piano. Yellow and white roses and tall white taper candles decorated the fireplace mantel, with a bowl of small pink roses on each end.

Lillian wore a pale-blue rayon organdy gown and held a bouquet of yellow rosebuds and bouvardia. Marie played the wedding march as Lillian's brother escorted her to the fireplace. Her maid of honor, a friend, stood by the mantel with a bouquet of pink lilies and blue ageratum in her hands. Dick waited at the fireplace for Lillian with his best man, Andrew, Betty's husband. Reverend Holly Jarvis officiated their vows. He had been the guest speaker during Religious Emphasis Week at Marie's Eastern Star meeting back in March.

A traditional tiered wedding cake, adorned with bride and groom figurines, was the focal point of their reception. Peggy and Patsy served the refreshments and kept punch glasses filled. Ice cream was also offered, which cooled their palates on this summer day. Dick and Lillian soon left for a honeymoon in Portland and had intentions to live in Lebanon.

Bill wasn't at his brother Dick's wedding, nor was he around when his niece, Katherine, was born. He had returned to his naval base in San Francisco. Aside from his tour in China and before his last furlough home, he had also been stationed in the Marshall Islands, a territory about halfway between Australia and Hawaii. His tours were completed, and he had served for almost two years. He would be honorably discharged in September to return home.

ON SEPTEMBER 16, the American Legion met, this time in a newly built American Legion hall, whereas before they usually met at the Masonic Lodge. They had a dedication ceremony for their new building, an installation for incoming post officers, and a discussion regarding a membership drive. Dinner duties for that year's Christmas party were also hashed out.

The Eastern Star also met in September, with the Marguerite chapter's social club resuming their monthly benefit card parties. In September, they met at Mrs. Gertrude Gleason's home. In October, their card parties returned to their regular meeting place at the Masonic Lodge, where on Wednesday, October 8, Marie was their hostess.

At the November 18 American Legion meeting, members discussed their upcoming Christmas party and how they would also help veterans. Marie, as Santiam Unit 51 finance chairman, asked that anyone attending bring a white elephant gift—that is, a gently used item that another member would appreciate—for their gift exchange. She also announced that they would have Santa and a tree at their Christmas party. In addition, a collection was started in which donated unwrapped presents would be given to the gift shop at the Veterans Hospital in Portland, which the gift shop would then wrap. Many posts and units in Oregon were contributing to this cause. They hoped for enough gifts to be received so that each veteran could choose a gift for each family member. Their unit was also helping a Lebanon family whose husband and father was sick and unable to work. They packed a Thanksgiving box for them.

It was a well-attended meeting, with many new members initiated and several visitors. Their recent past district auxiliary president, Mrs. Violet Larsen, who Marie had met at their summer picnic, accompanied by their current district auxiliary president, Mrs. Violet Updike, who lived in Toledo, were among the distinguished guests. Yes, like Marie, they both had the first name of Violet, although few people if any knew that Marie went by her middle name. Mrs. Updike gifted the unit with a symbolic handkerchief, commending them for their work. Their district had placed third in the state for membership, and the Santiam unit had helped make this happen. In response, they gave Mrs. Updike and Mrs. Larsen corsages, each made with a homegrown chrysanthemum.

The American Legion ended the year 1947 with their Christmas party on December 16, setting business aside. Clarence and Marie were among the 150 people served a turkey dinner. After dinner, they joined in together to sing Christmas carols, and Santa visited for their gift exchange. Lights were then dimmed as members danced by the glow of a tall lit Christmas tree.

Another Christmas celebration for Clarence and Marie was the arrival of her brother Frank and his family. Marie's youngest daughter, Patsy, reveled in the playtime to be had with her cousin Jack. Their family visited for a full week, through Christmas.

Clarence and Marie rang in the new year of 1948 as guests at a New Year's Day wedding. The bookkeeper at *The Lebanon Express*, Miss Betty Holm, was getting married. It was a large church wedding in the nearby city of Silverton. A Christmas tree flanked by candles stood tall in the sanctuary and added festivity to their religious ceremony. At the reception afterward, there was much mingling to do. Guests had come from all over the Willamette Valley. Several staff members from *The Lebanon Express*, as well as Peggy, Patsy, and Betty and her husband, Andrew, also attended the event.

Inside the next week, the first week of January, Marie attended the Lebanon PTA meeting. Although she wasn't an officer this school year, she remained quite active, serving on committees. More than sixty parents and teachers attended this Tuesday evening, January 6 meeting, held at Santiam School. An associate professor of psychology from the University of Oregon was their keynote speaker. He lectured on social hygiene, and a film, *Human Growth*, was shown. A discussion followed on the probability of teaching social hygiene in the public schools and at what age it should begin. It was a well-received agenda, but Marie looked forward to their February speaker.

At the start of the second week of January, Marie had an Eastern Star function. On Monday evening, January 12, the Marguerite chapter held a public installation for officers. Mrs. Berneice Duncan would be their worthy matron. Marie had been elected to be the warder, and Mr. Ronald Gilson to be the sentinel. Mr. Gilson had been in the skit that Marie performed back in March when their chapter had hosted the meeting for the Willamette Valley Matrons and Patrons Association. During regular meetings, the warder sat next to the door, on the inside of the meeting room, whereas the sentinel sat just on the other side of the door. Their job was to guard the meeting room.

The International Order of the Rainbow for Girls, a Masonic-related and fraternal organization, assisted in the ceremony. Two girls lit candles, which then gleamed among the greenery for their ceremonial rites. Three other girls sang a song in harmony with one another. A piano solo and another song presentation were also performed. Afterward, refreshments were served in the dining room. Each dining table was decorated with a miniature flower garden.

Early in the third week of the month, Marie had her birthday on Tuesday, January 20. She was forty-four years old and was becoming the worthy woman that she had set out to be when they first arrived in Lebanon years earlier. When her father died in 1945, she didn't stop her leadership or other civic roles. Rather, she was diligent in her work to show that as a woman, she could make a positive difference. And still, on this birthday, she knew there were more things to do. She was active in the Bid-Away Bridge Club, the firemen's auxiliary, and other organizations. Through these groups, she found encouragement from friends.

Her family life was likewise quite good. Bill lived at home now and helped Clarence at his newspaper job. He had turned twenty years old in November, celebrating it with friends on a weekend ski trip to the Hoodoo Bowl recreation area. As for her other son, Dick, well, she wished him well in his new marriage.

All her daughters pleased her. Betty was an adult and married, with two grandchildren for her. Peggy had turned eighteen years old in November, was in her last year of high school, and, according to school officials, was proceeding well in her apprenticeship. Patsy, her youngest child, was active in the Rainbow Girls.

Clarence was a fine husband and father. There was more to him than she had known when she married him. Back then, as an abandoned wife with two little children, she had only done what she knew she had to do for the sakes of Dick and Betty. As their family grew, she found that Clarence was the best loving man she could have ever dreamed of. He was there for the children when she was busy with her membership activities.

ON TUESDAY EVENING, February 3, Marie attended the monthly PTA meeting, where they had two guest speakers, the second of whom Marie was eager to hear from. It was Mr. A. A. Dodds, the coordinator for the Future Craftsmen Club that Peggy was a member of. He spoke of the increasing number of students seeking apprenticeships and said that more local firms were needed to support this trades and industry program. Mr. Dodds pointed out that all students currently in this club were maintaining high grades in their classes. Before closing, a brief service commemorated the fifty-first anniversary of the national PTA organization. Marie then helped on the Refreshments Committee, greeting attendees.

Marie also had an Eastern Star event in February, in which she again hosted a card party with their social club. In their business session, a decision was made to sponsor a series of lectures by Mr. Sam Gordon, a bridge expert, on March 25, 26, and 27. They would sell tickets to the lectures to raise money for charitable donations, with Marie as the event chairman. After their luncheon, they spent the rest of the afternoon playing cards.

On Thursday afternoon, February 12, Clarence was called away from work, as was Mr. Robert Penland, the newspaper's business manager. As volunteer firemen, they were needed at the home of an elderly couple, Mr. and Mrs. Campbell. They arrived on scene to find the house ablaze with flames that extended above the roof through the ground-floor windows. The nearest fire hydrant was dry, which proved to be a problem. It took them two hours to smother the flames and seal the roof.

Mr. Campbell had been in their backyard, and his wife away from home, when the fire started. They were safe from harm, but they lost all their possessions. Situations such as this were why Marie helped in philanthropic projects through the American Legion. She felt for their homeless predicament and was compelled to help more with worthy causes.

Lebanon's Red Cross fund drive was held in March each year. The money raised would help people who experienced loss from a fire, flood, or other calamity. Mr. Regis Foss was the Red Cross general chairman for their 1948 fund drive. He organized three teams to canvas Lebanon and appointed a chairman to each. One person was to head the business district, another one the industrial district, and Marie was to be the residential district chairman.

Their five-day fund drive netted over $4,300. It was little more than their $4,200 quota but much greater than the $3,300 raised in the prior year. The Red Cross Linn County executive secretary, Mrs. Virginia Faulkner, made an announcement to those who helped: "It takes a high place in state achievement records for this year. A very fine response by residents of the area and business and industrial concerns is reflected in my final report."

They had topped all other communities in Linn County. In response, Mr. Foss thanked his chairmen when he said, "It is impossible to personally thank the many who worked individually and in teams to make this drive so successful."

Marie must have felt a sense of accomplishment as Mr. Foss continued, "Lebanon's standing in the county and the state may well be a source of pride to these workers and to the individuals who so generously contributed funds to the cause."

On Thursday evening, March 11, Marie attended an Eastern Star event. She went with Mrs. Vada Whetstone and a few other Marguerite chapter members to the Willamette Valley Matrons and Patrons Association installation ceremony. The chapter in Jefferson, close to Salem, hosted it. Mrs. Berneice Duncan, the Marguerite chapter's worthy matron, was installed as vice president.

The March PTA meeting was mostly all business. Marie listened to hear that the room mothers had followed the example she had set in its first year of existence. Where Marie had once organized bake sales to fund the drinking fountain, the gymnasium heating system, and then the playground set, this year's room mothers were also raising money and making changes. Proceeds from rummage sales purchased band uniforms for high school students, a radio phonograph for Santiam School, and a still film library collection for Queen Anne School.

Come the April meeting for the PTA, officer elections were held, and Marie's committee work during that school year showed that she was a viable candidate. Marie's next commitment to the Lebanon PTA would be as their president for the 1948–49 school year. More than seventy voting members had elected her. The other officers elected were Mrs. Willa Huston as vice president, Mrs. Marie Chilcote as secretary, and Mrs. Alice Howard as treasurer.

ON FRIDAY AND SATURDAY night, April 16 and 17, the Veterans of Foreign Wars hosted a musical stage show, *Fun For You*, in the auditorium at Lebanon High School. Earlier that week, an article appeared in the local newspaper to let people know more about it. In it, the Veterans of Foreign Wars, or VFW as this civic group was commonly called, announced that awards would also be handed out. They asked for people to write letters to the VFW to name their favorite neighbor.

Marie attended the Saturday night show, and Clarence perhaps went with her. It featured local talent who impersonated radio stars. Television wasn't yet available for most of Oregon, but Portland was in a testing phase, with the promise that all Oregon residents would have television within a few years. Until then, aside from an occasional outing to the cinema, people were entertained by the radio. Family time often meant gathering together for a radio program to be immersed with drama, stories, and music from Bob Hope, Bing Crosby, Jack Benny, Jimmy Durante, Minnie Pearl, and other celebrities.

This VFW show brought laughter and enjoyment out of the sound box of radio to offer it live on stage to the audience. A skit with a barn scene and square dancing was one act. Prominent businessmen likewise entertained the audience with a burlesque show, impersonating Betty Grable, Lana Turner, Mae West, and Gypsy Rose Lee in a Hollywood breakfast scene. And the VFW even had someone dressed up as Frank Sinatra—he sang as best as he could, but he couldn't compete with this incredibly famous and talented singer and actor.

Midway through their show, awards were announced, as promised. Of these, a bouquet of orchids was given to the oldest lady in the audience, Mrs. George Gerhardt. In fun, one lady was recognized for having the goofiest hat. For the Good Neighbor Award, Lebanon residents had voted well: Marie received this award.

At the start of the new week, the Red Cross held their state conference for representatives and disaster workers on April 19 and 20. Marie must have felt that she could easily help the Red Cross with any other events they had planned. She attended the conference with Mrs. Virginia Faulkner, the Linn County executive secretary, who lived in Albany. At this conference, the Red Cross adopted a resolution to inform local governments of proper procedures and facilities available in case of a disaster. Little did they know then how valuable this information would soon become.

The PTA state convention was a week later, in Klamath Falls. Marie was one of four Lebanon delegates who attended this three-day assembly that began on April 26. The other three delegates were Mrs. Frank Wells, Mrs. Kenneth Clark, and Marie's incoming vice president for the next school year, Mrs. Willa Huston. The Linn County PTA president, Mrs. Mary Herron, went with them. In all, 460 delegates representing 270 PTA units in Oregon attended the convention.

Marie and the other delegates had several business sessions and heard from many speakers. One issue up for discussion was making voting privileges on school matters available to all Oregon citizens, whether or not they were property owners. They also emphasized how technological development and accrual of material things were focal in the need to bring about the well-being of all people, with the family unit as the basis for the promotion of this objective. A banquet on Wednesday evening gave them a social hour to unwind.

April had been a busy month for Marie with both the PTA and the Red Cross. Her daughters each had accomplishments and celebrations in April as well. Betty was general chairman for a "Style Revue Show" with the Junior Women's Club. The event was a modeling exhibition sponsored by local merchants in which Betty oversaw all arrangements, including music by Mrs. Dorothy Page. For her three-year-old son, Randy, she hosted a birthday party with eight neighborhood children. Peggy, who not only bowled but did competitive roller-skating, became the Lebanon Skate Club Secretary. In her bowling league, she was the high scorer in the women's division. And young Patsy would have her fourteenth birthday at the end of April.

With all the celebrations and achievements to be enjoyed in April, Marie's father, who had passed away three years ago this month, was not in the limelight. And yet, if only he could have seen Marie now. She and her daughters were well accomplished in all they set out to do.

ON FRIDAY, MAY 7, Marie hosted a birthday party for a friend, Mrs. Genevieve Hatfield. Genevieve's friends called her Peggy, her nickname, and she would become one of Marie's best friends. Marie decorated for this party using spring flowers and added a floral centerpiece to their luncheon table. She invited several ladies: Mrs. Virginia Faulkner from Albany; Mrs. Madge Mote of Cottage Grove; and Mrs. Leonard Wood, Mrs. E. H. Jacobson, and Mrs. Caton, who all lived in Lebanon. Marie's mother, Laura, and Peggy's mother also took part in the celebration.

The American Legion celebrated Poppy Day on Friday and Saturday of Memorial Day weekend, May 28 and 29, with a proclamation by Mayor Tweed. As in years before, the auxiliary had received the handmade paper flowers earlier in May from those in the Veterans Hospital in Portland. Marie assisted in the work done by Santiam Unit 51 for Poppy Day. However, Marie wouldn't be with Lebanon folk on Memorial Day weekend.

On May 26, Clarence's father passed away. His funeral would be on Tuesday, June 1. That Saturday, May 29, Clarence and Marie drove to Portland under heavy rain. Oregon was experiencing high rainfall this year. Throughout May, newspapers all over Oregon and parts of Washington and Idaho reported the ongoing struggle to add sandbags to floodwalls. Despite the terrible weather to drive through, Clarence had to be with his family during this loss. Close to Portland, another sadness was taking place on this holiday weekend.

The resolution that the Red Cross had adopted in the state conference in April proved its importance come the end of Memorial Day weekend. Rain fell so hard on Portland's neighboring city of Vanport that it was wiped out. Internationally, it came to be known as the Vanport Flood.

Vanport was just northwest of Portland and on the banks of the Columbia River. At the height of World War II, more than forty thousand people, many of whom were Black, had come to Oregon to work in the Portland shipyards. Public housing developments were quickly built for these workers and their families in a 648-acre complex named Vanport. It was the country's largest public housing project and Oregon's second largest city. After the war, some Vanport residents left Oregon. Coinciding with their departure, some war veterans settled in Vanport to use their G. I. Bill money at Vanport College.

Many residents stayed when the war ended, although shipyard work was limited. They thought there was no other place in Oregon for them to go where they would be welcomed. The Ku Klux Klan, which had been especially active in the 1920s and 1930s, had contributed to this prejudice. Oregon's prohibition of Black residents had recently ended; however, redlining limited where they could live. Homeownership and voting weren't included in their legal rights. Oregon remained a predominantly white state.

Vanport had been a city much larger than Lebanon. Its dams and dikes failed under the heavy rainfall. Schools were among the first buildings washed away. Soon, all else was swept up in rushing floodwaters. Community aid from all over Oregon crossed segregation boundaries to rescue them. Portland coordinated with local organizations and the Red Cross to feed, house, and give medical care to these residents.

Only a couple of days after returning home from his father's funeral, Clarence boarded a small commuter plane in Lebanon with Peggy on Friday, June 4. Their trip took them over Vanport to see its flood devastation. From their aerial view, they gained a better understanding of this disaster. Marie's committee work with both the Red Cross and the American Legion helped ease the loss borne by Vanport families.

On Monday, June 28, the Linn County Red Cross had its annual banquet at the Lebanon Presbyterian Church. Mr. Richard Gordan, disaster speaker for the Pacific area of the Red Cross, was their guest speaker, and it was open to the public. He gave an in-depth talk on the rehabilitation efforts and relief work that the Red Cross was extending to aid in the Vanport Flood. Reverend Holly Jarvis, who had officiated Dick's wedding vows, gave an invocation. Marie played the piano for their dinner music.

Even though the heavy downpour of rain had let up, the summer unfolded as a wet one. Yet the rain didn't stop people from gathering together. In the first week of July, Betty hosted a bridal shower in her home for one of her friends, with Marie as the cohost. Pink hues filled the party scene, and under a pink-and-white parasol, a table bore many gifts. Betty was thankful for her mom's help, and Marie glowed in this social time.

There were two more parties in July to be enjoyed. One was for Marie's granddaughter and the other for her mother, both to celebrate their birthdays. On Friday, July 23, Betty hosted a party for sixteen little boys and girls. She had made a cake, iced it, and added one candle to the top of it. The party was in honor of her daughter Katherine—or Kathi, as family and friends called her. So as not to impose on Kathi's special day, the next party was on Monday,

July 26. It was a surprise birthday party for Marie's mother, Laura. Betty hosted this party as well.

Before the summer ended, Marie again enjoyed fellowship with American Legion members Mrs. Violet Larsen and Mrs. Violet Updike, as well as with Mrs. Coyner from Bend. On Monday evening, August 23, the Albany and Sweet Home units cohosted Santiam Unit 51's meeting to honor an official visit from Mrs. Coyner, their state auxiliary president. An interesting talk was given to describe how their work in the Poppy Program and other commitments helped veterans, all in the true spirit of Americanism—one of the three principles of their organization.

As Marie was happy to be a part of birthday celebrations, she also enjoyed the fellowship in the organizations that she was a member of, such as the gathering with American Legion members. Only a week later, the new school year would begin, and with that, the start of her PTA presidency. She had countless events to look forward to.

Chapter 8

— ❀ —

To Follow Life's Lead
September 1948–May 1949

Marie stood poised and sported a houndstooth dress with an ascot scarf that flowed and dropped perfectly just below her neckline. Her polite smile, accentuated by red lipstick with rounded corners, conveyed a benevolent charm as she welcomed guests to a teacher's reception on Thursday evening, September 16. Parents and PTA members showed up in a record-breaking attendance to meet sixty-three teachers in the south wing of Lebanon High School. Parents were handed name tags to pin on their suit jackets, and teachers wore corsages.

Marie greeted each person as they walked in, and the total in attendance numbered more than two hundred. Once everyone was seated comfortably in the high school's Little Theater, Marie stepped up to the podium and introduced herself as the 1948–49 PTA president. Her attentive audience listened as she next introduced the superintendent of the Lebanon schools, Mr. James King.

Mr. King's speech emphasized the student population growth. They now had 950 grade school students, up from the previous year's 622. The high school was no exception in that it had increased to 1,620 students. He also gave mention to Green Acres School, which would soon open. With an expressed appreciation for all that the PTA was doing, Mr. King recognized that they had their hands full. In all plausibility, Marie held her head high and nodded with a can-do attitude.

It was a tall order, but she had successfully led a Red Cross fund drive as residential chairman and had managed the unit's finances with the American Legion. She was accustomed to organizing events and assuming responsibilities. She knew that this PTA presidential term would experience many firsts in their membership pool. They now had room mother presidents not only in the two grade schools but also in the high school, along with a greater number of committees and chairman positions. And, as Mr. King had said, another grade school would open later that school year, which meant even more room mothers for Marie and her officers to lead. She knew she could lead the PTA. If only her father could also have known that.

Mr. King concluded his speech and then presented the four school principals, three for the grade schools and one for the high school, who then in turn named their teachers. A musical ensemble with songs and piano music followed. Lastly, a skit was given as a prelude to an upcoming high school show, which would have an all-boys cast. The assembly was dismissed for refreshments to be served in the cafeteria. Marie then made the rounds to get to know everyone she could and say her hellos to those she already knew.

The teacher's reception was but one of many PTA functions for Marie in her first few weeks of presidency. On Monday, August 30, she had met with her officers—Mrs. Willa Huston, Mrs. Marie Chilcote, and Mrs. Alice Howard—scheduling their first regular PTA meeting for October 5. Students would return to school that first week of September.

The day after her officers' meeting, on Tuesday, August 31, Marie had attended the Linn County PTA convention, which had met under the direction of the Oregon PTA. This event was an all-day affair and was presided over by Mrs. Mary Herron, Linn County

PTA president. Aside from meetings for members and officers, which were full of excitement and discussion for upcoming school events countywide, they had heard from several speakers. Mrs. H. H. Hargraves, Oregon PTA president, had stressed in her speech that an important PTA policy was non-interference in school administration. "Make the teacher a part of community social life," she said.

Although busy with the PTA that month, Marie didn't slide on her other commitments, even when an event was on her wedding anniversary. Inside the very next week, the American Legion met on Tuesday evening, September 21, for an installation of officers. Mrs. Kee Buchanon Groves was installed as Santiam Unit 51 president, with the vice presidency going to Mrs. Willa Huston, Marie's PTA vice president.

Two days later, Marie had a social function with the Red Cross. The Riverside Sewing Circle met on Thursday, September 23, to celebrate their anniversary. They were the oldest sewing unit in Linn County, having sewn for the Red Cross and other charities for twenty-seven years. They invited four special guests, all from the Linn County Red Cross, to their potluck dinner in Mrs. Leonard Simons's home. Marie, who was now serving as Linn County membership chairman, attended. Mrs. Virginia Faulkner, Mrs. Peggy Hatfield, and Mrs. Ella Wood were the other three who were invited to share in their celebration.

Many ladies chose to don a floral print dress for this happy occasion. As one of the honored guests, Marie chose a dark three-piece suit. Mrs. Faulkner, Mrs. Hatfield, Mrs. Wood, and Marie presented the group with an attractively decorated anniversary cake. A picture was taken of Marie with three charter members, which later appeared in *The Lebanon Express*.

When Marie chaired the PTA meeting on October 5, she appointed chairpersons for new committees. Superintendent James King was present, who initiated discussion of the November elections. Like the year before, an important measure would be on the ballot—this time for an amendment to allow all voters, regardless of property ownership, to be able to cast ballots on all financial measures. Marie informed the room mothers that they had to encourage everyone to vote. It was furthermore decided that this year's school census would be linked to PTA objectives, which would show that the forthcoming legislation was vital to school operations. Before departing, they had a social hour with refreshments to greet many new members to their first meeting.

On Tuesday, October 19, the American Legion had their monthly dinner meeting. While officers had been installed back in September, committee chairpersons were selected on this night. Marie would be the May 1949 Poppy Committee chairman. It was then voted on and passed to order three thousand poppies. In other business, it was decided they would do as they had done before at Christmas: give gifts to the Veterans Hospital in Portland.

The next PTA meeting was on the first day of November. However, Marie had been admitted to Emanuel Hospital in Portland at the end of October. Clarence was at her side on the first day of her stay, then returned home until she was ready for release. A five-day treatment began for her on Wednesday, October 27. Documentation surrounding Marie's health situation is nearly nonexistent due to privacy laws in place today.

To know that she was treated in Portland and not in Lebanon isn't alarming. The hospital in Lebanon was quite small and lacked any modern amenities, from oxygen masks to blood storage. Other than for minor ailments or injuries, or for an immediate emergency, people were routinely referred to seek treatment in Albany or elsewhere.

Marie returned home from Emanuel Hospital to recover and then was admitted for an overnight stay at the hospital in Lebanon on November 11. Thereafter, information isn't available that uncovers other details. And in her older years, she didn't reveal that she had traveled to Portland for medical treatment. We must presume that Marie made a full recovery that didn't impede her in any way.

In Marie's absence from the November PTA meeting, Mrs. Willa Huston, PTA vice president, presided over their business session. The Hospitality Committee did their utmost to assist Mrs. Huston and to greet members and guests. The superintendent of the Eugene public schools had already been scheduled to speak at this meeting, and he gave a fine presentation on the talent of qualified teachers.

Marie didn't host the December PTA meeting either, although she was present and oversaw the business proceedings. Traditionally, fathers who were PTA members hosted their December meeting each year. It was voted on and passed to send a Christmas check to the room mothers at the new Green Acres School to help with their funding. Piano music, square dancing, and a generous lunch followed their business.

Marie and her family had started the year of 1948 as guests at the wedding of the bookkeeper at *The Lebanon Express*. Likewise, 1948 wound down with another wedding for them to attend. Lebanon residents Miss Bonna Cooper and Mr. Dean Ward were married at Lebanon's First Christian Church on December 11. Marie conducted their wedding march music from the piano. The sanctuary for their Saturday evening vows was decorated with candelabras and baskets of white chrysanthemums. While one lady lit the candles, Marie played the song "Ah, Sweet Mystery of Life" on the piano. Another lady sang "Always" and "I Love You Truly," while Marie continued to play the piano.

The first of two Christmas parties for Clarence and Marie was on Friday evening, December 17. Their daughter Peggy went with them to the staff Christmas dinner given by Mr. Robert Hayden, owner and publisher of *The Lebanon Express*, and his wife. Of course, no year was complete without the annual Christmas party with the American Legion. This year, the post—that is, the men— cooked the meal and managed all dinner preparations. It was a break for the auxiliary ladies who normally did the cooking. A gift exchange with Santa, as usual, was held. Then Clarence and Marie joined other couples on the dance floor to celebrate the holiday season on this evening of December 21.

———

MARIE'S ITINERARY FOR January 1949 was full, with something on the calendar each week. Some events were simpler than others, such as meeting friends over a cordial card game competition, while other events were more formal affairs. At the end of the third week, it was but a casual moment to observe her forty-fifth birthday. In other gatherings, she had to shine as she encouraged people to get involved.

In her PTA meeting on Tuesday, January 4, Marie introduced their guest speaker, Miss Marjorie Herr, a high school physical education teacher. Miss Herr spoke on the topic of social hygiene and showed them plastic models and other materials that she used in her classroom. They needed to prepare students for their conduct in society regarding relationships with the opposite sex, marriage, and the understanding of family as a basis for social life. A recreation session followed with a game to see who knew the most names of their fellow members. It was Vice President Mrs. Huston, not Marie, who won that game.

Marie had an Eastern Star event in the second week of the month: an installation ceremony with the Marguerite chapter on Monday evening, January 10. This year, Marie was an officer and again a star point, this time Electa. As if to complement not only Marie's glowing appearance with red hair and unmistakable red lipstick but also her personality, Electa is characterized by fervency, hospitality, and love. A ruby is Electa's jewel, and the red rose is her flower.

The International Order of the Rainbow for Girls had their installation ceremony a week later, on the day before Marie's birthday. Her youngest daughter, Patsy, was installed as page. Patsy was Marie's playful daughter, from the party host to the partygoer. She was the one who liked to have fun and would find fun even when more formal expectations were placed on her. She was in other groups too—the Scouts, for one—and had been a Rainbow Girl for a couple of years. This was the first time that she was an elected officer. Their local chapter, the Marguerite Assembly, was large in comparison to other community chapters. DeMolay International, a fraternal order for the sons and other boys related to the Masons, assisted in their ceremony.

It was an affair to get dressed up for. Girls made sure their hair was well styled and their dresses were the finest they had. Patsy wore a cream-colored pastel dress, detailed in lace and with short sleeves that were off her shoulders. Marie could have been wondering whether Patsy was growing up too fast, now that she was almost fifteen years old. Her daughter had set aside her kittenish personality to show that she also had a serious side.

The third week of January gave way for Marie's work with the Red Cross to become increasingly busy. On Monday, January 24, she attended the Linn County Red Cross board meeting in Sweet Home with Mrs. Peggy Hatfield. Mrs. Hatfield was the Linn County secretary, serving with Mrs. Virginia Faulkner, executive secretary. Marie was also a board member in her role as the Linn County membership chairman. She also represented the Lebanon Red Cross as their production manager. Sweet Home didn't have a local chapter, but several residents attended this board meeting as guests. Mrs. Faulkner described the foundational steps involved in a Red Cross organization. Marie interjected to urge the Sweet Home civic leaders to start a chapter.

After their Sweet Home visit, Marie next implored Lebanon residents to do their part. In her role as the Lebanon production manager to the Red Cross, she appealed to women's clubs to give quilts and other linens. A series of fires had depleted their bedding supply during this especially cold winter. Marie made sure people had her phone number should they have any questions on how to help.

Meanwhile, the annual fund drive in Lebanon for the Red Cross was being planned. They had a new general chairman this year, Mr. George Kingan. He was relatively new to their community through the acquisition of their local Firestone Tire Store. A quota had been set at an easy $4,000, and Marie was again the residential chairman. Their fund drive was scheduled to start on March 1.

On Monday, February 21, Marie presided over a tea party in Mrs. Russell Slocum's home to prepare for this fund drive. Guests included Mrs. Virginia Faulkner and Mrs. Fred Connet, the sister-in-law to Mmes. Madge and Florence Connet. Marie appointed captains to help. Mrs. Peggy Patchell, her friend in the Eastern Star, was one of the captains. Mrs. Alice Howard, the treasurer under Marie's presidency with the PTA, was another well-chosen captain. And yet another captain was also in the American Legion: Mrs. Carrie Nichols. This party was a social time so that they might get better acquainted with each other while learning about their commitment.

Other meetings that month for Marie included the American Legion meeting on Thursday, February 3, and the Eastern Star meeting on Monday, February 7, in celebration of their chapter's fiftieth anniversary. The firemen's auxiliary normally met on the second Monday of each month. This month, that Monday fell on Valentine's Day, and the auxiliary instead had its annual banquet dinner for the volunteer firemen. Three days later, Marie was at a reception dinner that preceded Patsy's Rainbow Girls meeting.

However, before the onslaught of her February meetings, she had presided over the PTA meeting on the first day of that month. Marie had welcomed the Oregon State librarian, her assistant, and a school reference librarian as guest speakers. The Queen Anne School secretary-treasurer, Mrs. Margaret Chisholm, also spoke to give a history of the Lebanon PTA in commemoration of Founders' Day. In the business session, Marie had appointed chairmen to three new committees. Their meeting had adjourned for refreshments and group singing.

Two PTA events were on the last weekend in February, on Friday and Saturday, February 25 and 26. One was a rummage sale given by the Queen Anne room mothers as a fundraiser. This granddaddy of all rummage sales, as it was described and advertised, was held at Crites Tire Shop, located at 593 Main Street in downtown. Two blocks over, at 754 Main Street, the Lebanon PTA held a bake sale at Bob and Jack's Market. This market often helped civic groups, serving as a drop-off place for donations. The American Legion, just the month before, had also had a bake sale here. With her can-do spirit of enthusiasm, Marie was at both PTA fundraisers on both days of this weekend.

An exchange student from India attending Oregon State College was the guest speaker at their PTA meeting on March 2. In their business session, Marie called on two chairpersons to give reports for their February fundraisers. Aside from rummage and bake sales, other events were complementary to their monthly meetings. Room mothers did well in their event organizing, and parents were quite involved. The relationship between students, teachers, and parents was much better and more welcoming than it had been only a couple of years before.

In March, Marie received a letter from the National Congress of Parents and Teachers, or the National PTA. In it, they thanked her for the substantial increase in membership. Local membership in the PTA had increased by 14 percent this school year, with 136 women and 35 men. The attendance at their monthly meetings was also noted, at 40 percent greater than the year before. The letter concluded with a congratulatory remark to all new members.

THE RED CROSS fund drive officially kicked off on Tuesday, March 1, the same day that Marie had her PTA meeting. While the fund drive in 1948 had exceeded their goal in only five days, this one needed more time to reach this year's quota of $4,000. Perhaps this was because they had a new general chairman, which could have meant a learning curve, or perhaps his chairmen needed more time to reach more people.

General Chairman Mr. Kingan announced in their next Red Cross meeting that they had more work to do. His industrial chairman had thus far only turned in 65 percent of his goal. The business chairman wasn't faring well either. And his residential chairman, Marie, was lagging well behind, at only 20 percent collected. Mr. Kingan, in an effort to intensify their fund drive, extended the end date to March 22. Marie and the other two chairmen agreed with Mr. Kingan at this meeting on the morning of Thursday, March 10.

On that same day, in the afternoon, radio station KWIL presented a special one-hour program to formally dedicate their new studio to the community. They aired the first half live from their new location, a soundproof studio on the mezzanine floor of the Lebanon Hotel, and the second half live through leaded wire from the auditorium at Lebanon High School. In the days leading up to this March broadcast, the newspaper printed the station's intentions, describing that listeners would hear from several Lebanon dignitaries interspersed with local talent.

The program's panel board of speakers comprised presidents from five well-respected civic organizations. One was Marie as the PTA president, with the others representing the Lions Club, the Kiwanis Club, the Business and Professional Women's Club, and the American Legion Auxiliary, Santiam Unit 51. To round out this lineup, listeners also heard from leaders who represented the Cascade Plywood Corporation, *The Lebanon Express* newspaper, and the board for the Strawberry Festival. Although listeners couldn't see their speakers, they were informed and enlightened as each person added their personality to their few minutes of stardom. The entertainment given by local talent consisted of a mixed chorus and a five-minute skit from high school students.

Returning to her Red Cross duties, it took only a few days for Marie and her team of captains to meet Mr. Kingan's wishes. By March 15, Marie had fully reached her mark in the residential district. The other two chairmen were close behind at 90 percent. Come March 22, an added $150 caused them to surpass what was proposed as an easy $4,000 quota.

In April, Marie attended the monthly meetings with the Eastern Star, the American Legion, and the firemen's auxiliary. She rarely skipped any meetings of organizations in which she was a member. Of course, her card clubs saw her often. This month, though, Marie mixed it up a bit. Other places saw the likes of her too, including the Girl Scouts, the Business and Professional Women's Club, and the Toastmistress Club.

On Friday afternoon, April 1, Marie attended a dessert card party, hosted by her daughter Betty, for Girl Scout mothers and leaders. Betty's fond memories of being a Girl Scout had motivated her to become a troop leader. Marie was one of two winners in their bridge game. The other winner was Mrs. Hayden, in town from Tacoma, Washington, for a visit with her son, Mr. Robert Hayden, Clarence's supervisor. Aside from playing cards, they were entertained by the girls, who performed a playlet with songs.

On Tuesday, April 5, Marie's PTA meeting highlighted a scholarship that they would give to a student leaving high school to pursue a degree in education. With only one more meeting in this school year, elections were held for the 1949–50 incoming officers. Two of Marie's officers would move up in rank, with Mrs. Huston becoming president and Mrs. Chilcote vice president. The installation for them and the other two officers would be in their May meeting. Lastly, Easter refreshments were served.

On Thursday, April 14, Marie attended a meeting with the Duplicate Bridge Club, hosted by Mrs. Peggy Patchell. This club was different from her Bid-Away Bridge Club in that they played in tournaments, hence the name Duplicate. She didn't win a score prize on this day, but she had in their meeting two weeks before.

Fresh-cut spring flowers were used in decorations for both meetings. This spring was proving to be bright and sunny, unlike the terrible rainstorms of a year before.

On Tuesday, April 19, the American Legion had their monthly dinner and meeting night. Marie gave a keynote speech to Santiam Unit 51 in anticipation of Poppy Day in May. She said, "Now, more than 25 million crepe-paper replicas of the Flanders Fields poppy are made every year by disabled veterans working under direction of the American Legion Auxiliary and are worn throughout the nation to pay tribute to the dead of both wars." As Marie drew in her fellow members to hear what she had to say, she continued. "Contributions given in exchange for the poppies are used in legion and auxiliary work for the welfare of the disabled and needy children of veterans."

On the next day, Wednesday, April 20, Marie attended the Business and Professional Women's Club—or the BPW, as their name was often shortened to. Marie wasn't a member but sometimes went as a guest to provide music, since they appreciated her piano playing. Their speaker was Mrs. Bernus, who lived in Albany. She spoke of her local chapter of the Toastmistress Club, as Albany was the nearest place to Lebanon that had a chapter. This club offered a supportive atmosphere for its members to become confident and skilled in public speaking through constructive feedback. It was an all-women's club tailored after the men's club, the Toastmasters. An open discussion followed her speech as to the steps needed to form a Toastmistress Club in Lebanon.

Come the next evening, Thursday, April 21, Albany's Toastmistress Club met for their annual public relations dinner at an upscale restaurant, The Hub. Marie attended it with her friend Mrs. Peggy Hatfield, who wasn't only in the Red Cross with her but was also a BPW member. Marie's daughter Betty and a friend of hers, Mrs. Jenette Witty, also went.

Their dinner event seated several out-of-town guests, many of whom were from Corvallis or Salem. From Albany, Mayor Mr.

Justin Miller, the mayor's wife, and the Albany chief of police, along with several other city officials, also attended. People from many different groups came to listen to the presentation from this Toastmistress Club. The Oregon State Mothers Club, the Albany BPW, the Albany chapter of the American Legion Auxiliary, the Twentieth Century Book Club, Oregon State College officials with student fraternity members, and many other groups—too numerous to name—were well represented with their presence. It was an ideal opportunity for Marie to meet leaders who spanned a wide-reaching area.

The PTA state convention was also in April, from the 26th through the 28th in Eugene. Marie was one of six Lebanon delegates who attended, up from four the previous year. This year's theme was "Cornerstones for Living in Home, School, Church, and Community." Convention leaders announced that the National Education Association highly commended the Oregon PTA for its generosity in tuition scholarships. Marie was justly proud of her local group's contribution to this program.

Only a few days later, on Tuesday, May 3, Marie chaired her last meeting as PTA president. Students would be on summer break from June through August, and then new PTA officers would start in September. Marie's meeting had a full agenda with several reports given, one for the recently attended state convention. In unfinished business, they voted to allocate remaining funds. The latter part of their meeting was dedicated to the installation of the officers who would serve the 1949–50 school year. To inaugurate Mrs. Huston as president and Mrs. Chilcote as vice president, as well as the other two officers, a musical program began the ceremony. Mrs. Dorothy Page played the piano while Mrs. Huston's husband sang a solo rendition of "There's a Tree in the Meadow."

To have Mrs. Page in attendance was meaningful. She and Marie occasionally played the piano together in other groups. On this night, though, Mrs. Page had to play the piano without Marie, and as always, she played beautifully. Her husband was still the high school athletics coach, not forgetting when Marie's son Bill had been on his football team.

Each officer received a corsage. In an impressive moment, the principal of Queen Anne School, Mr. Ernest Caldwell, presented Marie with her past president's pin. If only her father could have seen that his daughter, who was once a little girl like the students they were guiding, was taking an active role in where her life was leading.

Chapter 9

Don't Follow, Lead
May 1949–January 1950

Lebanon's mayor addressed the community on May 24 in an in-depth speech. In his conclusion, he said, "I, Peter Tweed, mayor of the city, do hereby proclaim Saturday, May 28, 1949, to be Poppy Day here in the city of Lebanon, and urge that all citizens observe the day by wearing the memorial poppy of the American Legion and Veterans of Foreign Wars and their auxiliaries."

Marie had volunteered with her auxiliary's Poppy Committee for several years. As this year's 1949 Poppy Committee chairman, she led the others when, in early May, they received their boxes of poppies from the Portland Veterans Hospital. Together, they counted the poppies and then distributed them in exchange for donations.

The reward for Marie when hearing Mayor Tweed make his announcement to city folk must have been momentous. She could see the strides her Poppy Committee members were making. Likewise, it could have been bittersweet as people stopped what they were doing to pause and reflect on their loved one, now gone. Marie was grateful that her husband, Clarence, had survived his combat in the first war.

The Linn County Red Cross met on Thursday evening, June 9, at the First Presbyterian Church in Albany. They had their annual banquet, in which the women from the church were in charge of dinner preparations. Their meeting opened with elections and business reports. Marie would take office as the volunteer service chairman and Mrs. Peggy Hatfield as the production chairman. Mrs. Hatfield and Mrs. Virginia Faulkner retained their roles as secretary and executive secretary, as their positions were salaried and not of a volunteer nature. Mr. Kingan, who had been the general chairman in Lebanon's recent fund drive, would also serve on the executive board.

It was reported that the final count had been completed for the Lebanon Red Cross fund drive and that it had increased funds by one-third over the preceding year. Marie reported on behalf of the Lebanon chapter to say that sixty garments went to Navajo children during their cold winter. Marie further informed them that area women had made 143 quilts, which were distributed to those in need. A guest speaker from the Portland-Multnomah chapter followed their business session and spoke about how the state's blood bank was used in emergencies. They ended with an entertainment program presented with singing and a clarinet solo.

In the American Legion, Marie and several other members went as Lebanon delegates to their 1949 state convention. It had been two years since Marie last attended. This year's convention was held in Salem, Oregon's capital, starting August 3 and lasting for four days. About three thousand members, statewide, attended. Each day started early with a morning breakfast at 6:30, and while the morning weather was cool, it soon warmed up. Clear, sunny, and warm skies saw them through the four days.

Each day went well into the evening hours, ending with a nightly dance at the armory. It was a full schedule of meetings and entertainment, and while not everyone attended everything, there was plenty to do at this convention and plenty to see in Salem. Many of their business sessions were held in the capital building. Oregon Governor Douglas McKay was one of the speakers.

For entertainment there was an air show, a Friday evening parade, and tours of the capital building. Several different bands and drum corps, and also a Scottish band with bagpipes, each took their turn to engage attendees. Radio star and country vocalist Eddie Dean also gave a concert. It was a successful convention, and Salem residents had extended a warm welcome. Marie returned home braced with ideas for Santiam Unit 51.

At the end of August, Clarence and daughter Peggy took a week-long vacation from their work with *The Lebanon Express*. Peggy had been promoted to a production operator position when she completed high school, and she had one year left of her apprenticeship. Earlier that summer, she had been a bridesmaid in a friend's wedding. She was often a wedding attendant for friends. Her time would come to get married, but for now, she was content to live at home and work for the newspaper. She was now nineteen years old, to turn twenty in November. She thrived in her bowling league and other activities and wasn't yet ready to settle down into a marriage. Peggy chose to spend her free week at home.

For Clarence's week of vacation, he went with Marie and his mother-in-law, Laura, to Pendleton, a city in the far northeastern corner of Oregon. Marie's brother Harry and his family now lived here. It was a long drive, at about five hours, with plenty of open countryside to sightsee. It also gave Marie and her mother uninterrupted time to visit and talk.

Marie was at ease, if not proud, to tell her mother about the many exciting things she was involved with. However, sharing with her mother about any apprehensions or uncertainties that she had when with her groups didn't come easy for Marie. When an older adult, Marie said that revealing her emotions to her mother wasn't something that happened. Their formal stance with each other had been set in place when she was a girl, brought on by the overshadowing nature of her father. A woman's role was to keep to the house and not worry about any matters outside of the home. That rule was set by her father, and a rule, when broken, not easy to talk about.

It wasn't like Marie to step away from her commitments for a full week. Nor was it like Clarence to take a vacation. He was constantly under deadlines to get the newspaper to print on time, often working well into the evening hours and past any closing time for the office. He also had a bad back, which often gave him shooting spurts of pain. He preferred to work through the pain rather than stop to rest.

While it may have seemed like a forced vacation, it was one that they found enjoyable. When in Pendleton, they all attended the annual Pendleton Round-Up, a rodeo show. Clarence and Marie stayed only a few days, whereas her mother would stay longer to visit with Harry and his family.

In the first week of September, Marie had several events, starting with an installation for the Rainbow Girls on Tuesday evening, September 6. Patsy was installed as decoration chairman, and Dewanda Hamilton as worthy advisor, who, of the elected officers, would be the one to lead their group. DeMolay International—the fraternal organization likened to the Rainbow Girls, but for boys—took part in the ceremony. One boy placed a tiara on Dewanda's head. Marie was pleased to see that her youngest daughter was happy with her membership in the Rainbow Girls. Perhaps, when older, Patsy would join the Eastern Star as many of its girls went on to do.

On Thursday, September 8, Marie attended a small bridge party in the home of her friend, Mrs. Grace Scroggin. This party was also a surprise baby shower for another friend Mrs. E. H. Jacobson. Mrs. Scroggin's home was filled with pink and blue flowers and other motif decorations. Marie was one of the winners in their card games.

Grace and Marie were good friends and close in age, with Grace less than a month older than Marie. Like Marie, Grace's middle name was also Marie, though she didn't go by her middle name as Marie did. She had two sons whom Marie's children knew from school. Her husband, a pilot, had been the judge in the airplane contest that Marie's son Bill had competed in and won when he was a little boy. Aside from frequent bridge parties, Grace and Marie were often beside each other in their volunteer activities.

Marie attended another party a few days later, on Sunday evening, September 11. It was a surprise housewarming party for fellow American Legion members Mr. and Mrs. Lloyd Lyon. Clarence most likely went with Marie. After their potluck dinner and several rounds of cards, Marie played the piano while the party folks enjoyed group singing.

Later in the week, it was Marie's turn to host the Duplicate Bridge Club. They met in her home on Thursday, September 15. Marie won a score prize, as did Mrs. Betty Ouderkirk, who had also been a delegate to the American Legion's state convention the month before. Marie took care to decorate the game tables, and they played well into the afternoon hours.

One might think that Marie was taking it easy now that her year as PTA president was over. On the contrary, she would show that this was far from the truth. For her, it was more a matter of what to do next and less about why to do it. When she did her grocery shopping, she saw people who struggled to buy enough food for family meals. Each time she went to the department store for a new suit, she knew that some families shopped at a discount store. Her ears perked up when Clarence would arrive home from a fire call, sharing stories of what happened to this family or that family. And God forbid there should ever be another disaster like the Vanport Flood in '48.

Her week away with Clarence had given her all the relaxation she could muster. Right before their Pendleton vacation, Marie had garnered useful ideas from the American Legion's state convention. Her heart tugged at her to help people who were less fortunate or had been met with a dire situation. She was well rested and ready to put those ideas into action.

In September, the American Legion resumed following their summer break. Daughter Peggy went with Clarence and Marie to their meeting this month. As it was an event for grown-ups, Patsy stayed home with her brother Bill, who like his brother, Dick, wasn't one to tag along to events. Elections for incoming post and unit officers had been held in their May meeting, and they would be installed on this night, following their dinner.

During dinner, all eyes were on Marie. She was their newly elected 1949–50 Santiam Unit 51 president. While the ladies smiled, Clarence had even more to smile about. He handed Marie an overflowing bouquet of flowers. It had to be overflowing—his wife wasn't only accepting a great honor, but he too felt honored on this night, because this wasn't just any night. There was yet another reason to celebrate. This was September 20, two days before his birthday and the day before their wedding anniversary. It was twenty-three years ago that Clarence had married Marie. Gratitude was in the air, with Marie grateful to have such a supportive family.

Their District 3 auxiliary president, Mrs. Vernice Schulz, who lived in Florence, was invited to perform the auxiliary's installation duties. Two unit members would assist her: Mrs. Blandena Wilson, their outgoing sergeant-at-arms; and their outgoing president, Mrs. Kee Buchanon Groves, who had written and directed the pageant for the 1947 Strawberry Festival. When the unit's installation ceremony began, Mrs. Schulz pinned a corsage on Marie's lapel and then proceeded to pin corsages on the other incoming officers. Mrs. Schulz then handed Marie the gavel and took a firm handshake in exchange. For Peggy, seeing joy in her mom's demeanor gave her a moment to set aside her favoritism toward her dad and recognize that her mom was also an important person.

Their auxiliary was one of the largest units in this part of Oregon, having grown in just the past few years to nearly two hundred members. As with any unit, it was led by seven elected officers, along with several chairpersons as appointed by the unit president. This unit was the perfect group of kindred members and friends for Marie to lead. Other officers installed were Mrs. Marjorie Long as sergeant-at-arms; Mrs. Ella Wood, who was also a Red Cross member, as chaplain; Mrs. Ruth Parton as treasurer; Mrs. Alice Youman as secretary; Mrs. Beatrice Crandall as second vice president; and Mrs. Betty Ouderkirk as Marie's first vice president. Marie looked forward to sharing a year of the legion's work with her new officers. She was ready for new challenges.

Mrs. Ouderkirk's husband, Mr. William Ouderkirk, would lead the men as post commander. Although Clarence was a member in good standing, he never pursued any opportunity to be an officer with the American Legion nor with the Elks Club, another fraternal group of which he was also a member. His work with the newspaper and as a volunteer fireman kept him busy, with only a little time left over for bowling.

The business sessions for the post and unit followed their installations. Marie reported on their recently attended state convention and then announced the committee chairmen whom she had appointed. Mrs. Vada Whetstone, Mrs. Opal Lyon, Mrs. Kee Buchanan Groves, Mrs. Maude Duncan, and Mrs. Peggy Patchell were among the members she had chosen to help her lead Santiam Unit 51. Several fellow members were also in the Eastern Star, alongside Marie.

Marie also stated that she and Mr. Ouderkirk, post commander, would jointly help Lincoln County's emergency fund drive to combat polio. Their county's funds were exhausted, and yet they had several active polio cases. Marie needed her chairpersons to help in this effort. Polio, short for poliomyelitis, is a viral disease that afflicted many people, and in 1949, there was no cure. It is a disease with myriad discomforts and comes with the risk of becoming irreversibly paralyzed.

In the Eastern Star, Mrs. Vada Whetstone and Marie went to the Willamette Valley Matrons and Patrons Association meeting on Saturday, October 8, this time hosted by the Stayton chapter. Although Stayton is southeast of Salem, they first had to drive north, then south again, as the only highway eastward to it was from Salem. Marie, who loved to travel and loved visiting people, didn't mind the drive. As such, she was a frequent guest at chapter meetings.

Marie was soon on another out-of-town visit, this time to an American Legion event. Mrs. Duncan, a unit chairman, went with her to the Willamette Council meeting on Sunday, October 16. This time, the district meeting was held in Oakridge, southeast of Eugene. It met monthly on a Sunday, Marie's family day, yet she set aside one Sunday a month for this council, for which she was now their secretary.

As AUTUMN LEAVES fell with a cold winter soon to follow, Lebanon residents took in two entertainment events. A third event would come in the midst of winter, in February. Likened to when Marie was in her girlhood days and performed at the Hippodrome and the Liberty Theater in Bend, so too would she be among the performers in both of these fall events.

The first was a variety show with the Veterans of Foreign Wars, or VFW. Similar to their April '48 *Fun For You* show, which had included impersonations of radio stars and at which Marie had won the Good Neighbor Award, this show was a newspaper revue to bring the newspaper to life. It was held in the high school auditorium, an event space to accommodate a large audience.

Marie was the pianist for this show, called *Laff It Off*, which was performed on both Friday and Saturday evening, October 21 and 22. It had ten scenes, and each scene depicted a newspaper section. Orphan Annie, Blondie, Popeye, and Dick Tracy were impersonated for the comics section. Throughout the show, when music was needed, Marie was on stage playing the piano.

Before the month's end, Marie traveled to another Eastern Star event. Mrs. Peggy Patchell and Mrs. Abbie Leckband, their chapter's recent past worthy matron, went with her to a chapter meeting in Independence on October 29. This was a reception dinner in honor of grand officers.

Then, the Elks Club performed *Go West*, with Mr. Delmar Clem as their show's announcer and Marie in one of the leading roles. This was a three-night charity minstrel show starting on Thursday, November 3, at the Elks Temple. The all-white cast of actors had their faces painted black to act for any Black American characters. Although this entertainment choice is offensive today, it was widely accepted and enjoyed in that era. The show opened with a can-can dance; then the first skit was given, a factual portrayal of Captain Gray's Oregon exploration up through the Willamette and Santiam rivers. He was white, as was his wife, played by Marie. Their faces, therefore, weren't painted black. They captured people's attention as Marie clutched Mr. Ed Thompson as Captain Gray, and he shouted, "Port ho!"

Two other performances given were a skit about a pickpocket, portrayed as an African piece of lore, and "That Lucky Old Sun," a popular 1949 song by the Black American Louis Armstrong. Witty jokes, clever skits, and blackface antics were strung together to make the audience laugh. It was a packed house with the audience at full capacity. Money raised by the Elks from ticket sales would support charities.

After a day at home with the family that Sunday, Marie began her next full week, starting with a Girl Scout meeting on Monday, November 7. She played the piano for their after-school meeting in the Girl Scout leader's home. Marie's daughter Betty, who had been the troop leader for the prior school year, remained active in it.

Later that same week, Marie returned to her events with the American Legion. On Thursday, November 10, Marie assisted Mr. Ouderkirk, post commander, at an Armistice Day assembly at Lebanon High School. The high school's band played an opening number. Reverend Harvey Schmidt began the assembly with prayer and then introduced Student Body President Don Anthony. After this student gave a few words to welcome everyone, he introduced Marie and Mr. Ouderkirk.

Marie spoke to a full auditorium of teenagers as she described the American Legion's work. She explained how they could help with Poppy Day by buying a poppy and then wearing it. She then described their Christmas projects in which they would send gifts to benefit the patients in the Portland Veterans Hospital. An Oregon state representative, Mr. Warren Gill, who was also a Linn County resident, was their main speaker. Mr. Gill emphasized that the students of today were the leaders of tomorrow. Reverend Carl Wachter gave a closing prayer. A high school senior concluded the assembly by playing "Taps" on the bugle.

Their American Legion meeting that month was on Tuesday evening, November 15. They had an initiation ceremony for new members following their potluck dinner. Marie's daughter Peggy, whose twentieth birthday was only two days away, was one of the many new members. In their auxiliary's business session, Marie, as their unit president, thanked the ladies for their outpouring of gifts for the veterans.

Earlier on that same day, Marie had been a speaker at a Red Cross tea party. The Lebanon chapter had begun plans to bring the bloodmobile to their city, hopefully in December. People most often traveled to Portland to give blood. This would be the first time the Red Cross bloodmobile would include Linn County in their stops, with Lebanon as their chosen city. Mr. Kingan, who had been the general chairman on the fund drive earlier that year, was appointed to be the chairman for this bloodmobile.

Marie cohosted this tea party with Mrs. Grace Scroggin to garner interest from women's groups. Their social affair brought in such a large crowd that one could have wondered how Mrs. Scroggin's home accommodated so many people at one time. No less than twenty organizations were represented by their presidents and other members. Many Red Cross members also attended, with Mrs. Virginia Faulkner and Mrs. Peggy Hatfield giving short but informative speeches. Marie's brief speech emphasized how important it was to have a bloodmobile. Their fourth speaker explained how the blood was collected, processed, typed, and distributed. Committee work was also discussed, concluding with a date to schedule the bloodmobile.

On the next day, Wednesday, November 16, the regional group of the Red Cross met in Portland. Marie went with Mrs. Faulkner, Mrs. Hatfield, and Mr. Kingan to the meeting. Mr. Kingan announced to the regional members that they had set a date for the bloodmobile, December 16, and that they were ready for it.

A radio program that aired a few days earlier on Sunday, November 13, had heightened enthusiasm. Dr. Frank Girod, president of the Linn County Medical Association, spoke during a KWIL radio station program. He pleaded with his listeners to get involved, donate blood, and let others know that the Red Cross bloodmobile was coming to town.

One thing that had hindered Lebanon was its lack of an adequate hospital to receive, store, and refrigerate blood in such great quantity. Oftentimes when patients needed blood, they were sent to another hospital. Red Cross workers started what they called a weekly milk run to show their capability. Every Monday, a driver from Portland brought blood as needed in a refrigerated container to their hospital. In the same manner, they transported donated blood from Lebanon to Albany and Sweet Home medical centers for storage. At the same time, plans were evolving to build a new hospital.

As the Linn County Red Cross volunteer service chairman, Marie and other county volunteers helped their Lebanon chapter to prepare for the bloodmobile's visit. They recruited and then trained volunteers and created committees. Marie served as their contact person and received many telephone calls and house visits. In all, she recruited forty volunteers, six nurses, and several physicians. These volunteers included typists for the donor cards, telephone receptionists, canteen workers, nursery attendants to care for children while their mothers donated, and others who could help.

District 3 of the American Legion had its annual conference at the Veterans Memorial Building in Eugene on Sunday, November 27. Mr. Ouderkirk, Lebanon's post commander, and Marie, as Santiam Unit 51 president, attended. Mrs. Schulz, District 3 auxiliary president, presided over the business meetings for auxiliary members and presidents. Mr. Samuel Bowe, state commander, addressed all members during their banquet dinner and said that the American Legion was the largest veterans organization in the world, with 3.5 million members. Oregon members from sixteen cities in four counties attended this conference.

Tuesday, November 29, was the day for the American Legion to deliver Christmas gifts to the Veterans Hospital in Portland. Marie and her second vice president, Mrs. Beatrice Crandall, would make the trip with the Junction City unit president, Mrs. Earl Tyler. They took account of their donations as they loaded up the car. There were lots of dolls, complete with wardrobes, and other toys for the veterans to give their children.

Not only did they have a carful of family gifts for the veterans to choose from, but they also had a display cart for the gift shop to use to show a sampling. The Cascade Plywood Mill from Lebanon had donated supplies to make the cart, which was handcrafted by a Lebanon organization. Marie's son-in-law, Andrew, had then hand-painted it. Thanksgiving had just passed, and while many housewives were planning what Santa would bring their children, Marie could only be pleased that she was helping those less fortunate.

It was a cloudy day on Friday, December 16, with rain showers forecasted. This was far from a cloudy time, though, for the long line of people on the corner of Oak Street and stretching down Grove Street. People anxiously waited in front of the VFW hall for the three o'clock hour when the bloodmobile would open its doors. Their first donor, Mr. William Baldwin, the Santiam School principal, couldn't be happier that he didn't have to travel to Portland to donate blood as he had done many times before.

Every volunteer showed up, and nurses stayed well past the seven o'clock closing hour. No one was turned away. It rained at 6 p.m., but these nurses were too busy to pay attention to threatening weather. The newspaper out of Albany would report the next day that a record-smashing 150 blood donors turned up for Linn County's first contribution to the Red Cross blood program. This set a new state record in a zone that covered not only Oregon but also counties in southwest Washington. Six months earlier, another Oregon city, The Dalles, had broken the record with 147 pints of donated blood. Lebanon surpassed that with their 150 pints.

The Red Cross Center from Portland, who had helped coordinate the milk runs, praised their success, with considerable credit given to just two Red Cross workers. One was the donor recruitment chairman, Mrs. Ruth Parton, who was also the treasurer under Marie's presidency with Santiam Unit 51. The other noteworthy praise was extended to the volunteer recruitment chairman, Marie.

Following that weekend, come Monday, December 19, Marie went with Mrs. Peggy Patchell and Mrs. Vada Whetstone to a White Shrine of Jerusalem meeting in Salem. Mrs. Patchell and Marie had also been to the Brownsville chapter with the Eastern Star chapter a few days earlier, on December 14, to assist in installation duties. The White Shrine of Jerusalem is a fraternal organization, with Eastern Star membership as a requirement to join in 1949. Marie and some of the Marguerite chapter members in the Eastern Star occasionally attended their meetings, and as Eastern Star members, they were always welcomed. The purpose of the White Shrine of Jerusalem is threefold, with charitable and fraternal being two facets. Foremost, they are spiritual, and the word "white" in their name is used to mean purity in its spiritual component.

Like the Eastern Star, which has a special emphasis on five biblical heroines, the White Shrine of Jerusalem also has an emphasis: the biblical story of the three wise men and the gifts they bestowed. Although biblical tenets are expressed in these groups, religion is irrelevant. Rather, the spirituality found through fostering friendships and community relations is of importance. It was to these groups—the Eastern Star and the White Shrine of Jerusalem—that Marie turned for spiritual guidance rather than the congregation in a church.

The White Shrine of Jerusalem also met regularly and had social events and fundraisers for community charities. The Salem chapter, which was the closest chapter to Lebanon, met on the third Monday of each month. On this night, December 19, Mrs. Patchell, Mrs. Whetstone, and Marie were three of twelve people initiated as new members.

Clarence and Marie closed out the year of 1949 much like they had the year before. Their daughter Peggy went with them to two Christmas parties. The first was the annual staff Christmas dinner with Mr. and Mrs. Robert Hayden of *The Lebanon Express* on Sunday evening, December 18. This time it was held at Melody Lane, a popular place in town for dinner parties and after-dinner music for dancing. The other party was on the evening after Marie's initiation into the White Shrine of Jerusalem. On Tuesday evening, December 20, the American Legion met for their annual Christmas dinner. Turkey and all the trimmings fed more than 150 members in attendance. One guest was from the San-Vets organization, which had recently disbanded. On behalf of his group, he gave the American Legion a handful of belongings and several pieces of furniture.

During their business session, discussion ensued to describe how successful the Red Cross bloodmobile had been, not forgetting how busy Marie was in recruiting volunteers. A recap was also given for their trip to the Veterans Hospital with the gift donations. Aside from the party on this night, they had also given a Christmas party for the children of veterans three days earlier, on Saturday. A recap was given for that too. Additionally, their work to fill Christmas baskets for needy families in Lebanon was ongoing, with plans set as to who would fulfill the deliveries.

Santa officiated their gift exchange; then the music and dancing began. One member played the accordion, some gave piano solos, and some gave extended song performances. With guests to greet, members to say hello to, and event planning for the new year to be discussed when engaged in conversation, Marie wasn't among the piano players.

Marie's commitments in the new year of 1950 began with a PTA meeting on Tuesday, January 3. Mrs. Willa Huston, PTA president, called on Marie to share about the recent Lebanon Red Cross bloodmobile. Marie used this opportunity to thank all the PTA members who had helped to make it a success. Before their next meeting, scheduled for February 7, Marie would first be with the Crowfoot PTA. That chapter served a small countryside town near Lebanon. They would have an evening event on Friday, February 3, with a box dinner and square dance, and Marie agreed to be their pianist for it.

A surprise housewarming party was given by the American Legion for two members, Mr. and Mrs. Bert Morsch, on Saturday, January 7. This large gathering had guests who were also in the Eastern Star and other groups. Two ladies were in charge of refreshments, and Marie helped them to serve the attendees. Cards were played, and gifts were given to the couple. Their next meeting with the American Legion would be on Tuesday, January 18. With that meeting, they would vote to donate an American flag and flagpole to the nearby Sodaville grade school.

In the Eastern Star, the Marguerite chapter had their installation on Monday evening, January 9. Mrs. Alice Kimes was installed as worthy matron and Mr. Ronald Gilson as worthy patron. When, in 1948, Marie had been their warder, or inner guard, Mr. Gilson had been their outer guard as sentinel. For 1950, Marie was again an officer, to serve a second year as Electa, a star point. Marie's next visit to an Eastern Star chapter was with Mrs. Peggy Patchell two days later, on January 11, in Sweet Home. Like with the Brownsville chapter visit in December, Marie and Mrs. Patchell helped with ceremonial duties.

The parties and celebrations that the new decade had opened with would lead into a full year with commitments beyond anything Marie could envision. With these commitments, even greater celebrations would come, celebrations to include more people than she could imagine. Marie braced herself for the 1950s with a mindset to do as she had done through the 1940s. She would tackle the next obstacle, overcome the next hurdle, lead her neighbors and friends, meet new people, and do her part in the many groups she was a member of. What she did not know in the early days of 1950 is that by doing these things, she would inevitably change her community not only for the better but also forevermore.

Chapter 10

— ❀ —

Needs of the Needy
February 1950–May 1950

Marie's two roles in the Red Cross in 1950—one as the Linn County volunteer service chairman, and the other as the Lebanon production manager—overlapped in their need for donations. In January, two newspaper articles were printed, one in *The Lebanon Express* and the other in the *Salem Capital Journal* in Marion County. Each was worded differently, but both informed residents that Linn County was experiencing a shortage of bedding donations for needy families. To help women's groups, the Red Cross would furnish batting for any sewers to make quilts for this cause. In both articles, Marie's phone number and address were given. She wanted to make sure that people knew how to reach her, leaving no room for an excuse not to help.

Several factors caused people to be less fortunate. Although the war was over, many veterans had returned home with injuries that kept them from their full-career capacity, adversely affecting their income potential. As Clarence could attest, house fires were common. The fireplaces, kitchen appliances, and electrical wiring used in homes were far from the modern home standards of today, which, through no real fault of the homeowners, put residents at risk.

To compound these issues, Lebanon was again in another bad winter. When the Red Cross article appeared in the Lebanon newspaper, one could read on the same page that the city streets were caked in a layer of ice. Countryside schools were closed until the snow and sleet subsided. Warm bedding was a must-have, and yet some people couldn't afford this basic need. Marie had to do more than just wait for an answer.

In February, Marie went to print on her own accord. The very first article on page 3 in the February 3, 1950, issue of *The Lebanon Express* had a heading in big bold letters that read, "Needs Of The Needy By Polly Potter." Her first letter in what would become a long-running column shared the troubles of a woman afflicted with polio. Through both the Red Cross and the American Legion, Marie was keenly aware of many polio cases.

We don't know how or why Marie chose Polly Potter to be her pen name. Speculation could abound. In biblical times, priests had paid pot makers, whose land was rich with clay, to bury their poor people. Since then, communities have continued to bury anyone who dies poor or unknown in what they call a potter's field. Or Potter could have been in remembrance of her childhood books. Beatrix Potter was a well-regarded author of tales for children in Marie's girlhood days, with *The Tale of Peter Rabbit* as one of her more famous stories. As for the name Polly, we are left to guess. A girl or woman who is especially optimistic, often foolishly so, can be characterized as being a Pollyanna, as was seen in the 1920 feature film *Pollyanna*, starring Mary Pickford. As a popular star, her films were often shown at the Liberty Theater in Bend during the same years that Marie performed there as a pianist.

Under this article's heading, an editor's note was given to let readers know that many requests had come to the attention of *The Lebanon Express* for assistance. In part, it read:

Recognizant of the fact that many individuals and organizations are willing to give assistance to these cases if the circumstances are known, this method has been suggested to bring them to the attention of the community. Polly Potter will receive written requests for help and after investigation will turn the letter over to interested organizations and individuals. Address all correspondence to Polly Potter, Box 365, Lebanon.

Polly's letter followed.

> Of particular appeal is the case of a mother and her three children living in a rural area. The mother, a victim of polio, is unable to work and barely able to do the housework in their small home. The father deserted the family long ago and the small support check that the law requires him to send is inadequate and uncertain. There is one girl, 8, a girl, 5, and a boy, 3. The mother whose size is 14, as well as the children need warm clothing. There is also a need for food.

As Marie tended to her newfound calling as Polly Potter, her leadership with the American Legion and her dedication to all her memberships were unwavering. Another civic group to name in which Marie was an active member was the Linn County Concert Association, headquartered in Albany. It took little of her time to help this group recruit musicians, some famous at the national level. They performed in concert in Linn County, often in Albany or Lebanon. On average, they booked five musicians a year.

In 1949, Marie had been cochairman with Mrs. Douglas Waddell in their membership drive. In that year, one of their concert series was with the New York-famed Miss Susan Reed, an Appalachian folk singer. For February 1950, they scheduled the much-sought-after opera singer and radio sensation Mr. John Carter. On Tuesday evening, February 21, people came to the high school auditorium in Albany, dressed in their finest suits and gowns, for Mr. Carter. Renditions of Mozart, Bach, and Chopin were in his band's lineup of music as he sang tenor. A reception followed, held in the Cascade Room at the Albany Hotel and by invitation only.

Marie, in a long black cocktail dress accentuated by a V-neck front, joined Mrs. Waddell and three other ladies from the Linn County Concert Association to dine with Mr. Carter. *The Lebanon Express* later covered the story of his Albany concert, complete with a group photograph. Marie is pictured with a small group of ladies standing next to radio star Mr. Carter, who is clad in a tuxedo. They appear relaxed and happy.

Another social function for Marie was on the very next night. As if to outdo the recent performances given by the VFW and the Elks Club, the Jaycees Club was next in line. Their opening night of *The Burlesk Show* was on Wednesday, February 22. It was a two-night one-hour burlesque show, as its title implied, and held at the Park Theater.

Although Marie wasn't a Jaycees member, she was their pianist for the event, dressed for fun in a Kentucky Derby men's suit. If she missed any notes on the piano, it was overlooked, as everyone's laughter was nonstop. One hilarious ruse after another was acted out in fun for an adults-only audience. All the cast members were dolled up in costumes of their own choosing, described by some as ridiculous but amusing. In true burlesque fashion, the male entertainers showed their hairy legs in their dance and song rou-tines. One male actor was disrobed by another and left standing in long red wooly underwear. Money raised from ticket sales was earmarked for local civic projects.

Meanwhile, the Red Cross was formulating their plans for their annual fund drive, scheduled for March, as well as another bloodmobile visit in April. This year's general chairman for the fund drive was Mr. Delmar Clem. As a member of the Elks Club, he had been the announcer for their show back in November. For the third year in a row, Marie was the residential district chairman.

On Thursday afternoon, February 23, and the day after her evening with the Jaycees, Marie cohosted a Red Cross tea party at the home of Mayor Peter Tweed with his wife. Marie's team, an all-woman team that numbered thirty, along with team captains, were their guests. They discussed organizational plans to reach this year's quota of $4,100.

On the next day, Friday, the fourth weekly letter from Polly Potter appeared in the newspaper. She began by thanking a kind-hearted woman who had come forward to help with many hand-made baby clothes. Her baby had died from being born too early. Polly next shared about one family's troubling situation, in which she asked for furniture and for groups to put together kits of basic household items. In Polly's plea for help for this woman, she ended by causing her readers to picture a scenario.

> My special worry this week is a family, a mother, father, and six children, who have lost their home and possessions by fire. Through the Red Cross and kind friends they have been provided with shelter, food, and bedding.

> Imagine yourself bereft of every household article that is such a part of your daily life. Not even the familiar needle and thread left to darn the boy's socks or mend a tear in Sally's sweater.

On Monday, March 13, Marie visited the monthly meeting of the Lebanon Senior Women's Club. They discussed their upcoming style and fashion show, just in time for Easter. It was concluded that Marie would be their pianist for this event. In other business, Marie spoke of the need for used clothing, furniture, and food for impoverished community members. It was then decided that their club would sponsor a project to supply baby clothes and layettes for the needy. In all, eighteen members and a few visitors were present.

In the American Legion, Marie, as Santiam Unit 51 president, was directing several chairmen in volunteer work to help combat polio. Back in February, they had sponsored a March of Dimes dance at the high school as part of a fundraiser for this. Marie had been the pianist for their old-time square dance at that event. Other fraternal organizations and the Girl Scouts were also involved with volunteering, donations, and fund drives.

Their auxiliary now extended their efforts to help in the fight against tuberculosis. TB, as the disease name is often shortened to, was another problem not yet under control. It is caused by a bacterium that usually attacks the lungs. A chest X-ray is the best-known way of early detection, and then timely treatment is administered. In cooperation with three Linn County government health organizations, they started a survey in February to last up until early May, when the county's TB chest X-ray mobile unit would be in Lebanon. This survey, under the chairmanship of Mrs. Carrie Nichols, involved house-to-house visits to acquaint residents with the free services to be offered by this mobile unit. Their goal was to schedule no less than 80 percent of adult Lebanon residents for an X-ray.

The American Legion's birthday was given special recognition at their dinner meeting on Tuesday evening, March 21. On behalf of her unit, Marie presented a large birthday cake to Mr. Ouderkirk, post commander. In celebration, Mrs. Vada Whetstone, Mrs. Peggy Patchell, and Mrs. Cora Harden, who were all dressed in old-fashioned costumes, performed the song "Memories."

Marie presided over the auxiliary's business to discuss the upcoming Poppy Day. They also agreed to place Easter plants in the Roseburg Hospital. Of greater excitement up for discussion was the open installation for Junior Girls to the American Legion, scheduled for the next weekend. Junior Girls was a brand-new organization, never before done in their unit, to bring girls whose parents were members into their membership.

The Senior Women's Club Style Show took place two days later, on Thursday, March 23, and was held at Melody Lane, the same place that *The Lebanon Express* had had their dinner party in December. Dining tables were grouped around a spotlighted stage, and the revue was set to begin after the serving of dessert. Proceeds of their sold-out event would go into a community aid fund. Marie sat at the piano, back center on stage for the show. Twenty women and girls each took their turn modeling Easter dresses and other spring fashion, jewelry, and accessories that could be purchased in Lebanon's downtown shopping district. Local merchants, J. C. Penney for one, provided their attire. As each new garment was modeled, Marie's piano playing changed the tempo to accentuate the mood. Easter was right around the corner, on April 9 that year.

On the next day, Friday, Patsy left for a two-day Rainbow Girls grand assembly, their state convention, in Corvallis. Four chaperones accompanied Patsy and several other girls. Their chapter's worthy advisor, Miss Dewanda Hamilton, also went. A Saturday evening dance with their local DeMolay boys concluded it. Arriving home, Patsy had another big event come the next day.

On Sunday evening, March 26, the American Legion held the public initiation for Junior Girls. Marie's daughter Patsy and twenty-one other girls were welcomed into the American Legion through a candlelight ceremony. Yellow daffodils and forsythia were the chosen decorations for this patriotic and happy occasion. An installation followed their initiation ceremony. Of the twenty-two girls, six were installed as Junior Girl officers, and of these six, Patsy was installed as chaplain. Marie couldn't have been prouder of her two youngest daughters. She was pleased when Peggy recently became an American Legion member. Now her youngest daughter, who would be sixteen years old the next month, was a Junior Girls member and officer.

Meanwhile, the total funds received from Lebanon's annual Red Cross fund drive had been tabulated. Following a kick-off breakfast for chairmen that Marie had attended on March 10, she had been quite active in leading her team captains. As residential chairman, she had raised more funds than she had in the two prior years. In all, the three chairmen more than met their $4,100 quota, and without any difficulty this year. Marie would also be on scene for the Red Cross bloodmobile visit on Friday, April 7, as the volunteer service chairman.

Following the bloodmobile visit, Marie had two American Legion events, with a card club meeting in between the two, all inside the next week. The first event was held at city hall on Tuesday, April 11. No less than sixty Lebanon residents showed up at two o'clock in the afternoon to hear what could be done about TB. Although Marie had been leading auxiliary ladies with a house-to-house survey since February, they needed a better response and a greater level of community involvement.

At that event, Marie represented the American Legion on an eight-person panel with individuals from the Oregon Tuberculosis Association, the Oregon State Department of Health, and the Linn County Health and Tuberculosis Association. Each person spoke with an imploring message to get organized. They needed people to be callers who would conduct house-to-house visitations to schedule appointments for each adult to receive a chest X-ray. A TB chest X-ray mobile unit would visit Lebanon from May 1 until May 12 to provide services for tuberculosis screening. The second American Legion event scheduled that week was a District 3 dinner party.

Two days after the event at city hall, Marie hosted the Duplicate Bridge Club meeting. She went all out with decorations in her home for this Thursday afternoon get-together. Artistic floral arrangements with red tulips, grape hyacinths, and yellow daisies adorned her fireplace mantel. Miniature baskets of bridal wreath blossoms were centered on each of three card tables. Window drapes in her spacious living room were open to let in the abundant sunshine on this early spring day.

At the end of the week, Marie's first grandchild, Randy, turned five years old on Saturday, April 15. While in all likelihood Marie stopped in at her daughter Betty's home to wish her grandson a happy birthday, she was soon on the road again. Mr. and Mrs.

Whetstone and Mr. and Mrs. Gleason joined Clarence and Marie to travel to the American Legion District 3 meeting and dinner party. As their district secretary, Marie always attended their monthly meetings. This time, it was held in Taft, an oceanfront hamlet of Lincoln City. On this night, they honored past district commanders and auxiliary presidents. Following their business, they had a dance with music performed by gleemen and a local band.

Come Monday, April 17, the Salem chapter of the White Shrine of Jerusalem had its annual installation. It had been only five months since Marie and her friends Mrs. Peggy Patchell and Mrs. Vada Whetstone were initiated. Marie's mother, Laura, attended it as well, along with two other Eastern Star members from Lebanon: Mrs. Eva Craig and Mrs. Julia Lytle. Marie was one of the many officers installed. She was their elected organist, to be their pianist for their meetings. Mrs. Patchell and Mrs. Whetstone were also installed as elected officers, to be queen's attendants. A musical program with a trombone solo accompanied their ceremony, and a reception followed. Both the Eastern Star and the White Shrine of Jerusalem would take a summer break and resume meetings in September. Even without the formal meetings, Marie stayed in close contact with fellow members. It was in these two groups that Marie found guidance to foster her spiritual beliefs.

The Business and Professional Women's Club met two nights later, on Wednesday, April 19. Marie had again been invited to be their pianist. Marie's good friend Mrs. Peggy Hatfield was their president, and she could have been any one of a number of members to invite her back. Mrs. Vada Whetstone was also a member. It was a club that gave professional women a group setting in which to discuss their business ideals and celebrate their accomplishments. Like other groups, they also supported many worthy causes. The national organization had a lengthy history, dating back to 1919 and earlier. Their Lebanon chapter started in late 1946, with their first regular meeting officiated in early 1947. Their annual highlight was the National Business Women's Week in October.

When Marie stepped into the meeting room, she was greeted by many familiar faces and handed a corsage to pin on her suit jacket. All visitors received corsages. Room decorations showed that great attention was given to detail and lent a sweep of elegance. While Marie was sophisticated, the grand affair with lavish arrangements was fancier than those found in the meetings that she regularly attended. Frisking paper lambs with miniature cutout parasols easily caught one's eye as people stepped up to the display table for a program brochure. Bowls of lavender-hued French heather greeted them at their dining tables. A vase of yellow and white daisies sat next to each dinner plate. Marie found time to eat while their guest speaker gave a talk about Oregon tree farms. Until then, she played the piano for their dinner music.

On Sunday, April 22, the American Legion Junior Girls District 3 conference was held in nearby Toledo. Of the twenty-two girls installed into their Lebanon unit, Patsy and one other girl attended it. Patsy served as chaplain during their afternoon meeting at this all-day event.

On May 16, the American Legion honored Gold Star Mothers at their monthly dinner meeting. A cakewalk followed, and then the post and the unit parted ways for their business meetings. This was Marie's last meeting as Santiam Unit 51 president. She called on chairpersons for reports. They heard from Mrs. Carrie Nichols, the TB survey chairman. They had fallen short of their goal of having 80 percent of Lebanon residents receive an X-ray during the mobile unit visit. However, it was still seen as a success, with more than four thousand residents communitywide receiving an X-ray.

They also heard from Mrs. Ruth Parton, poppy chairman, who said they were ready for Poppy Day on May 26 and 27. Another agenda item was for the Strawberry Festival in June. Each year, the American Legion took an active role in it, with the unit president serving as the chaperone for the festival queen and her princesses, who were all carefully selected high school girls.

Lastly, elections were held. Mrs. Beatrice Crandall, Marie's second vice president, would be their new unit president. Although Marie had been installed in September, following last year's summer break, this year they would have their installation in June for the new officers. With but a month left of her presidency, Marie had more work to do before her term officially ended. Marie would see her auxiliary through the Strawberry Festival.

Two days later, Marie chaperoned ten Strawberry Festival princesses to a meeting with the Jaycees Club in Sweet Home. The Jaycees Club, for which Marie had been the pianist at their show in February, is a civic group for young adults that focuses on leadership and business development through social service activities. Marie and her princesses were their honored guests, and they heard from a University of Oregon speech group who gave a symposium. Marie and four of her princesses provided the musical interlude.

On Friday and Saturday, May 26 and 27, Marie assisted Mrs. Parton on Poppy Day. There were many people and businesses to visit to extend encouragement. It was a full weekend of American Legion events for Marie, as she had a district meeting to attend on Sunday.

The Willamette Council meeting of the American Legion met in Springfield that Sunday evening, May 28. Clarence and Patsy, as a Junior Girl, went with Marie, as did Mrs. Vada Whetstone and Mrs. Maude Duncan, who was related to Mrs. Berneice Duncan. This council oversaw Willamette Valley district officers, meeting on a regular basis, and, like the district officers, alternated in their meeting place.

Marie's one-year term as District 3 secretary was also ending. In a token of appreciation, Marie presented the District 3 group a gift of a hand-crocheted tablecloth that her mother, Laura, had made for them. The council announced that Marie was a viable candidate for District 3 president. Her year as the Santiam Unit 51 president and as the District 3 secretary had made her worthy of this consideration.

A few days before that meeting, Marie had assisted her daughter Betty with her Girl Scout troop. On Thursday, May 25, the Girl

Scout leaders had an afternoon teakettle card party as a fundraiser, and Marie had taken charge of the game tables as scorekeeper. It was the second event that month at which Marie and Betty had both helped. On Saturday, May 13, one of Betty's friends had gotten married. Marie had been the pianist for their wedding, and Betty had been a hostess, in charge of the guest book. Whenever Marie's schedule was free to help Betty at an event, she was happy to do so.

Marie was quite proud of her oldest daughter for her community involvement. Betty had grown up to be a fine young woman, turning twenty-five years old at the end of this month. Marie recalled all too well the uncertainty she'd had when, twenty-five years ago, she hadn't known what was to come of her newborn daughter without a father. And she remembered her father's disapproval of her failed marriage, as if it were her fault. She had known then that it wasn't her fault, despite her father's insistence that it was a woman's duty to keep a marriage intact. Back then, her intuition and gutsy determination set her out to prove both of them culpable of wrongdoing—her first husband for his actions, and her father for his illogical beliefs. One could question whether in doing so, her anger ever really dissipated.

The May 23, 1950, issue of the newspaper had another letter in the "Needs of the Needy" column. It gave an account in Polly Potter's words of a woman eerily similar to the woman Marie had been twenty-five years earlier. Polly also pleaded on the woman's behalf, saying she needed bedding and other household items. After stating her needs, Polly lastly described in detail what she thought of this woman's predicament.

> This week brought me another deserted mother with a problem. She has two adorable children, and she is a fine mother. Her husband just walked out of her life two months before her youngest child was born. I wonder how many women under the same circumstances would manage as well as this woman does.

As to fathers who desert families, I am sure there is not enough space for me to express my contempt for these men. They assume obligations so lightly and when things become difficult they just walk out on all their responsibilities. Maybe someday a law will be put into effect that will punish them as they deserve. I don't see how any man could resist such darling children as these two. I am sure any of my readers would admire the courage of this mother in bringing these two babies up properly under such difficult circumstances.

Chapter 11

Don't Just Lead, Build
June 1950–October 1950

Marie traipsed through soggy grass as she crossed the schoolyard with ten Strawberry Festival princesses in tow. Ardeth, Alice, Joan, Adelie, Jackie, Jane, Dewanda, Betty, Mary, and Elaine were all high school girls. Dewanda was in the International Order of the Rainbow for Girls alongside Patsy, Marie's daughter, serving as their worthy adviser. Mary was the daughter of Mrs. Waddell, the Linn County Concert Association's president, with which Marie helped with fundraising. Marie was officially still the American Legion Auxiliary president, and as such, their chaperone.

They took their place on stage, next to three judges. It was Friday morning, June 9, and people were gathered on the high school lawn to hear who the judges had chosen as queen for the 1950 Lebanon Strawberry Festival. The grass was wet, as it had been raining off and on that day and the day before, so people remained standing. It was a small panel of judges, representing different Lebanon civic groups, with their chairman being an Oregon State University professor.

Up until 1950, this event's official title had simply been the Strawberry Festival. The senior royalty court for its parade had comprised one girl from each high school in Linn County to serve as a princess. This year, 1950, that changed. It became the Lebanon Strawberry Festival, and the royalty court girls were all chosen from Lebanon High School. Their 1950 parade would have nine princesses, with one of the ten original princesses to be queen, as chosen by the judges.

One judge made the announcement. They chose high school senior and valedictorian Miss Dewanda Hamilton. In surprise at hearing her name, Miss Hamilton became too weak to stand, but Marie took hold of her and clutched her in a strong hug for this tear-jerking moment. Under a light rain shower, the coronation ceremony began. Marie didn't let go of her. Dewanda needed Marie's strength. Mayor Peter Tweed placed the crown on her head. Clouds then moved aside, and the rain parted ways.

An hour later, the grand parade began, a two-mile-long procession of vehicles and floats. First in line was a city police car, and then a fire truck. Four chauffeured cars followed with Queen Dewanda, nine princesses, and their chaperone, Marie. Next in line was the float with what the residents proudly called the largest strawberry shortcake in the world. The high school band marched behind the strawberry shortcake. Others followed as they went south on Main Street. Marie and the girls waved to bystanders for a full hour.

Prizes were awarded for first, second, and third place for the floats in the parade. The Rainbow Girls took second place. After the parade, Queen Dewanda made the first cut to slice the strawberry shortcake, and then each resident who wanted a slice had their fill. Other events carried the festival through to the end of the day and the next day. Horse racing was featured on both afternoons, and lastly, a square dance was held on Saturday night.

Marie was given her past president's pin during their next American Legion meeting, on Tuesday evening, June 20. It was the night to install officers, with Mrs. Beatrice Crandall becoming the new Santiam Unit 51 president. Patsy and the other girls in the Junior Girls sang two songs. When Mrs. Crandall presided over their auxiliary's business session, Marie was chosen as a delegate to attend the state convention in early September with her. Marie would attend it not only as their delegate but also as District 3 president. The Willamette Council had elected Marie as president in an unopposed and unanimous vote.

Come the next evening, Wednesday, June 21, Marie was at the meeting for the Business and Professional Women's Club, or BPW, its better-known name. Tonight's meeting was at the First Methodist Church with dinner in its dining hall, and the church ladies had prepared the meal. Table lighting was provided by tall taper candles. Bowls with Paul's Scarlet roses accentuated each dinner place setting. They had an installation ceremony for incoming officers instead of a guest speaker. Mrs. Margaret Grahm became president, and tribute was paid to Mrs. Peggy Hatfield for her service as president for the past year. Two ladies sang a solo as Marie played the piano for their ceremony.

Marie wasn't a guest at their meeting this time. Two weeks earlier, Marie had been one of three new members initiated into their group. To be a member of the BPW was naturally the next best step for Marie. She had plans to start a local business office for the Welcome Wagon, and with that, she was officially a career woman. While she had encouraging support from fellow members of the American Legion and the Red Cross, this business venture could use any extra push she could give it so that it would have a good start. Any contacts gained would prove beneficial, she reasoned in agreement with her friend Mrs. Hatfield and others.

The Welcome Wagon was a public relations service that acquainted new residents with their local businesses. In 1950, it operated in over nine hundred communities nationwide. Lebanon didn't yet have a chapter, but Marie would start one. She first had to take the weeklong session of courses that the organization offered, and was scheduled to do so in September.

To better understand what the Welcome Wagon was, one can read what Eleanor Roosevelt, the First Lady from 1933 to

1945, wrote, which was printed in the *Los Angeles Daily News* on June 2, 1950. Mrs. Roosevelt makes mention of her attendance at a meeting when detailing her Memorial Day activities, which also included visiting her husband's grave and her sons and their families.

Monday evening, I went to a small meeting of an organization called The Welcome Wagon. This organization has hostesses who call on newcomers to a city or an area and try to bring them quickly into the life of the community. They sign them up as volunteers in various activities, such as hospitals, bring gifts from the merchants and introduce them to the various shops in town, tell them how to get in touch with Boy and Girl Scouts, the Ys and schools, and once a month they hold a meeting, sometimes educational and sometimes purely social. In this way, people grow more quickly into the life of the community and have a neighborly feeling.

Meanwhile, Marie never missed a beat to write her "Needs of the Needy" weekly column. Issue after issue showed someone in need. Marie didn't have to look far to see that many fellow members in the groups she was involved with had it comparatively good. In this observation, there was also plenty for her to hear. Some women commended her for her good works. Others may have instead questioned her. The June 13, 1950, issue of the newspaper gave another letter from Polly Potter, and she seemed to respond to any such questions.

So many people are afraid that I will not investigate these cases and that I will help someone who does not deserve it. I feel sorry for anyone who feels that way as they evidently do not have the spirit of charity which all need to make us human. How much better to help someone who is not deserving than to not help someone who is. Who is to judge whether or not anyone is deserving of help?

Maybe a man does not have the ability to support his family, maybe a man is even lazy but should the families of men like these suffer, and these children are the future of our country, and we want them to have decent education and at least the necessary things of life. But to relieve the minds of those who are worrying, I do investigate every case. A great many are referred to me by the Red Cross and most veterans cases from the Legion auxiliary but of course many come to me through this column.

In these summer months, the Eastern Star, the White Shrine of Jerusalem, and the PTA were on summer break. The Red Cross continued to meet, and Marie attended their June meeting as their newly elected Linn County home nursing chairman. In this chairman role, she would recruit nurses and make arrangements for them to travel to Corvallis for training.

The American Legion saw no break in their work. The auxiliary never seemed to rest, save for their annual picnic on Sunday, July 9. Clarence, Marie, and daughters Peggy and Patsy went to the picnic, following their meeting attendance with the Willamette Council in nearby Florence.

While the summer months were usually less bustling with business and activities for the American Legion, Mrs. Beatrice Crandall, their auxiliary president, was asked to form a committee to help the fundraising efforts for a new hospital. Plans and hopeful wishes had begun in 1947 toward the building of a new hospital in Lebanon. Their needed capital was being met with hesitancy. In the summer of 1950, and under the leadership and presidency of Mr. John Nylund, 130 businessmen formed a fundraising campaign group. These businessmen had to overcome myriad obstacles to raise this capital. They decided to meet daily before their workday began. That meant it had to be an early morning hour and furthermore, they would need breakfast.

Mr. Nylund asked Mrs. Crandall whether her auxiliary could help, and she obliged by creating a Breakfast Committee. She would be the chairman but needed a vice chairman, and Marie didn't hesitate to be that can-do person. After that restful Sunday picnic in early July, the hard work began. Only a couple of days into the new week, Marie and the other committee members were on-site with Mrs. Crandall at the Lebanon High School cafeteria even before the sun rose on that summer day.

Mr. Wesley Hickey, a navy veteran, had arrived two hours earlier, cooking since before four o'clock that morning. The Breakfast Committee helped him with final preparations, and then he left to go to his job as a cook in a local restaurant. Marie and the other ladies served all 130 men a hot breakfast at six thirty that morning. This was only the first day. The campaign group returned the next morning and the next. They returned every morning for six weeks, six days a week, with only Sundays off. Mr. Hickey was there every morning to cook.

Some ladies may have missed a day or two out of sickness, oversleeping, or a family obligation. Not Marie. She didn't miss a day helping in their Breakfast Committee. She rose early every morning, tended to her daily hygiene, and carefully selected an outfit. Then she was out the door and to the high school. She had men to meet and a hospital to build.

The campaign group's meetings were chaired by Mr. Louis Barr, who was a politician from California. Mr. Nylund chose Mr. Barr for his expertise in hospital financial management in both California and Oregon. The men in this group represented a fair cross section of the Lebanon area. Some were employers with offices and businesses to run. Some were men who later in the morning would be on an assembly line or in a production job with any one of the mills. They were church leaders, labor leaders, industrial workers, and husbands and fathers. They began each meeting by tabulating the results of the previous day's solicitation, with soliciting groups divided into six teams, each with a captain. Under the inspiring direction of Mr. Barr, remedial advice was given, and effective plans were discussed. They depended on the Breakfast Committee not only for breakfast but also for a much-needed morale builder.

Marie's smile and charm, along with the hospitality extended by the other ladies, gave the men an energy boost as they toiled toward victory. These ladies recalled all too well how their hospital hadn't been equipped to store blood for their Red Cross bloodmobile drive last December. Their hospital wasn't keeping pace with other medical centers for modern amenities. Community members needed a place in their city to serve emergency and surgical needs.

Lebanon's history concerning a hospital had been rocky. It had gone through several changes, all with private management by nurses, even in its recent past. In 1917, the city's first established hospital, an eight-bed facility, was in the spacious Montague Home. Staffed by Dr. Joel Booth and other physicians, it moved in 1919 to the Scroggin House. Dr. Booth was also a longtime Eastern Star member whom Marie was well acquainted with. Mrs. Grace Scroggin's father-in-law owned the Scroggin House.

In 1922, sisters Martha and Mary Schuler, who were registered nurses and Mennonite members, assumed business management of the hospital. The Schuler sisters also cleaned and cooked. They kept a dairy cow and tended to a vegetable garden in the yard of the Scroggin House to help feed patients. In 1936, a sixteen-bed hospital in a stucco building was erected on the same lot. Then, in 1947, the Schuler sisters wanted to retire and demanded that Dr. Booth and the other physicians pay them for their investment. They had bought medical equipment and wanted $20,000 in return. The doctors were reluctant to comply. The Pacific Coast Mennonite Mission Board in Albany intervened. After more than a year of business haggling, the end result was that Lebanon again needed a new hospital. The sisters were terminated from their duties and responsibilities, and the physicians paid them as requested.

Next, the mission board hired an administrator to oversee the building operations. It was Bishop Allen Erb, a Mennonite from Colorado, who was well experienced in this line of work. During the ensuing eighteen months, the old place continued business while the administration and financing for the new hospital was planned out. Only a small fraction of the needed funds was initially raised. From there, they began meeting daily at the Lebanon High School with the Breakfast Committee, formed by the American Legion Auxiliary, to serve them breakfast.

WHILE MARIE KNEW where to start her day, she likewise tended to her other activities and commitments. Her bridge clubs saw her regularly, and she won a high-score award in a late July meeting. On July 23, a Sunday that year, her mother had another birthday, as did her granddaughter, Kathi, who turned three years old.

Marie also joined forces with her daughter Betty in some of her functions. Betty, who was evermore dedicated to leading the Girl Scouts in any role given to her, hosted a farewell party for one of the leaders on Wednesday, August 2. It was for Mrs. Frank Wells, who had served for three years as Girl Scouts district chairman. She was soon relocating to Hermiston. Marie and two other ladies helped Betty with party arrangements. It was a tea social held on the terrace of a garden at the home of another scout leader.

Shortly into August, the nearby city of Sweet Home had an event called Frontier Days. Likened to the Lebanon Strawberry Festival, this was an annual event, although it had only recently begun, with the weekend of August 12 and 13 this year marking its third year held. Lebanon, Albany, and other nearby cities participated in and attended this festival. Marie was one of two judges in the women's division for a costume contest that was part of the festivities. Contestants wore treasured garb of bygone days, and Mrs. Peggy Patchell won first prize. Although on a smaller scale than the festival in Lebanon, Frontier Days too had a parade, a horse show, and other fun activities to fill the weekend.

Meanwhile, the hospital campaign group determined that while the Mennonites could continue managing the old hospital, there had to be an ownership change. The new hospital had to be community owned, financed, and controlled. Only then would the Lebanon residents be willing to finance the needed capital. Mr. Nylund and Mr. Erb made it happen.

Mr. Nylund, with the help of Mr. Barr, also directed other final activities as the campaign was coming to a close. A twenty-one-member hospital board and a physician advisory board were formed to oversee all needed arrangements as they moved forward. A Founders' Service Organization was created in August, composed of all campaign workers. And the work for the Breakfast Committee ended in the third week of August. They had served thirty-six breakfasts during the six weeks of meetings. The campaign group had been successful.

On Tuesday, August 22, the Founders' Service Organization had a smorgasbord luncheon, also in the high school cafeteria. The buffet table was attractively laid with white lacy tablecloths. Autumn flowers adorned the dining tables. The lunch was in appreciation for all those who had thus far worked so hard toward the goal of building a new hospital. Meal preparation and decorations fell into the hands of the Rainbow Girls. Marie's youngest daughter, Patsy, at sixteen years old, remained active in this organization.

The American Legion Auxiliary and the wives of those who had been in the fundraising campaign group were the honored guests. Women wore their finest suits, and some also wore matching hats. Mrs. Crandall and Marie were invited to sit at the speakers' table with their keynote speaker, Mr. Barr. A fourth person, Mrs. Mary Herron, joined them. Mrs. Herron was also active in civic volunteering. She had been the Linn County PTA president during the time that Marie was the Lebanon PTA president. Her husband, Dr. Ralph Herron, was a surgeon and was on the physician advisory board.

During his speech, Mr. Barr spoke about the need for a women's auxiliary to help in the foundation of this hospital. He expressed that their board members were focused on business matters, which limited their scope, whereas this new auxiliary would give women the important role of keeping them grounded in humanitarian principles, on which the auxiliary should be founded. His suggestion was met with enthusiasm from the women, who then signed membership cards.

As their luncheon meeting continued, the physician advisory board next selected a fifteen-member hospital auxiliary board, which would formulate policies and guide physicians in their decision-making process. Mrs. Katherine Harris, whom Marie knew as a writer with *The Lebanon Express*, and Mrs. Hatfield were among the fifteen women chosen for the board, as was Marie. And they had over one hundred charter members to help them. The next order of business before their meeting concluded was to elect officers from those fifteen women. Marie was their first hospital auxiliary board president, with Mrs. Vada Whetstone as vice president and Mrs. Marilyn Hayes as secretary. With both lunch and business matters done for the day, everyone cheered together in triumphant exhilaration.

Marie would do her utmost as a founding leader. If only her father could have seen her now. He had never built a hospital. She would show him, even if he had to roll over in his grave, that she could build something—something great to help people. So many sad cases came to her in her role as Polly Potter, including many who were afflicted with illness. Marie envisioned a hospital that would be a sanctuary for the healing of the spirit as well as the body. She wanted its doors to be open always to persons of all creeds, races, and walks of life, whether being born or sick or on their deathbeds. No one should be turned away for lack of money, and their care should be personalized with kindliness, warmth, understanding, and love. Marie was resolute in making her dream come true.

Five letters from Polly Potter appeared in the newspaper in August, one for each week. The second letter alluded to the reminder that Lebanon needed an adequate hospital, one that was caring and giving.

> Does someone have a baby bassinet they no longer use? An expectant mother needs one badly. There will be no place for the baby to sleep except with its parents if some sort of bassinet cannot be found. They are barely able to save enough from his small wages to pay for the hospital and doctor so there is no money for extras. I do hope someone can give this baby a basket or bassinet.

SEPTEMBER OPENED WITH a wedding for a Lebanon couple, and Marie was the pianist for their ceremony. It was an evening candle-light event on Saturday, September 2, in a countryside house, home to relatives of the bride, Miss Edris Lanning. Edris was a young woman, recently graduated, whom Patsy knew from high school. Marie played the piano for their wedding march.

On Wednesday, September 6, Marie's daughter Betty and Betty's husband, Andrew, left for a three-week vacation to visit Andrew's mother in Cresco, Iowa. They took their children with them so they could get to know their other grandma. A scenic trip home was planned, with a visit to Yellowstone National Park in Wyoming. Although their daughter, Kathi, was quite young, both she and their son, Randy, who was now five years old, would surely find this park to be a sight to be enjoyed and one that was much different from their Lebanon backyard.

While Betty was traveling, so too was Marie. The American Legion state conference, a four-day event, was in Grants Pass with opening ceremonies on September 6, the same day that Betty left for her trip. Marie was one of several women in her auxiliary who went with Mrs. Beatrice Crandall, their auxiliary president. Mrs. Vada Whetstone and Mrs. Marilyn Hayes, who were now Marie's vice president and secretary with the hospital auxiliary board, also went, as well as Mrs. Betty Ouderkirk and Mrs. Kee Buchanan Groves.

Marie served as the convention musician. Although this involved piano playing, it also involved making arrangements for others to provide music, with a fifty-member accordion band from Grants Pass High School as a well-received addition to their musical entertainment. Mrs. Whetstone and Mrs. Groves also served as convention chairmen.

Before the post and the unit separated ways for their meetings, they heard from several speakers. Governor Douglas McKay was one of them, same as the year before. Another speaker was the national commander who lived in Kansas. He informed members of America's part in the Korean War, which had started in June. An awards ceremony and then later an installation of incoming state officers were on the agenda. Many units from all across Oregon were recognized for their committee work. Of these, Marie accepted a first-place award on behalf of Santiam Unit 51 for child welfare activities.

Marie would have attended the American Legion's dinner meeting in September, but she was out of town. This was during the same week that she was in Hollywood, California, for her training to start a Welcome Wagon chapter for Lebanon. Their meeting had two speakers, with one who talked about the Korean War. There had been lots of talk of that lately in all of Marie's circles, however, so it was okay for her to miss his speech. The other speaker was Mrs. Beatrice Crandall, Santiam Unit 51 president. She shared that when they were in Grants Pass for the state convention, she took a side trip to Camp White. She explained that, unlike the veterans hospitals in Portland and Roseburg, this was a home for disabled and indigent veterans. They agreed to include Camp White in their charitable donations.

In other business for their meeting, reports were given to show that Santiam Post 51 and its auxiliary had again been successful in a membership drive. In all, they had gained 452 members during the past year. And again, Mrs. Vada Whetstone was awarded for the most unit members drawn in.

They also read a letter received from Mr. John Nylund, the hospital board president, thanking the auxiliary for their work with the Breakfast Committee. In his written words, he furthermore stated that "a special plaque, the only plaque to be awarded to any organization for distinctive community service, will be placed permanently in the lobby of the hospital when it is completed. The only other plaque will be one dedicated to those who served their country in war."

The groundbreaking ceremony for the new hospital was on Sunday, October 15, at three o'clock in the afternoon. Under clearing skies on a chilly day, about five hundred people showed up to witness the start of their dig in the dirt to build their new hospital. Marie wasn't able to attend. Try as she might, she just couldn't be in two places at the same time on this day. There were times when she was able to do just that, such as when she was the Lebanon PTA president and had been at two rummage sales happening simultaneously—one as a fundraiser for the Lebanon PTA, and the other as a fundraiser for Queen Anne School. However, on the afternoon of October 15, she had a prior commitment.

About two hundred people instead attended a mid-afternoon church wedding for a young Lebanon couple, for which Marie was one of the hostesses. Reverend Harvey Schmidt officiated at the wedding, and Mrs. Dorothy Page played the piano for their ceremony. The youngest wedding attendant was Mrs. Blandena Wilson's little girl, who was the trainbearer for the bride's wedding march. Mrs. Wilson was in the American Legion Auxiliary alongside Marie. Guests were received in the church parlor for the reception afterward. The serving table was laid with a lace tablecloth, handmade by the bride's grandmother. Marie tended to the guest book at a table, which was adorned with yellow chrysanthemums. She greeted each guest as they signed their name in the book.

It was Marie's second event that day. First thing that morning, she had joined fellow members from the Business and Professional Women's Club at Lebanon's Baptist Church. Although Marie wasn't a regular churchgoer, this was different. Sunday was the kick-off day for the National Business Women's Week, and to attend church together was the first of many BPW events for this weeklong observation.

Mr. Delmar Clem was master of ceremonies for the hospital's groundbreaking ceremony. He had been the Red Cross fund drive general chairman last March. Although Marie wasn't there, Mrs. Beatrice Crandall was and presided over the event. Mr. Nylund turned the first shovel of dirt. In a loud and direct voice, he said, "Only in America is a project such as we are undertaking possible. Here in the Willamette Valley, there is more opportunity than anyplace in the world."

The local radio station, KWIL, tape-recorded everything. Architects from Portland were ready. Capital money had been raised and secured and then supplemented through a federal fund, the Hill-Burton Act. The new hospital would be a one-story building, wrapped around a grassy courtyard. It could take as long as two years to build, and they needed everyone's support and encouragement. It would have central heating and air-conditioning and be of earthquake-proof and fireproof construction. This would be a fifty-bed facility, with two operating rooms and a nursery. Patient rooms would have an intercom system and piped-in oxygen as needed. It would also have a modern and fully equipped laboratory, as well as a blood bank where whole blood and plasma could be stored for emergency uses.

Furthermore, Lebanon Community Hospital would have a living memorial to honor the American Legion Auxiliary. Mrs. Crandall gave the concluding remarks when she said, "Our members hope to join with the other women of the community in making the auxiliary of the new hospital a powerful working organization."

Many other groups had also seen Marie in October. Earlier that month, on October 4, she had attended a dinner meeting with the BPW. When at that meeting, they had decided to start this week together at church in observance of National Business Women's Week. They had also needed more member information for a newspaper article to highlight professional Lebanon women. Marie had given a brief biographical sketch of herself to interviewer Mrs. Helen Myers. Two other members had also helped in this regard.

In other business at that meeting, Mr. William Thomas had been their keynote speaker. As a local attorney, and of more importance, a school board member, he had given information pertaining to a school support measure. It was a bill being proposed for enactment and to be voted on in November. Marie had been keenly interested to hear what he had to say. She was still active with the PTA.

Their article, written by Mrs. Doris Gunderson, would be printed in the Tuesday, October 17, issue of *The Lebanon Express*. Its opening words called for people's attention: "With women in the spotlight during National Business Women's Week, let's take more than a passing glance at members of Lebanon's Business and Professional Women's organization. Here are some women who merit the spotlight."

Marie was acquainted with each woman Mrs. Gunderson made mention of, with some being close friends. Mrs. Peggy Hatfield's biographical sketch described her tireless Red Cross work. Mrs. Vada Whetstone was described as an insurance professional who was quite involved with the Eastern Star. Mrs. Margaret Grahm was named not only as the BPW president but also as a high school and college science teacher. And Mrs. Katherine Harris gained a worthy note for her work with their local newspaper. Those were but a small sampling of the many women named.

Mrs. Gunderson also included a biographical sketch of Marie: "Marie Conner, now District President of the American Legion Auxiliary, is at present pioneering the Welcome Wagon movement in this community. Her work with the county Red Cross, plus her own private charities, occupies much of her time."

Chapter 12

Leading Lady
October 1950

Marie had begun the third week of October with a spirit of comradeship when she had attended the Baptist Church with fellow members of the Business and Professional Women's Club. It was the start of the weeklong observance of National Business Women's Week, with other events scheduled to carry them through. Their featured event would be on Wednesday, October 18, 1950, with a public affairs banquet.

Lebanon wasn't alone in this honorary week, nor was Oregon. To this day, and dating back to 1928, cities all across America have continued to participate. Today, we can see that big cities from New York City to Los Angeles, and from Seattle to Cincinnati, observe this event. Likewise, smaller cities from Yakima, Washington, to McComb, Mississippi, and many more do the same. The designated week is usually in October or mid-March, or, as it was in its early days, mid-April. Often, a woman merits an award as Woman of the Year for their city or community, and sometimes more than one woman is chosen as worthy of this title.

Historically, the city's local BPW is granted the sponsorship of National Business Women's Week by their civic groups and mayor. As we've moved into the twenty-first century, groups other than the BPW have stepped forward to act as sponsors. In 1950, when Marie and others observed this week, local chapters of the National Federation of Business and Professional Women's Clubs were usually the sponsors.

This federation has a history that shows its full capability of organizing and conducting any functions related to this observance. It sponsored the first annual week from April 15 to 22, 1928, with local chapters nationwide participating. In the following year, 1929, the federation began observing it with greater emphasis placed on how businesswomen promoted community welfare. In 1936, President Franklin Delano Roosevelt formally launched the week with a letter to the federation's executive secretary in which he praised women's contributions to the economic life of the nation, resulting in twenty out of the then forty-eight states issuing state proclamations for their observance of it.

At the same time, in 1936, First Lady Mrs. Roosevelt was on the radio with a public broadcast from the White House to promote this observance. Mrs. Roosevelt and Mrs. Charl Ormond Williams, the president of the National Federation of Business and Professional Women's Clubs, discussed the topic of "Women's Responsibility for Effective Democracy." In their conversation, Mrs. Williams asked Mrs. Roosevelt if women could help assure a democracy. Mrs. Roosevelt ended her response with the words, "Women can take the lead in assuming the responsibility for encouraging interest in civic and governmental affairs."

When Mrs. Williams questioned Mrs. Roosevelt as to how she became interested in housing conditions, adequate wages, and reasonable working hours, Mrs. Roosevelt described her own experience. When she was younger, her travels abroad in Europe led her to teach classes. She summarized her experience when she said, "All of one's interests are really a gradual growth, and the moving force is the fact that somewhere along the line, you have learned to grasp every opportunity that comes to you for new experience and new knowledge and above everything else, you realize that no individuals and no conditions must remain foreign to you. Only in this way can you become a really helpful citizen."

Although this radio conversation was before the days when Marie was making her indelible mark, she was doing as Mrs. Roosevelt had advised. In the 1920s, Marie had had a rough marriage with a bootlegger, and she had been abandoned by this man, only to remarry. She couldn't change the fact that she had been the one to break the family tradition in that no one in all the previous generations that could be accounted for had remarried. She had overlooked her father's disappointment when her family's status quo had been broken. Her resilience had shown her success as a wife and mother, all while the country suffered from the Great Depression. She had experienced hardships, and yet she pushed on, into the 1940s and a new community that welcomed her. She had found that she had an understanding of her fellow citizens when they were faced with difficulties. Marie had risen above her difficult times. She had become the "really helpful citizen" that, in 1936, Mrs. Roosevelt had described.

In 1950, President Harry Truman likewise took an affirmative step when he commended this federation with a letter that he wrote to them:

> I know that the members of National Federation of Business and Professional Women's Clubs wish to be judged on the basis of competence in doing their jobs. They do not wish to be the objects of adverse discrimination nor the subjects of special favoritism because of their sex.
>
> I am happy to give encouragement to the theme, "Measure Up for Full Partnership," which you have chosen for National Business Women's Week. I believe that the steps which lead to success on the job are basically the same for both men and women. The most successful men and women I know have set their goals high and have worked

hard toward them. Successful people know that creative imagination as well as technical ability is necessary for adequate preparation for real partnership in the world's work.

I am glad that American women are rising to their opportunities for work in business and the professions. Their participation in their activities, offices, conference rooms, and legislative halls is good for the country. I am sure that the members of your organization will be increasingly successful in the everyday job of living up to your theme for 1950.

CLOSER TO HOME for Marie, the Oregon governor had made a proclamation on Saturday, October 14, the day before this week officially began. This proclamation was printed in the local newspapers in nearby Albany, their county seat, and in Salem, their capital city.

National Business Women's Week has become an American institution in the nearly quarter-century of its observance. The 23rd Annual Week, October 15–21, will be celebrated in all of the 48 states with arrangements geared to the theme, "Measure Up for Full Partnership."

I am gratified to have received the opportunity to lend the support of my office to the approximately 3,000 members of the Oregon Federation of Business and Professional Women's Club of Oregon, Incorporated, in their acknowledgement of this occasion.

The theme, "Measure Up for Full Partnership," is an inspiring one. Those words constitute a new, concise and forceful renunciation of an old code, a code that has underlain decade and decade of progress toward equal rights for women in the United States.

This year, the sponsors of National Business Women's Week are reiterating, in effect, that women do not want, need, or expect special concessions, conditions, or privileges to assure them appropriate placement in the American pattern of life. Far from desiring to be objects of favoritism, they intend to let competence, intelligence, and understanding speak their richly-deserved testimonial.

This has been the foundation of their movement toward securing the opportunities merited by their abilities, and I take great pleasure in encouraging continued success in this sphere by designating the week of October 15–21, 1950, as National Business Women's Week in this state, say I, Douglas McKay, Governor.

Governor McKay next spoke to the Salem Chamber of Commerce during a luncheon on Tuesday, October 17. His speech, "You and the Future," acknowledged the importance of National Business Women's Week. On that same Tuesday, Mrs. Gunderson's article appeared in the Lebanon newspaper, which spotlighted Marie and other local women in observance of this week.

Marie was also at a luncheon that day, but not with the governor. She was Electa in the Marguerite chapter of the Eastern Star, and as an officer was given a corsage by their hostess, Mrs. Vale Kimes, worthy matron. Mrs. Kimes gave all her women officers chrysanthemum corsages. Following their lunch at twelve thirty, they played pinochle at tables decorated in fall flowers. Marie's playing earned her a prize for the high score. That evening, Marie had dinner with fellow American Legion members at their monthly meeting.

Meanwhile, Marie kept at her weekly writing. A letter from Polly Potter was in their newspaper on that same day, Tuesday. Of greater interest, however, is the letter that appeared the week before. The "Needs of the Needy" column shared two noteworthy stories on Tuesday, October 10. One was about a family wanting to buy a house, and the other about a teacher whose students were making fabric squares for quilt making. Those quilts would become warm bedding for people in need. Polly had also shared her own experience.

> One of my best friends said she thought it must be so depressing to work with needy people so much. I only wish I could make her understand the deep satisfaction I derive from helping someone who does not know which way to turn for help and I am sure it would be a much harder hearted person than I to say "no" to them when they say, "Polly, I didn't know where else to go for help."

THE BPW IN LEBANON had been meeting regularly since its inception back in early 1947. In their 1949 observance of National Business Women's Week, and with a membership growth of more than sixty women, Mrs. Katherine Harris was the first recipient of the Woman of the Year award. It was later decided that this recognition would become an annual event.

Mrs. Harris secured her career position as the society editor with *The Lebanon Express* in September 1945. That along with her volunteer work with the Community Chest, a charitable organization, had helped her earn this honor. Most recently, she had been selected to serve on the fifteen-member hospital auxiliary board with Marie as president. Before Marie had become a BPW member a few months earlier, she had often been a guest at their meetings, usually as their piano player.

At their meetings, they exchanged ideas on how best to serve their community through their work. They helped each other through problems and celebrated each individual accomplishment. Charity work was also recognized, with many members involved in philanthropic activities. They voted and were activists who challenged any laws or policies that weren't advantageous for the professional or working woman.

To be a woman and a business owner in 1950 was a difficult feat stemming from restrictions placed on women by the banks that offered business loans. For the many women who weren't business owners but instead were dependent on employers, their salaries didn't keep pace with that of businessmen. Although the laws were the same for both men and women, it was common practice for a woman to be overlooked in matters concerning promotions and salary increases.

Of interest, in January 1950, President Truman had raised the federal minimum wage to seventy-five cents an hour for the first forty-four hours worked in a week, or about nine and a half dollars in today's money. This was a sizable increase from when it had last been changed, in late 1945, to forty cents an hour. Some states had even higher minimum wages, but Oregon wasn't one of them. Men often earned a dollar or more per hour while women were held back. Unknown at that time, it would be 1961, or eleven years later, when the minimum wage would again be raised.

In preparation for the 1950 observance of National Business Women's Week, Mrs. Margaret Grahm, BPW president, created a committee to oversee the selection of the 1950 Woman of the Year. The three-person committee was composed of Mrs. Peggy Hatfield, BPW junior past president; Mrs. Katherine Harris, the 1949 award recipient; and Mrs. Vada Whetstone, who would serve as chairman. The committee reached out to every known civic group in town in request for them to name a woman whom they would like to see be honored with this title. The Junior Women's Club, of which Marie wasn't a member, was one of six civic groups that unanimously selected her.

However, there were set standards for the committee to use to reach their decision. The woman chosen by those civic groups next had to be judged by the committee on six important criteria. Her activities achieved through organizations and how they were a benefit to the community was one criterion. She also had to have versatile civic accomplishments, responsible leadership, and a willingness to serve her community. Her recognition in her business or profession had to be outstanding. The last criterion, and of no less importance, was that her personality and character also had to be outstanding.

The three committee members were all good friends with Marie. However, their decision had to be reached not based on friendship but on worthiness. It had to be a woman who met or exceeded the set standards. It had to be a woman who, according to this year's slogan, measured up. And they had to consult with Mayor Peter Tweed for his approval. The BPW was, after all, only the sponsor and as such was acting on behalf of all of Lebanon in its decision of who would be Lebanon's Woman of the Year.

Marie wasn't alone in the fierce and friendly competition, nor the only ideal woman. After a careful review of all nominations and then a final determination, the committee and Mayor Tweed had to keep their decision hush-hush, even among their closest friends. This decision couldn't be revealed just yet. The Woman of the Year would be announced at their Wednesday night public affairs banquet. Invitations to this affair were sent to each service club and civic group, the mayor, and other city government officials, and were extended to husbands of BPW members. At shortly after two o'clock on Wednesday afternoon, KRUL radio station out of Corvallis brought attention to this event. Its program consisted of a short speech by a BPW member, a short skit, and a replay of Governor McKay's proclamation.

MARIE APPROACHED THE STEPS to the Lebanon Methodist Church. Clarence was beside her, and their daughter Betty was with them. Marie wore a black pencil dress with a deep V-neckline. Button earrings and a smile with perfect red lipstick brought attention to her face. Her hair was styled in a poodle cut with front-facing voluminous curls. Marie's polished look caused her to shine with a friendly confidence as they stepped up to the church's front entrance.

This church had two notable mentions this month. Not only was it where the Woman of the Year award would be presented on this night, Wednesday, October 18, it was also celebrating its centennial anniversary, with the church's founding one hundred years ago this month. It frequently served as a gathering place for area groups and their functions. A rotunda gallantly faced forward to look out onto the street and was to the left of its doors. A tall stained-glass window was on the right side of the two-story brick building, and a full chord window was above the foyer. It was a grand sight and a friendly sanctuary on the corner of Vine and Park that catered to many families in Marie's neighborhood.

It was a pleasant fall season, with temperatures hovering around sixty degrees all that day. It had been a little drizzly that morning, but no rain was in sight as they stepped under the covered entryway. The sun would set soon, and the public affairs banquet in honor of National Business Women's Week was set to begin at six thirty. Inside, people mingled and chatted freely in merriment, all in anticipation to hear who would become the 1950 Woman of the Year.

With people seated and as dinner ended, their event's chairman, Mrs. Vada Whetstone, stepped on stage and garnered everyone's attention. After welcoming remarks and notable mentions of some people in attendance, she introduced a few people. Miss Carolyn Landy, BPW Girl of the Month, was presented by Mrs. Violette Olstad, a home economics teacher. The Girl of the Month program had been started earlier in October, and Miss Landy was the first selected girl. She was a high school senior and led the Junior Girls in the American Legion. Mrs. Katherine Harris was also brought on stage, worthy of introduction as the 1949 Woman of the Year.

Mrs. Whetstone then informed people that they would hear from several speakers, but first Mrs. Peggy Hatfield had an announcement to make. Mrs. Hatfield, BPW junior past president, stepped up to the standing microphone. Newspaper articles from

Lebanon, Albany, and Salem give us the context of how the ceremony proceeded and the plausible spoken words. Mrs. Hatfield knew her fellow members well, and she knew her friend Marie in particular quite well—they put in countless hours of Red Cross work together, they played cards together, and Marie had recently hosted a birthday party for her. Mrs. Hatfield was a good-natured woman, hardworking and happy to recognize the hard work of others as she spoke to the audience.

This year's theme for National Business Women's Week is "Measure Up for Full Partnership." Our individual members carry on at their jobs this week, just as they have during the entire year. The many BPW women who are owners or co-owners of their businesses are an example of the part they play in the business life of Lebanon. Their occupations range widely in business, industry, and the professions.

Members of this organization have earned respected places in the working world by knowledge of their jobs and faithful performance of them. By the same method, they have given attention to local problems, helping the community to grow with integrity. In contributing to individual jobs and civic life, they have already measured up to full partnership.

There is one woman who has been active in civic affairs. She heads the new hospital auxiliary board of directors, assuring us a new five-million-dollar medical center, and is now organizing the Welcome Wagon project here and is a member of the Order of Eastern Star and White Shrine. She has participated in and occupied offices in the city PTA and the American Legion Auxiliary and at present is district president.

Active in Red Cross work, she is chairman of the home nursing division of the Linn County chapter. Among other outstanding interests, she is Polly Potter and collects food and clothing for needy families, as well as writes a weekly column in the local paper, telling of her work. She is a member of the BPW.

Three members of her family work in the composing room of *The Lebanon Express* including her husband, Clarence, son Bill, and daughter Peggy. A younger daughter, Patsy, attends high school. Another son, Dick, lives here in Lebanon. Two grandchildren also seek her attention. And she has a married daughter, Mrs. Andrew Peckham, who is here to share her mother's honor.

Mrs. Hatfield waved her arm in a gesture to invite Marie up on stage. In her final words and forgoing any formality, Mrs. Hatfield added, "Marie has measured up."

Marie wasn't at all shy to step up on stage. If only her father could have seen her now. He had wanted his boys to grow up to be fine men. He hadn't wanted a girl. She had grown up and was now a woman who was proud to receive this honor. Her father had been an intelligent and sharp man and even perceptive, although shrewd. Marie and her father were much alike in more ways than not. She had used her opportunities to reach this advantageous milestone, though unlike her father, she hadn't put anyone in the dirt in doing so. Marie wasn't ready to admit that she had turned out much like him. She was, though, ready to be the 1950 Woman of the Year for her Lebanon community.

Mrs. Hatfield handed Marie a gift from their club. It was a silver platter, engraved with her name, the year, and her honorary title. Marie smiled big as Mrs. Hatfield pinned an orchid corsage on her dress. In an announcement to the audience, Mrs. Hatfield said, "I introduce to you Lebanon's Leading Lady for this year."

People stood and clapped. The standing ovation continued as Mrs. Hazel McCracken, a fellow BPW member and close friend and neighbor to Marie, took a seat at the piano. Mrs. Ella Bahner led the audience in group singing as Mrs. McCracken played the piano. Other music followed with three members who each sang a solo, one in a baritone.

While the musical program proceeded, Marie rejoined her family. When Mrs. Whetstone returned to the microphone, she began the next segment, introducing their first speaker. Representatives from the Chamber of Commerce; the Kiwanis, Lions, and Junior Women's clubs; and the VFW and the American Legion and their auxiliaries each gave short talks. Another speaker was heard from, and that was Marie, representing the hospital auxiliary board.

Their last speaker was Mrs. Denice Holmes, BPW president and charter member, who spoke on the history of their club. Mrs. Holmes then called on all twenty charter members to each receive a corsage. She also gave the last business of the night: a brief report for each of their committees. The formal meeting adjourned, and those in attendance returned to their mingling and merriment.

Marie soaked in this social hour and couldn't be happier that Clarence was at her side. More often than not, he wasn't with her at her events, as he had other obligations, one being his responsibilities with the newspaper. This was different, though. It was a great honor for Marie to become the Woman of the Year.

She had an Eastern Star event in her datebook for the next night. The Marguerite chapter was again hosting the meeting for the Willamette Valley Matrons and Patrons Association. Like last time, she would be in a skit for its entertainment portion. Clarence likely wouldn't be with her for that, as it was on a Thursday evening, and with the newspaper going to print on Friday morning, Clarence would stay until it was ready. He worked long hours to make sure the paper always got out on time.

His frequent absence made the times that she did have him with her all the more sweet. With Clarence beside her, Marie brought her attention back to this evening. She was Lebanon's leading lady.

Part 3

*Marie Conner (at right) and Peggy Hatfield (at left) plan
the March of Dimes campaign, Lebanon, Oregon.*

Image Credit: *The Lebanon Express*, February 1, 1952.
(Eggen Photo)

Chapter 13

Polly Potter
October 1950–October 1951

"Our children are our future!"
—MARIE CONNER, 1951

There were four and a half weeks in October 1950, and with that, five issues of the "Needs of the Needy" column, one for each Tuesday. Her column only gave her pen name, but those who either already knew Marie or who would meet her through that charity project knew that Polly Potter and Marie were one and the same. While Marie's sentence structure and grammar usage wouldn't pass muster in a high school English class, her choice words, heartfelt messages, and gratitude, pleas, and criticisms were well received by Lebanon folks through her Polly Potter letters. Her letter on October 31, in its entirety, displayed those varied characteristics.

I have a few requests for aid this week as everyone has been more than generous. Thanks go to several people and clubs who gave lovely new baby things. I would have enough to make up 3 or 4 nice layettes if there were more diapers. That is the only thing needed now for the layettes and also blankets to be used as covering for little beds. There are pinning blankets but no heavier ones. These could be made out of old wool blankets and finished in some way around the edge.

Another use for old wool blankets is to use them inside quilts instead of cotton batts. The sewing groups making these quilts say this would make better quilts than the cotton batts. So, please look and see if you can find an old blanket no matter how worn or ragged but above all, clean, and let me know and I will see that one of these groups get it so that they can finish up some quilts. It looks like as though we will have a hard winter and I would like as much bedding as possible on hand for when it is needed.

I am again pleading with anyone who wishes to get in touch with me to please write to me. I will try so hard to answer every message. I receive so much correspondence that once in a while a letter or card is mislaid and I wish to apologize to anyone who has not received an answer. I simply do not have time to answer the phone and as this is absolutely volunteer work which I try to take care of in my spare moments, it will make it much easier on me if you will write instead of phoning. And I do beg of you to give things that are wearable even if you have to give fewer things. The most of you do that but you'd be surprised if you could see what some people consider wearable, and boxes of absolute junk are brought to my home. If I had time to sort this out, probably some use could be made of it, but I haven't the time.

I received a letter from a club asking if I could tell them of a baby in a needy family for Christmas time. I am sure that I can and if they will go ahead and carry out their plans, I will find the baby for them. How wonderful it is to have these groups that are willing to work together and do so good. Some of them are very small but they want to do their share.

I want to add my plea to that in the Thursday paper, for the little Hand boy suffering from leukemia. This is such a heartbreaking thing and anyone who would like to help in any way should contact his parents who live south of Lebanon in the Knot Hole service station area. They will be most appreciative of any help.

On Wednesday, November 1, Marie made a house call to Mrs. Robert Clark and her firstborn baby. Mrs. Clark offered Marie coffee, and Marie gave her a Welcome Wagon gift basket. It was filled to the brim with items from fifteen Lebanon merchants, and a colorful ribbon was tied to its handle. Mrs. Clark was one of four new mothers and one of eight housewives that Marie called on that week, with the others of the four being new residents of Lebanon.

When Marie had returned from her weeklong training classes in Hollywood, California, in September, her first duty as a Welcome Wagon hostess had been to garner participation from business owners. Each merchant that Marie recruited paid Welcome Wagon a fee, and Marie, in turn, received a commission. The more people became aware of their business, the more sales they had. For Marie, the benefit was less about her commission, which was small, and more about meeting new people and making new friends.

Each merchant filled gift baskets with a wide array of samples, from soap to silverware, from baby clothing to linens, and from food to stationary supplies. Marie then made a house call to those new to town and to expectant and new mothers to give the housewife a gift basket. Marie informed them about grocery stores, shopping places, businesses, societies, and churches. When she told them about the schools, she made mention of the PTA. And she told them about the annual Lebanon Strawberry Festival. Those who were new to Lebanon didn't have to build their civic and social life all over from scratch. Marie was their introduction to what Lebanon had to offer.

Later that month, Marie met with a Welcome Wagon administrator from Eugene in downtown Lebanon. Marie was on several errands that day, and when she came out of a meat market with a turkey, she put it on the back seat of her visitor's car. In their shared excitement at the coffee shop about the Welcome Wagon, they forgot all about the turkey. When their visit ended, the administrator returned to her office. Hours later, Marie made a special trip to Eugene—an hour's drive away. She needed her turkey. Thanksgiving was the next day.

The American Legion was also on Marie's calendar many times as 1950 wrapped up. She had numerous units to visit as much as possible during her District 3 tenure. On Monday evening, November 27, it was a covered-dish dinner meeting with the Albany unit. In early December, it would be with the Corvallis unit to speak about the American Legion's work. Before and after her Corvallis visit, Marie had two meetings closer to home.

The Willamette Council met on Sunday afternoon, December 3, for business and to enjoy a turkey dinner. Marie's Lebanon unit, Santiam Unit 51, hosted it. The district commander and vice district commander and their wives were in attendance, along with other district officers. Mrs. Vada Whetstone and Mrs. Marilyn Hayes were on the Dinner Committee with Mrs. Beatrice Crandall, unit president. Several reports were given, and Marie reported on membership. It was also announced that the district conference would be in February in Toledo, and Marie added that to her appointment book. A few high school girls provided the after-dinner music.

The Christmas party for Santiam Unit 51 was on Sunday, December 17, and again with a turkey dinner. Marie attended that, as did several district officers. Gold Star Mothers were the unit's honored guests on that night. For music, Mrs. Lois Abrell led group singing while Marie played the piano. Two young girls with accordions almost as big as they were performed two songs, and Santa officiated the white elephant gift exchange.

Marie enjoyed those social gatherings. She also thought of people who were less fortunate. Her last Polly Potter letter in 1950 detailed ongoing needs and expressed her gratitude.

> Many, many thanks to all the fine people who helped to make Christmas a very happy day for so many needy families. I am sure that every one of you who made the day brighter for others must have had the true feeling of "Peace on earth, Good will to men." I know these people were grateful although they do not have the ability to express themselves as others do. The look on one child's face when I handed her a few used toys was enough to make me happy through and through.
>
> I was asked how many needy families I had reported to me at Christmas time and when I said 43, they were amazed and didn't seem to think there could possibly be that many. When I convinced them that there was, they couldn't see why there were so many. But it all comes back to these men who just walk out on their wife's children without a thought as to who could care for them.

MARIE'S SON BILL and daughter Peggy had had birthdays during her busy holiday season. Bill was now twenty-three years old, and Peggy was twenty-one. They had been working beside each other in the production room at *The Lebanon Express*, with Bill as a general apprentice and Peggy as their addressograph operator. The printing business, though, wasn't Bill's career calling—the navy was.

Bill left home on the first day of 1951. He had reenlisted in the navy, and his induction was on Tuesday, January 2, in Seattle, a little more than three years after his honorable discharge. America had been in the Korean War since June, and with that, Marie worried about her good son. *The Lebanon Express* hired Mr. Gerald

Holbert to replace him. People called him Jerry, and right away Peggy took a liking to him. Mr. Holbert was from a small town in upstate Washington, with a Canadian town being the only nearby city, and his parents still lived there. After two years in the navy, he had left his hometown behind in search of a promising future. He didn't know where he wanted to live, but Lebanon was a good starting point. His brother lived there.

While Bill was building waves on the open sea, Marie was building a new hospital. The hospital auxiliary board met each month, usually on the last Wednesday in the Central Lane Office. Mr. John Nylund and other hospital officials also met here for their meetings, and they often took turns speaking to the auxiliary board. Marie had two officers at her side, Mrs. Vada Whetstone as vice president and Mrs. Marilyn Hayes as secretary, as well as twelve other members who sat on their board. And their fifteen-member board had one hundred charter members to assist with committee work. They guided hospital officials in their decision-making process and voiced any needed suggestions. They kept them grounded in humanitarian principles, as they had promised when their board was first created.

In mid-January, auxiliary members came together one evening to help with the March of Dimes campaign. They inserted, sealed, and stamped seventeen thousand donation cards to be later mailed. It took them three and a half hours. This was not related to their hospital work, but they were happy to do it. Many civic groups helped in Lebanon's annual fundraising for this national campaign. It had started in 1938 and encouraged each person to give ten cents in the polio fight.

Lebanon's next big fundraiser was for the Red Cross in March. Their annual drive had a new chairman, Mr. Herb Wymore. Marie wasn't the residential chairman that year, but she assisted Mrs. Margaret Grahm, the BPW president. From tea parties to choosing captains, Mrs. Grahm followed Marie's lead, doing as Marie had done in the past three years, and Marie was on call to help.

On Friday evening, March 15, the Hospital Founders' Service Organization hosted a get-together dinner for all the hospital workers. As Marie mingled and socialized, talk was nonstop about the many new and exciting things that were in the works for the new hospital. Their musical entertainment was provided by a barbershop quartet from Eugene, Four-Tune Four.

Polly Potter's letter in the "Needs of the Needy" column on March 20 drew attention to her new clothing room, located in the American Legion hall. It had started in January and was open on Monday afternoons. Polly emphasized that it was the place to drop off donations and the place to come to for help. Of course, Marie also received many donations on her doorstep at home. She had several volunteers, some of whom were from church groups and one being her good friend Mrs. Peggy Hatfield. The room was an unheated space where she and her volunteers sorted and distributed clothing and household goods.

There was no formal application process for someone in need. Marie felt that if someone was brave enough to ask for help, they were desperate enough to need that help. The March 20 letter was printed on the Tuesday before Easter Sunday.

I would like my readers to picture if you will what it would be like to have just barely enough income to pay the rent for a tiny little house and to pay the light and water bill and the barest food necessities. We who worry about a new Easter bonnet or whether our shoes and purses match, please stop and think what it would be like to not have even the simplest of new clothes. Always someone's cast-offs. And then something happens, like the 60th wedding anniversary of a couple who has been mother and father to us. How nice it would be to attend this affair. Now, remember we are nice people just like other people but through a great deal of sickness we have been reduced to living on a welfare check. I hope I have made the picture clear.

In April, Marie had two American Legion events. One was an official visit to the McKenzie River unit near Eugene on Wednesday evening, April 11, at which she gave a keynote speech on Americanism. In the next week, Santiam Unit 51 and its post met on Tuesday evening, April 17. Past presidents were honored on that night.

In May, the hospital auxiliary board lost two members by resignation. One was Marie's secretary, Mrs. Marilyn Hayes. Mrs. Mary Beth Smithley was elected to fill that vacancy. The other was Marie's friend Mrs. Peggy Hatfield, who had other commitments. They elected Mrs. Betty Woods and Mrs. Grace Scroggin to the board to bring it back up to fifteen members. Marie and Grace were dear friends through their shared volunteer work and often played cards together. Grace's husband was on the Building Committee with the hospital board. Next, they created a new officer position of treasurer and elected Mrs. Helen Gustine to serve. Their annual elections would be in September, when new officers would succeed them.

When in her Polly Potter role or as the Welcome Wagon lady, Marie doted on newborns and little children. In June, she was asked to offer her home as a foster home for two young children. Mrs. Patricia Ramsey had filed for divorce. Her husband and she were fellow members of the American Legion, and Mrs. Ramsey had been their 1947 Poppy Committee chairman. Mrs. Ramsey got a court order for the children to be removed from the family home and sent to Marie's house, where she was now staying.

Other family and home front changes likewise happened in June. For one, Marie's daughter Betty also filed for divorce. Marie's first grandchild was now six years old, and her granddaughter almost four. While Marie lost one son-in-law, she gained another that month.

Marie's daughter Peggy and the new apprentice at *The Lebanon Express*, Mr. Jerry Holbert, gathered many friends and family members together at a quaint little congregational church in Tonasket, Washington, for their wedding. Their ceremony was on Saturday, June 24, at four o'clock in the afternoon in commemoration of her grandmother. Marie's mother, Laura, had been married at the same hour on the same day in 1894 in Kansas.

Several carloads of people drove from the Lebanon area to be with them on their special day. Unfortunately, Marie's sons, Bill and Dick, couldn't be with them. Dick and his wife lived in Texarkana, Texas, and it was too soon for Bill to be granted another furlough from the navy. Bill had come home only a month earlier for a one-day visit. He had arrived at three in the morning, then returned to his base later that same day. No one had received much notice when Jerry, who had been in Lebanon less than six months, and Peggy had announced their engagement.

Peggy's older sister, Betty, was her maid of honor while Patsy, Peggy's younger sister, was a bridesmaid. Her sisters wore blue gowns, with Patsy's dress being of a taffeta material and having a wide flowing skirt. They carried pink carnations tied with yellow ribbons. Peggy's best friend, who was a teammate in her bowling league, played the piano for the wedding march and other music. There were many wedding attendants. Some were Jerry's friends and family members who lived in Washington.

Marie wore a long gown in a dark hue of wood violet. Pink earrings and a hat in a blended deep mix of blue and purple accessorized her dress. Jerry's mother wore a brown suit with chartreuse embellishments. Pink corsages adorned their outfits. Bouquets were fastened to the end of the pews with white satin bows. People were seated and the wedding march music began.

Clarence was at Peggy's side, and they walked arm in arm as he escorted her down the aisle. She wore a long white satin bridal gown, accentuated by imported Belgian lace, with a long bridal train that followed. Pear orange blossoms fastened to a headpiece kept her veil in place. She carried a white Bible upon which lay a spray of pink orchids tied together with white satin streamers.

Ahead, the altar was flanked by a lit candelabra and baskets of flowers in pastel shades of pink, blue, and yellow. The church's reverend officiated the vows.

Following their daylong celebration, Peggy and Jerry left for a seaside honeymoon from Washington through Oregon and into California, where they were relocating. They wouldn't return to Lebanon anytime soon. Marie, though, was soon back in Lebanon. She had only one day to get a "Needs of the Needy" column to print by Tuesday.

I am now back and hope I will not be gone again soon. Last week's appeal for things for the little family who lost their home, and their husband and father was not very successful. Evidently many people thought, "Oh well, somebody else will give them the things they need." It's too bad so many seem to forget that a thing like that, a fire, can happen to anyone.

They have received some clothing but there are so many things that are needed in a home. If every reader of this column would give just one article, I am sure they would have what they need. Towels, pillowcases, sheets, bedding of all kinds, dishes, and furniture are all needed. I will be home so if you would like to give anything, I could pick it up. Just call me and I will be so glad to pick up anything and if you have a piece of furniture you could spare, I also can get a truck to pick it up.

Please try to find time in your busy day to think of this sweet girl who lost so much and see if you can spare a few linens or something for her home. She will make the most of whatever is given her. How nice it would be if each person reading this would think, "Now surely, I have something nice I could give this little mother to help make her day a little brighter" and not have it something that you have discarded and that is shabby. I am so often thrilled when someone brings something to me for some unfortunate person that is really nice and is given because the giver has the real spirit of giving.

We are very much in need of large size dresses at the clothing room. You may either leave them at my house or take them to the room on Monday afternoons when it is open. This room is located behind Dr. Elvin's office on Second Street with the entrance in the alley.

Marie had recently moved the clothing room from the American Legion hall to a free space offered by that doctor. Unlike the old room, it was heated. And it was on the ground floor, making it easy for people with mobility issues to enter.

Marie and several friends attended the American Legion's state convention in Seaside on Saturday, September 15. It was a three-hour drive from Lebanon to this coastal town, northwest of Portland. Their all-day session of business meetings included an election for new officers at the state level and for all Oregon districts. Marie's one-year term as District 3 president ended, and Mrs. Frank Walters from Albany succeeded her. In Marie's service to District 3, she was next appointed as their Child Welfare chairman.

One breakout business session at that convention was for the 8 et 40. This was an arm of the American Legion and an honorary group whose members were accepted by invitation only. Today, this group is an independent organization and more commonly known as the Forty and Eight. Marie was accepted into it, then elected as its state musician.

Mere days later, on Tuesday, September 18, Santiam Unit 51 met. The unit gave Marie a gift and thanked her for her year as their District 3 president. Marie's daughter Patsy was one of three girls who gave an informative speech about their recent American

Legion Junior Girls state convention. Patsy was in her senior year of high school. Marie was proud of her. She thrived in both the Junior Girls and the Rainbow Girls.

On Friday, that same week, September 21, Clarence and Marie celebrated a milestone: They had been married for twenty-five years. Staff at *The Lebanon Express* honored Clarence with a cake for two celebrations, one for his birthday and the other for his silver wedding anniversary.

Marie most plausibly met the significance of that milestone with a sense of awareness. Her volunteer work as Polly Potter was her daily reminder of what could have been a pitiful and destitute existence with two young children. Clarence had given her a good home life, and she credited him for it. Yet it was Marie, not Clarence, who had built her life. He just happened to be at her side with love and encouragement as she paved her way. She had fought against her father, who had spoken aloud that she was meant to stay home. Instead, she had stepped out and into her community.

The last week of September 1951 was recognized in Lebanon as Business Professional Women's Week. Inside that week, the hospital auxiliary board met midday on Wednesday, September 26. Marie had been their president since August of the year before, when their board had been formed. Elections were held for incumbent officers to a one-year term. Marie remained on the fifteen-member board while Mrs. Vada Whetstone moved up in rank from vice president to president. Mrs. Whetstone said, "A busy time is anticipated for the auxiliary this year inasmuch as the actual construction of the hospital is underway."

That evening, Mrs. Whetstone, Marie, and many other ladies from the hospital auxiliary board attended the public affairs banquet hosted by the BPW. The year before, Mrs. Peggy Hatfield had given the awards speech to name the Woman of the Year. This year, the tables were turned. Marie gave the speech and handed Mrs. Hatfield a silver platter engraved with her name and the words "Woman of the Year, 1951." Marie's good friend Peggy was a tireless worker in the Red Cross, and she often spent countless hours with her in the Polly Potter clothing room.

Polly Potter's letter that same week shared an experience that could lead Marie to later help in other worthy causes. Her presidencies with District 3 of the American Legion and the hospital auxiliary board were over. Although she was busy in all she did, she had two voids to fill if she wished. The first part of Polly's letter, which had been printed on September 25, told of that worthy cause, while the last part informed readers of current needs.

"…And a little child shall lead them." I was reminded of this phrase from the scriptures while attending a two day meeting of the Oregon Society for Crippled Children and Adults. As I listened to the fine talks by men who have made human afflictions their life study, I was impressed and thrilled to know that there are people who do care for the unfortunate and afflicted.

The strides made in the last few years in medical research are overwhelming. A few years ago, a child born with an affliction was considered queer by all but his parents and either pitied or shunned by others. Now, something is done for them, and they are able to take their place in society and be treated as an equal. Such courage and cheerfulness shown by the crippled children who were present at this meeting could be a lesson to many adults who are perfectly normal.

The crippled children's school in Eugene is supported by this society and is one of the finest schools of its kind in the United States. So much is being done there for children who have afflictions of one kind or another. It would be an inspiration to anyone to visit this school and see what they are accomplishing there by the fine staff of teachers and therapists. Please remember what is being done by this society when you receive your Easter Seals next spring and donate generously to this cause. Who knows, one of their children might be one who will need help some day. Our children are our future!

Yesterday I was visited by a young woman who is a mother of two lovely children. She had been deserted by her husband and she is an orphan. There was no one for her to turn to for help. She had been living in a furnished apartment as her husband had never provided too well for her and she had nothing of her own to keep house with. Now her money is gone, and she has had to move, and I found a cheap unfurnished place for her, and she will receive just enough to provide food and rent from welfare.

She needs everything to keep house with and would be so appreciative of anything that is given to her. Just a few dishes and cooking utensils, towels, bedding, and does anyone have an old electric iron they no longer need? Both of her children are girls, and she likes to keep them clean. She is very sensitive and was desperate when she came to me. If she could just have enough things until she can go to work and earn money.

Please call 2812 and let me know if you have anything for her. She needs a chest of drawers or dresser to keep the children's things in and said she wouldn't care what condition it was in as she would be glad to paint it and fix it up. She has a bed and stove, and I was able to find an old davenport for her. I do hope someone has a few pieces of old silverware or dishes they will give this plucky little mother.

Marie's appointment book for October had many things penciled in. She had meetings to attend with the American Legion, the 8 et 40, the BPW, the PTA, the Eastern Star, the White Shrine of Jerusalem, the Red Cross, and the firemen's auxiliary. And the annual weeklong membership drive for the Linn County Concert Association was always in October.

She also looked forward to her card games with her bridge clubs and had a board meeting with the hospital auxiliary. There was more to do to help build the new hospital that her community desperately needed. She had house calls to make as the Welcome Wagon lady. She had people to help as Polly Potter. Lunches with her good friends Peggy and Grace were also squeezed into her appointment book. Two of Clarence's brothers—one from Portland and the other, Don, from Bend—were also due to visit them that month. She had things to do and meetings and visits and errands to run.

Thursday, October 4, started like many other days. Marie's appointment book showed that she had many things to see to, which could put her home later than usual. Clarence wouldn't be home anytime soon either. It wasn't unusual for him to work late, even several hours past dark, on Mondays and Thursdays to make sure the newspaper was ready to print the next morning on the two days a week that it was published. He never left the production floor until it was done, no matter how late it was, even if it put him into the wee hours of the next morning.

Marie was on an errand that Thursday afternoon. She drove east on Vine Street, and as she crossed Williams Street, a fuel truck collided with her car. The driver, Mr. Arley Hornish, who lived and worked in Lebanon, applied his brakes as his heavy load slammed into the front driver's side of her car. It was rare in 1951 for cars to have seatbelts, and Marie's car was no exception. The next twenty feet was a rough ride for Marie. She was stuck between her seat and the steering wheel as the fuel truck pushed her car up and over a curb, where it finally came to rest on the sidewalk. The truck landed nearby and upside down.

Residents at the intersection of Vine and Williams rushed out of their houses to help. Mr. Hornish was visibly shaken up but otherwise unscathed. Marie remained in her car and was in obvious shock. She had noticeable cuts, bruises, and possibly internal injuries. An ambulance arrived soon, and after immediate first aid was given, she was rushed to Lebanon's hospital. It was the nearest hospital. It had to do.

Chapter 14

The Hospital
October 1951–July 1952

"Let your light shine."
—Marie Conner, 1952

The "Needs of the Needy" column had been printed on Tuesday, October 2, 1951, two days before Marie's car accident. It was three weeks later, on October 23, that readers again heard from Polly Potter. Her letter began with a plea for a woman needing work while her husband recovered from illness. The concluding request was for household items on behalf of two elderly women who lived together. In between those two stories, Polly informed people of her recovery.

I am sorry that this column has been missing for several editions due to the fact that I was in a very serious car accident. Although I am better, I am still unable to do much of anything, but I simply can't bear to be out of touch with all of you wonderful friends and there are so many who need help and only through the column are we able to secure help for them.

The generosity of all you readers is what gives the help for these unfortunate people. Through the marvelous cooperation of a very good woman, I will be able to pick up or deliver things. She has been carrying on while I was hospitalized but without the column she could not reach all of you who supply the things needed so badly by these people. Consequently, the clothing room which she kept open every Monday afternoon is almost completely depleted. There have been several desperate cases, and she has helped the best she could. Her phone number is 6241 and if you have anything to contribute, please call her and she will arrange to pick them up.

As Marie healed, she wanted to be at the next event and in the next meeting. Thus, she tried to pick up where she had left off on that early October afternoon. And thanks to that car accident, she had all the more of an incentive to see Lebanon's new hospital become a reality. Their hospital auxiliary board met the day after her October 23 Polly Potter letter.

Marie's recovery was painstakingly slow, so people rallied together to help in her volunteer work and with the Welcome Wagon. She also had her daughter Betty nearby. Betty had moved back home with her children when she had filed for divorce. With Marie's mother living in their cottage, or the guest house as they now called it, Betty and her children stayed in the house.

Marie's grandchildren rarely voluntarily offered her a quiet moment. She cherished her first grandchild, Randy, now almost seven years old, but also expected him and his little sister to behave, be quiet, and be respectful. Her home was her sanctuary, and in her recovery from bruises and sore bones, she especially needed quiet time. She didn't allow unnecessary noisemaking or for her home to be strewn with toys and clutter. Marie had no tolerance for unruly children. She never had and never would.

At the next hospital auxiliary board meeting, which was on Wednesday, November 28, they heard from a guest speaker from the hospital board, Mr. Richard Davis, Equipment Committee chairman. Mr. Davis reported that approximately $50,000 worth of equipment had been or was presently being ordered. They would have all new surgical and X-ray equipment in the new hospital, whereas beds, dressers, and other patient room furniture would be moved from the old hospital to save on expenses. When he concluded his report, Mrs. Vada Whetstone, president, opened the meeting for discussion and questions. After Mr. Davis replied to questions from Marie and others, they adjourned to meet again in January instead of December as it conflicted with Christmas.

While the hospital auxiliary board took a break in December, so did Marie. She had to rest if she were to fully recover without complications. But she wasn't one to sit at home and do nothing. So she took a vacation to Southern California to visit for a few weeks with her daughter Peggy and her new husband. Marie returned home in late December, in time to attend the annual newspaper staff Christmas party with Clarence, given by Mr. and Mrs. Robert Hayden.

In 1952, the hospital board first met on Thursday, January 17, chaired by Mr. John Nylund, president. More than two hundred people showed up for their annual elections and to hear updates, so they moved their meeting from the Central Lane Office to a larger space at city hall. All the officers on their twenty-one-member hospital board of directors were reelected.

Several updates were given in that meeting. Mr. Ralph Scroggin's building report showed that more than 40 percent of the construction work was completed and the roofing was finished. Mr. Richard Davis reported much as he had at the hospital auxiliary board meeting back in November. He gave an accounting of hospital furnishings thus far purchased and what remained to be bought. He also stated that the hospital auxiliary board had a committee to make new curtains and draperies. Mr. Robert Johnson, Plaque Committee chairman, reported that samples and estimates were being received for the Founders Plaque to bear the thirty-two hundred names of contributors. Dr. N. E. Irvine stressed that the

Hill-Burton Act, which they were partially funded by, carried no government control of their hospital. Rather, the control was completely in their hands and under the guidance and direction of the hospital auxiliary board.

Marie's next week was a busy one. It began in celebration of her forty-eighth birthday on Sunday, her family day. She was healing well with many of her bruises nearly gone. The warm winter days in California had done her good. On Wednesday, she attended the hospital auxiliary board meeting, and then on Thursday, she hosted the meeting for her Duplicate Bridge Club. The next day, Friday, she was with her youngest daughter, Patsy, at a Rainbow Girls potluck dinner.

Mondays had been clothing day for her Polly Potter work in which free household items were handed out from their clothing room each week. However, the day after her birthday, she had instead been at the brand-new Polly Potter Thrift Shop. Her shop had opened that month and, like at the clothing room, was staffed by volunteers. It depended on donations to support its operating expenses and to help those in need. Just as with the clothing room, Marie and her volunteers didn't say no to anyone. If someone needed a household item that was in their store but didn't have the money to buy it, they received it for free.

In 1952, there were many legal barriers that kept women from owning a business. It would be more than thirty-five years later when the Women's Business Ownership Act of 1988 would pass to help businesswomen. However, Marie's store was a nonprofit incorporation and she didn't need to secure a loan to own and operate it. Those two factors were in her favor and prevented her business from legal obstacles.

THE ANNUAL MARCH of Dimes campaign was underway to happen in January in cities all across America. The civic groups in

Lebanon, though, were slow in their commitment and fundraising organization. Mrs. Vada Whetstone, the hospital auxiliary board president, felt other pressing issues took precedence, and so, unlike in the year before, they wouldn't manage the donation letters.

Proceeds from the annual campaign would in part help the Oregon Society for Crippled Children and Adults. Marie recalled her recent visit there and had shared about it in her column a few months earlier. Her heartstrings tugged at her. Then Mr. Longfellow, who was the Linn County March of Dimes chairman and whose office was in Albany, expressed an urgent need for Lebanon to get involved. Marie came forward.

She was given little time to bring people together, but she did it. She appointed her friend Mrs. Peggy Hatfield as her cochairman. They prepared and mailed donation letters to nearly every resident listed in Lebanon's phone book. It was an exhaustive feat for only two people. Under short notice, some people mailed in their donations, and some didn't. Marie also visited the PTA and other area groups while Peggy enlisted team captains. Word of mouth was the fastest approach for Marie. Mr. Longfellow's appointment of her had been on such short notice that the newspaper barely had time to alert residents. An article was printed on Tuesday, January 29, that informed residents to leave their porch light on in the evening of Thursday, January 31, if they wished to donate but hadn't yet.

On that same Tuesday morning, the "Needs of the Needy" column also included a reminder of their March of Dimes fundraiser.

> I feel we can be proud of our community because of the wonderful spirit which seems to pervade it, of wanting to help one another. I sincerely hope that each and every one of you who is able will contribute to the March of Dimes because if you have ever seen a child who has suffered from this disease, I am sure you will be willing to help. Let your light shine.

More than one hundred ladies joined Marie and Peggy on that Thursday evening for their citywide canvass. They were bundled up in heavy coats to ward off the blustery wind that cut at them on that cold winter night. In only an hour, from seven o'clock until eight o'clock, they had stopped at every Lebanon home that had a porch light on.

The visit Marie had made to the crippled children's home had left a lasting impression on her, and she was ever so grateful that their campaign was successful. Aside from thanking as many people as she could in person, her gratitude also appeared in the newspaper, with more than fifty women credited by name. She penned her heartfelt thanks to those who had given to that cause when she wrote, "These contributions will help children walk again."

In Mr. Longfellow's final reports, he remarked on Marie's fortitude. He described it as one of the biggest organizational efforts ever attempted in the county. Marie, in turn, expressed appreciation for the response she had received, saying, "It has been most gratifying. The march represents unity of purpose, unity of all faiths, and unity in a common cause."

Polly Potter's first request in her letter, printed on Tuesday, February 12, was for herself. After that, she pleaded for several young mothers with differing needs. The opening of her letter used an exclamation point twice, leading us to conclude that her homelife with Betty and the children must have been taxing.

This week, Polly Potter is making a plea for herself! Imagine that! But it is true. I have finally been forced to admit that I cannot go on indefinitely doing everything that I am doing without a little assistance. What I want is a girl to live in my home and help me with my housework. I could give her a good home and wages. I have found help for so many women in the position that I find myself, but now I have no more girls who need work so please let me know if you would care for this sort of job and I will interview you and see if we can't come to an agreement.

I prefer a girl who is out of school and could be here all day to answer the phone. The work is light as I have all electrical conveniences. She must like children as I have two grandchildren living with me at this time. I hope I can find a girl who really needs a home, and I could help her a great deal if she needed it. Write or call me at 2812.

One week later, on Tuesday, February 19, Marie was the guest speaker at the Business and Professional Women's Club in Springfield, held at their American Legion hall. BPW members were interested in how Lebanon had conducted its fundraising campaign to build a new hospital. Members from the McKenzie-Willamette Hospital Guild and other community leaders also attended their dinner meeting. They too wanted a new hospital and were enthralled to hear about Marie's experience.

Come the next Tuesday, February 26, the "Needs of the Needy" column gave an update in Marie's search for a live-in housekeeper. That letter also alerted readers of ongoing clothing needs. As far as bedding needs went, a beautiful hand-pieced quilt had recently been given by the Ladies Aid Society. That group had had an all-day potluck get-together at which they made the quilt for Polly Potter to give to someone in need. Many civic and social groups did likewise. Marie had been a luncheon guest for one of those groups, where they gave her several handmade layettes. In her February 26 Polly Potter letter, she didn't hesitate to share her good news.

I am very happy to say that I was fortunate in finding a good girl to stay in my home and help me out. I felt sure that my plea would be answered, and it was. The other home that needed help also has someone. There are always so many who need work so it is just a matter of finding the right one although I was beginning to be discouraged but now I feel that I can do so many more things to help others. I know my home will be well cared for. Having someone here to answer my phone will help so much and those who want to get in touch with me may do so now.

While Betty might have wanted a more permanent solution for her and her children, Marie's less-than-perfect son Dick was also having marital problems. His marriage was falling apart, and they had no children. Same as when he had lived in Lebanon, he had been working odd jobs in Texarkana. At the end of February, Marie got word that he'd left his wife and enlisted in the army. That meant that both of Marie's sons were in the military, with Dick in the army and Bill in the navy.

Bill was a gunner's mate, responsible for the operation and maintenance of guided missile launching systems and gun mounts and guns. Bill and another young man from Lebanon both served on the USS *Essex*, an attack aircraft carrier in Korean waters. Another shipmate was Mr. Neil Armstrong, who, unknown at that time, would go on to become an astronaut. He was a naval aviator commissioned aboard the *Essex* from the summer of 1951 until March 1952. Marie was disappointed by Dick's choices and worried about Bill's. She prayed for her good son to come home in one piece from the war.

THE ANNUAL RED CROSS fund drive began in early March. Again, Lebanon had a new general chairman, Mr. Ed Bilyeu. He was also the president of the Hospital Founders' Service Organization. That year, Mrs. Ruth Parton and Marie shared the duty of covering the residential district as cochairmen. They knew each other well through their memberships in the PTA, the hospital auxiliary board, and the American Legion.

Mrs. Peggy Hatfield, as the Red Cross Linn County secretary, had several speaking engagements to garner interest for their fundraising. She also spoke for personal enjoyment, and Marie was proud of her friend for her award-winning speech, "Let's Be Friends." In February, it earned an award at the county level with the Toastmistress Club, the women's club that promoted leadership through the practice of articulate public speaking.

On Wednesday, March 11, Marie and Ruth cohosted a Red Cross tea party in Mrs. Herb Wymore's home. They used spring flowers and candles for decorations. Mrs. Virginia Faulkner, Linn County executive secretary, and other Red Cross officers gave informative speeches. Marie and Ruth then appointed Mayor Tweed's wife and other ladies in attendance as captains to canvass the residential area. $5,200 was their fundraising goal, an increase from prior years, but Marie had always been successful in those fund drives, and she would be again.

As March wound down from that fund drive, Marie had another important engagement before the month's end. State delegates with the American Legion convened in Springfield. Aside from their business sessions and a banquet, each district presented a speaker. Marie spoke for District 3 when she gave an informative talk related to her work as chairman with their Child Welfare Program.

On April 25, Bill's ship docked in San Diego. He was given a thirty-day furlough and came home to visit for a few weeks. At the end of April, Marie's youngest child, Patsy, turned eighteen years old. She would graduate from high school in early June and then leave for California to attend San Jose State College near her sister Peggy.

Before Bill's furlough ended, his sister Peggy and her family also came home to visit. Not only did Marie have two of her children back home for a nice visit, but she also welcomed her third grand-child. Jerry and Peggy's first child, a girl, had been born in April.

At the same time, Marie's oldest daughter, Betty, was making plans to relocate that summer. Marie's first grandchild and his sister would be moving far away, to Southern California. There can only be one first grandchild, and Marie didn't want to let him go. Any sadness, though, was lifted in the joyful spirit found in her Polly Potter work.

One of her letters was printed on Tuesday, April 29, the seven-year anniversary of her father's passing. When Marie's home had been bustling with family members in April, thoughts of her father could have surfaced. She had loved him dearly, although she had not agreed with him on many issues. Had he been alive, he certainly wouldn't have accepted her choice to be a business owner rather than a stay-at-home housewife. However, the rewards that she felt from her charitable work made her certain that she was doing the right thing. Her April 29 letter expressed her confidence in this decision.

> Last week, a very nice young mother came into the shop and said that it meant so much to these mothers who must bring up their families on such a small income. She made me feel that it was all so worthwhile even though it takes so much of my time. These women select their purchases as though they were in the best store, and they have a good feeling of paying their way. I really enjoy meeting these people and I want them to feel as if I was a friend and that I am willing to help them in any way I can.

ON SATURDAY EVENING, May 17, the Hospital Founders' Service Organization presented a musical program at the high school. Their community concert featured barbershop choruses and quartets. Proceeds from ticket sales were to support their work. That was the last big fundraiser before the hospital's grand opening. Meanwhile, the hospital's board of directors sold the old hospital building for $25,000 to the city library with part of its land to be used as a city park.

As final provisions ensued for the new hospital, writers and photographers with *The Saturday Evening Post*, a national publication, came for a visit. They were so overly impressed with how the small American town of Lebanon, Oregon, worked together to finance and build a new hospital. Readers could learn from Lebanon residents what it took to achieve such an accomplishment and be motivated to do the same. Eighty photographs were taken during their visit to accurately portray all the work that was involved, including one or more pictures of Marie and other ladies who had been on the Breakfast Committee. But only a few pictures made the final cut, none of which were of Marie. Lebanon's story was later highlighted and published as a full-length article in the September 13, 1952, issue of *The Saturday Evening Post*.

In May, the hospital board of directors met with city councilmen. The new hospital needed sewer lines, and it needed the streets that it sat on to be paved. That hadn't been done yet, and the board officers stressed that timeliness was of prime importance. The board also met with the Mennonite Board of Missions and Charities in May. They discussed and then drew up a contract for management. The Mennonites had continued to manage the old hospital while the new hospital was being built, with the understanding that there would come a time for an ownership change. Lebanon doctors had been the sole owners of all the real and personal property under the Mennonites' management until 1951, when they deeded their property to the hospital board.

The contract was named the "Memorandum of Contract" and detailed that the new Lebanon Community Hospital was a non-profit organization. It was to have safeguards and protections in place to ensure that it was a community-owned hospital under the management of a second party, the Mennonite Board of Missions and Charities. And as Marie had both hoped and fought for, their hospital would turn no one away. The exact wording of that provision was given in *The Lebanon Express* on May 23, 1952.

It is intended that the second party shall at all times maintain diligent businesslike collection methods and a fee schedule commensurate with current conditions and reasonably related to the services rendered, provided, however, that the second party is to receive all patients without respect to class, creed, or color, and shall not deny admission to anyone to the hospital for the sole reason of said individual's inability to pay the required fees and charges.

In the June meeting for the hospital auxiliary board, discussion evolved to be ready for their hospital's grand opening in late July. They were ready. The Sewing Committee had completed the window curtains and cubicle drapes. The Flowers Committee had selected the flowers that would greet visitors. The Social Program Committee had drafted brochures and tour pamphlets, and those had been printed and were ready for use. Marie and her good friend Mrs. Grace Scroggin were on the Public Relations Committee. They had done their part to keep residents informed and had advertised in the newspaper and other places. As outgoing as Marie was, the advertisements were more of an afterthought. In all that Marie did, she spread the word.

On Sunday afternoon, July 20, Mr. Nylund, hospital board president, opened the doors to the brand-new Lebanon Community Hospital. A ribbon was cut to begin their dedication ceremony. Mr. Delmar Clem was again master of ceremonies, same as he had been for their groundbreaking ceremony back in October 1950. No ceremony is complete without music, and none other than Mrs. Dorothy Page officiated as their organist. There had been many times that Marie and Mrs. Page had played the piano together at events. At this event, Marie was instead a tour guide. Their ceremony included the introduction of several prominent leaders, along with a few short speeches. Then, the tours began.

Marie and other women on the hospital auxiliary board conducted tours under the guidance of Mr. Ed Bilyeu, president of the

Hospital Founders' Service Organization. People saw the patient rooms, the administrative quarters, and even its boiler room where the heating system was kept. Aside from modern heating, the new hospital also had air-conditioning, and it was in use on that warm midsummer day. The laboratories where the blood storage unit was located were another not-to-miss area. Hospital and surgical equipment were also pointed out. All four wings were beautifully decorated with flowers and handsewn draperies. It was a brightly lit and well-modernized facility. Come seven o'clock that evening, more than three thousand people had taken a tour.

Marie could look back over the last two years that had brought her to that day. She had led women in the Breakfast Committee to ensure the men on the campaign fundraiser started their day with smiles and encouragement. She had been the first president of the hospital auxiliary board, calling men out when they fell wayward of their goal to make it an all-inclusive hospital. She had supported Mrs. Vada Whetstone as the new auxiliary president through her committee work. And she had proudly given people tours of their new hospital. It was a hospital by the people and for the people. Patients would soon be moved from the old hospital.

Marie could also look back on her young life in Bend. There, she had attended many civic group meetings, where she had come to understand that one had to show up and then do whatever it took to make needed changes. She recalled that her father had discouraged her from any such participation. She was a girl then. She was to grow up, get married, and build a family life. Nothing more. Yet she had defied him: She had helped build a hospital.

Chapter 15

Love

August 1952–December 1953

*"Love for our fellow man is larger
than any building or any faith."*
—MARIE CONNER, 1952

As the summer of 1952 ended, the lively activities of children and grandchildren in Marie's home also ended. Her oldest daughter, Betty, had moved to California with her children. Marie's youngest daughter, Patsy, was also in California, as a student at San Jose State College. Peggy, Marie's middle daughter, had a family of her own and lived in San Jose as well. The boys, Bill and Dick, were away in military service.

Marie's memberships with the PTA, the Eastern Star, and the White Shrine of Jerusalem were on their summer break, but other groups were active. The hospital auxiliary board, the firemen's auxiliary, the Red Cross, and the American Legion continued to meet monthly. When she met with her Duplicate Bridge Club for a luncheon on Tuesday, August 19, both she and Mrs. Grace Scroggin were awarded high honors in their scores.

On the next day, Marie attended another luncheon, this time with the Business and Professional Women's Club. They met at the home of a fellow BPW member for a picnic to see her extensive gladiola garden. Talk was in the air for two upcoming and exciting events: their annual awards banquet and a national dedication for their new hospital. Many ladies who were at that picnic were also members of the hospital auxiliary, if not as board members, then as charter members who helped in committee work.

On Wednesday evening, September 24, the BPW named Mrs. Mary Herron as Lebanon's 1952 Woman of the Year. Mrs. Herron was in the PTA and had been its Linn County president when Marie had been the Lebanon president. Her husband was a surgeon who practiced at their new hospital. Mrs. Peggy Hatfield was honored to give the awards speech, and it was a well-attended event with a guest speaker, dinner, and music.

The hospital auxiliary board had their September meeting in the hospital as the Central Lane Office location was no longer needed. The national dedication for Lebanon Community Hospital was set for October 12 in recognition of the one hundredth project completed under the Hill-Burton Act. It was now in full operation for patients and had earned federal acclaim. Marie and other hospital auxiliary board members were in charge of the dedication's program itinerary. The U.S. Surgeon General and members of the Oregon State Board of Health and their wives, along with Governor McKay and several other state and federal government officials, were expected for it. President Harry Truman had also been invited.

Marie had healed from her injuries from her car accident of almost a year before and was back in action for those two events and many other activities. Not only did she have a new car, as the old one had been wrecked, but she also now had a pickup truck to use for her store. It was an older, well-used truck with no heat. It had holes in its floorboard that whistled when air blew through, which in the summertime made it feel as if it did have heat. In the winter months, it was more of an icicle. Still, it did her good in the many donations that she picked up and then delivered.

Polly Potter Thrift Shop moved in September from a small room to its own building at the edge of downtown. As Marie managed her Welcome Wagon business and stayed active in the many groups that she was a member of, the Polly Potter work was the one place that her heart always brought her back to. To help others was her focus and one that she tended to with a fervent drive of ambition. She also increased her working hours at the store that same month, from one afternoon a week to several days a week. The "Needs of the Needy" column that was printed on Tuesday, September 9, expressed her gratitude.

How happy I am to be able to tell my readers that I now have a home for my Polly Potter clothing room! This new home has ample space for the large assortment of articles that are given by all of you generous people. Through the kindness of many men and women I will have all remodeling done that is necessary. Materials have been donated and busy people have given of their time so that none of the small funds from this project needs to be touched for remodeling expenses.

My heart was very full today as each person that I approached agreed to do whatever I asked. At last, I have realized just how many good people we have in our town. They are from different churches and faiths, so this proves that there is good people in every church no matter if they are not of our faith. It also proves that love for our fellow man is larger than any building or any faith. I hope that everyone who has helped in this work knows just how grateful I am for what they have done.

We should be completely moved into our new home by next week. The new location is 1329 South Main, next to the skating rink. How nice if this could be the last time we need to move.

In December, the American Legion hosted a Christmas party for children. They had also donated many new items for Marie to give as Christmas gifts at her Polly Potter Thrift Shop. Grade school students had collected gift items for that same cause. Marie's heart was gladdened to have their support.

She looked forward to Christmas week, not only to help folks but also to welcome her youngest daughter, Patsy, home from college for a visit during her winter break. Marie's son Bill couldn't be home for Christmas. His next furlough would be in the spring. He was still fighting in Korean waters and had recently advanced in his naval ranking. *The Lebanon Express* printed an article on December 16, which, in part, described his naval work aboard the ship he was on.

> Famous since World War II as the "Fightin'est Ship in the Fleet," the *Essex* has been in almost continual combat operations since her recommissioning on January 15, 1951. The famed flattop began her second tour of Korean duty on August 1, 1952, operating with two Panther jet squadrons, one F4U Corsair squadron, and one AD Skyrader contingent.
>
> Aircraft from the *Essex* killed over 2,600 communist troops, destroyed more than 200 North Korean bridges, and made some 3,139 rail cuts along with the destruction of many rail cars, locomotives, and trucks on the carrier's Korean tour.

For Marie, thinking about Bill and his navy career could send her into frets and worrying. So, she didn't stop to think about it. Instead, she stayed ever more involved in her Polly Potter work. She, Clarence, and their daughter Patsy would be warmed by a festive fire in their fireplace on Christmas morning, and she wanted to make sure others also had warmth and blessings during that cold winter season in Lebanon. She set aside thoughts of Bill, and as her column on one December Tuesday morning described, she set about to make it happen.

I opened the shop at 10:30. The first thing of course is building a fire in a wood heater. The wood is rather wet, no kindling and no axe. But we always get it started. By this time, we have quite a group of people in the shop. They are there for various reasons. Saturday, 89 people came to the shop. Some came for help, some out of curiosity, and some to buy. Today the first thing I must do is drive nearly to Berlin to aid a lovely old couple. It is nearly 1 p.m. when I arrive back in Lebanon.

We prepare a hasty lunch in our little kitchen and as I try to eat a few bites I receive the most wonderful gift that could have come to the shop. Our telephone had arrived. Nothing was ever needed more. The number is 7042. I felt my day had been full. Also, during this time, I interviewed three people while I was at a cup of tea and a sandwich, trying to get a bite in now and then. I was able to help all three people due to those who had made purchases during the morning. You see, the shop is a place to help one another. The one who pays helps the one who needs and the one who gives the articles helps the other two and I am sure the giver is repaid by the joy she brings.

Since the opening of the shop, I have had a dream of a sewing room, but we have never had time to get the room cleaned out because it was the room where things needing repair or cleaning was kept. Now the barn that is directly behind the shop has been almost completed so that we were able to remove these things to there. With one helper and so many to wait on it seemed an impossible task. But again, a wonderful thing happened. A mother and daughter who are old friends of mine walked in and offered to help. We certainly could use them, and they worked all afternoon.

Several old people without transportation wanted boxes of things delivered so my trusty pick-up and I were out in the rain off and on all afternoon, so you can imagine how time flies when we are that busy. My closing time came only too soon. We had not completed the renovation of the room needed for sewing. I went to the home of a helper who had to stay home all day with two grandchildren. Her daughter relieved her of this job in the evening, so she and I went back down after a bite to eat, and at 12 midnight, we had the room in apple pie order and now my dream has come true. Anyone who has an hour or so to spare and wants to drop in and do some mending or tie quilts will now be able to do so. Of course, all I need now is a sewing machine and ironing board for this room. I purchased a nice machine from a woman who needed money, but someone needed the machine so badly and of course I now do not have one.

Saturday, a beautifully dressed person came in and looked around and asked, "What is this place?"

She understood what I meant when I answered her. "It is the heart of Lebanon."

As 1953 BEGAN, Marie's work in her Polly Potter Thrift Shop was ever more of a help to those in need. In February, sixty-two families were served with free household items. When her shop could have faced depletion, a Girl Scout troop came forward with a hefty donation. The girls visited Marie in her shop on a Saturday morning to personally hand her several items.

On Saturday, March 21, Marie attended an American Legion event in Salem. It was the official Oregon visit by the National American Legion Auxiliary president, Mrs. Rae Ashton, from Utah. A social hour and dinner preceded the meeting and was held at an upscale hotel restaurant. The Oregon governor and his wife were among the distinguished guests. Marie, who loved to travel and meet people from other places, decided that if not that year, then sometime soon, she would attend a national convention for it or for another group that she was in.

In April, District 3 of the American Cancer Society held a Cancer Education Campaign. Out of several counties in the district, Linn County didn't have any officers or official leaders. Marie assisted Mrs. Graham, District 3 commander, for their county's campaign, which brought awareness of cancer, its research, and how it affected a person, their family, and their community.

In May, Marie took office as the Linn County commander for the American Cancer Society when they held a fundraiser. That campaign and the one before it stressed the importance of early detection and treatment of cancer. Funds raised provided scholarships for professional education, public awareness, medical grants, and research. Marie enlisted several county residents to serve as team captains and to help in other ways. Her volunteers were a new group of ladies to her. In other fundraisers that she had helped with, such as for the Red Cross, Marie had worked with fellow members from the American Legion and other groups with whom she was well acquainted.

In June, Marie's devotion to children found a place in the American Legion. She wholeheartedly believed that children were our future, and she showed that as a chaperone to two girls. Their Junior Girls group, which had started in 1950, had grown in membership enough to send two Lebanon delegates to their state convention. Officially named as their counselor, Marie escorted them for a weeklong conclave at Willamette University in Salem. Their opening sessions on Monday, June 8, concluded with an evening dinner and social hour. The convention had 225 girls and their counselors in attendance. All the girls were teenagers, excited to be away from home for several days even though it was to learn about patriotism.

Marie undoubtedly chose to wear business suits for the meetings during this formal gathering. The girls, though, stuck to the modern fashions of the day. Some wore cotton dresses, while others opted for the comfort look in pedal pushers, which were tight-fitting slacks that fell to a couple of inches above the ankle. Throughout the week they heard from several speakers. The convention leaders had a goal in that they wanted the girls to return home at its conclusion as model citizens and with the true spirit of Americanism.

In mid-July, Marie went with her two best friends, Mrs. Peggy Hatfield and Mrs. Grace Scroggin, to the Toastmistress International Convention, with the Oregon city of Portland as its chosen location. Nearly one thousand members attended, with some women coming from as far away as Alaska, Scotland, and Japan. Same as any chapter meeting that offered the opportunity for one or more members to practice their public-speaking skills, this four-day conference had a full lineup of engaging presenters, as well as instructional sessions. Lebanon had recently started a local chapter. Peggy was its president, with Marie and Grace as committee members under her presidency. With Marie and Grace at her side, Peggy was given a charter for their Lebanon club to be officially recognized as a chapter.

However, Marie tried to be at home whenever she could spare a moment that summer. The summer before had been quiet at home with all the children moving away. The summer of '53 was different. Her youngest daughter, Patsy, was home on summer break from college. And Betty's children were also in town, spending the summer with their father who still lived in Lebanon. Marie could not get enough of her first grandchild, Randy. He was the one she was most proud to introduce to her new friends and to shop clerks when out on errands. There could only be one first grandchild. Her sons, Bill and Dick, though, were still away. The Korean War ended in July, but Bill was content in his navy work, with no intention to leave his career. And Dick had several more months left until his discharge from the army.

On Wednesday evening, July 27, Marie's mother, Laura, was honored by neighborhood friends with a potluck lawn party. Her eighty-second birthday had been a few days earlier. Marie took her granddaughter Kathi, who shared the same birthday, with her to wish her mother a happy birthday. Marie had other good news to share with the neighbors: On July 24, the day after her mother's birthday, Marie's daughter Peggy had another baby girl.

While Marie had many things going on, some old and some new, Clarence stuck to his usual routine, even without his daughter Peggy at his side. He was dedicated to *The Lebanon Express* and attended the Elks Lodge meetings and occasionally the meetings with the American Legion and the Masons. He had his bowling league that he enjoyed, and he hoped that Peggy had time to bowl in her young motherhood role, as she too loved the sport. And all too often, he was called to duty as a volunteer fireman. Whenever he battled yet another house fire, Marie was reminded of her reasons to help others—not that she needed any reminder.

Marie wasn't the only person who knew she liked to help others. It was a part of her well-regarded reputation in town among Lebanon folk. In August, the post office received a letter with a postage stamp; however, it didn't bear the address of where to send it to. It only read "Polly" on the addressee line, and only one line of information appeared below it: "Lebanon, Oregon." The mailman, though, knew well where to deliver it. When Marie opened the envelope, there was no letter to be had, only a ten-dollar money order payable to "Polly." The bank didn't question it. They knew Marie Conner was Polly.

In mid-August, Marie hosted a bridal shower in her home for a former classmate of her daughter Patsy. She used bouquets of deep red gladioli to decorate for the party. A large white cake with orange blossoms and ice cream was served to the eighteen young women who attended. Little did Marie know that there would soon be another bridal shower for her to host.

In September, she and Clarence took a short vacation to California to see Peggy's newborn daughter, their newest grandchild. It was a family road trip. Randy and his sister needed to return home to their mother, Betty. Patsy also needed to return for college—even if for only one more term, as they were soon to find out. When in California, Patsy introduced her boyfriend, Frank Piggot, to Clarence and Marie. She had met him in college. With her introduction, Patsy and Frank became officially engaged to be married.

Frank and his mother lived in Palo Alto, California, about thirty miles north of San Francisco. He had finished high school there before enrolling in college to become an electrical engineer. Tall and slender, Frank towered over Patsy, who was short and bubbly in stature. They planned to live in Palo Alto after their January wedding.

When in Palo Alto to meet Mrs. Piggot, Marie and Patsy visited their local American Legion unit. That unit treated them as honored guests for their past officer roles in Oregon, with Marie as past District 3 president and Patsy as a past officer for the Junior Girls. Patsy agreed to become a member of their unit once married and living there.

Following their return home, Marie quickly resumed her work as Polly Potter. Volunteers had overseen her operations while she had been away. She also had meetings with the Eastern Star and the White Shrine of Jerusalem, which had reconvened for their new year and fall-time meetings. Aside from the many obligations that Marie had, one important thing she needed to do was handle preparations for Patsy's wedding in Lebanon in early 1954. Mrs. Vada Whetstone and other friends were happy to help Marie with wedding plans.

On Wednesday evening, October 14, Marie attended the annual awards ceremony sponsored by the Business and Professional Women's Club, where Mrs. Vada Whetstone was honored as their 1953 Woman of the Year. The BPW president, Mrs. Grace Scroggin, presided over their ceremony, beginning with the introduction of Mrs. Mary Herron to a full room of members, visitors, and guests. Mrs. Herron then gave a short speech and named Vada for the honorary title. Vada's tireless work with the Red Cross was among her qualities.

On Monday evening, November 1, Marie and her mother attended the meeting for the Marguerite chapter of the Eastern Star. Her mother, Laura, was their honored guest in recognition of her fifty years as an Eastern Star member. She had joined Eastern Star as a charter member in 1903 in Jennings, Oklahoma, transferring her membership to an Oregon chapter when the family had relocated.

In this observance, and with more than one hundred members and guests in attendance, their meeting proceeded with ceremonial precision. Laura was escorted from the west end of the room under an archway of yellow chrysanthemums. Mrs. Dorothy Page, Mrs. Alice Youman, Mrs. Violet Olin, and five other women followed closely behind, each carrying a bouquet of flowers. At the east end of the room, they were met by their chapter's worthy matron, Mrs. Willa Huston, who handed Laura a bouquet of golden-toned chrysanthemum blooms.

Marie played the piano for the music that followed. First, a solo was performed by one member, and then the choir sang "In the Gloaming," with some of its words substituted with Laura's name. The five officers who represented biblical heroines each pinned a paper star on Laura's dress, each one a different color—red, blue, green, yellow, and white—and dependent on the heroine or star point. Each paper star was large, at about ten inches in height and width, and had ribbons that streamed downward. The stars overlapped a bit to fit across her bodice. When done, Laura's lacy pink dress was adorned as if she were wearing a sash from her left shoulder down to her right hip. She gleamed with colorful stars and ribbons. To conclude the music for this portion of the meeting, they had one more singer, who performed the Glen Chandler song "Silver Threads Among the Gold" while Marie played the piano.

The reception after their meeting was no less lively. Marie's brother Harold and his wife had traveled far to be with their mother on her special night. They gifted her with a set of china.

It was Marie who was well known in many groups, whereas for Laura, the Eastern Star was the one place that she gave her full devotion to. And on this night, Marie surely doted on her mother with well-deserved attention.

As Marie and her friends set about making arrangements for Patsy's wedding, 1953 ended with several holiday parties. The Eastern Star and the American Legion each had their annual dinner gatherings and gift exchanges. Then there was the staff dinner for *The Lebanon Express* that Clarence and Marie attended. Her bridge club meetings were also not to be missed. On the first Thursday in December, she hosted the Duplicate Bridge Club meeting and then, at the end of December, cohosted their luncheon Christmas party, also with a gift exchange.

Clarence and Marie were home alone for Christmas in 1953. Yet they had each other, and love was in the air with their joy over Patsy's engagement. It was a Christmas to cherish her alone time with Clarence. She couldn't foresee what was to come, but later she would look back on that day with heartfelt gratitude for her Christmas Day and other times with him. If only Marie's father could know how happy she was. She had a special place in her heart for her children even though they couldn't be with them that Christmas. Polly Potter's words a few days earlier in her column had expressed her sentiment with a gentle reminder that when people help others, it is for the sake of children.

I was delivering Christmas baskets through mud and snow, and I was getting tired and weary at the end of the day. I had one more to deliver and although it was dark I felt I must find strength to finish my work.

As I approached the home where I was to leave the basket I thought, "how can anyone live in such a place?" I knew the mother of the three children living there was not morally a good woman. I had pleaded with her to move to better surroundings and to be a good mother, but she would not listen. I know how some of you probably feel as you enter such a home and I felt that evening that maybe I shouldn't have come.

But I took the large box I had for them into the filth and squalor of that place and on top were three little toys for these children. One toy fell to the floor and a sweet little blonde girl about five years old stooped to pick it up and as she raised her eyes to me, and they were shining, she said, "Oh Christmas." The wonder in her voice made me cry.

Chapter 16

Clarence

January 1954–May 1956

*"The service we give to humanity is
the rent we pay for occupying a place on earth."*
—MARIE CONNER, 1954

Clarence was again arm in arm with one of his daughters for a trip down the wedding aisle. To pat her hand and then squeeze it tight showed that he didn't want to let his youngest girl go. Patsy was the baby of the family and always would be, no matter how grown up she was on that winter day in early 1954. Clarence had to tilt his head to smile at her. Her chosen gown fit her short and plump physique well. It was of ballerina length with a full skirt and formal bodice.

As his daughter, she was beautiful. Her gown was made of alençon lace and net over taffeta. Alençon may have been too fancy of a word for him. It was a delicate lace with a floral design, and the bottom edge of her dress was scalloped. A sweet strand of pearls lay at her neckline. Frank had gifted her the pearl strand, and he waited for her at the altar.

Marie surely walked the room to greet guests as they arrived. She had no doubt already fussed with Patsy's hair and made sure she had on the right shade of lipstick. First Christian Church in Lebanon had a large sanctuary, ideal for the many extended family members and friends who were with them on that Sunday afternoon of January 3. One couldn't fail to spot the mother of the bride among the many guests, with her metallic blue hat that accessorized her rose-beige dress.

Mrs. Hazel McCracken played the organ as two young men, Mr. Richard Connet and Mr. Tony Hayden, ushered people to their seats. The Conner, McCracken, and Connet families had become fast friends back in 1937, when Clarence had moved his family onto Park Street. Their children had been playmates when younger. Mr. Tony Hayden was the son of Clarence's supervisor. The wedding march began with Mrs. McCracken's fingers on the organ keys.

As Clarence walked Patsy down the aisle, a ring bearer and two flower girls followed them. Patsy's niece Kathi was one flower girl, and the ring bearer was Patsy's nephew, Randy. Marie was proud of her first grandchild, Randy, and envisioned that he would grow up to be a fine young man with a bride of his own. She returned her attention to her youngest child. Patsy carried an orchid bouquet with stephanotis, flowers similar to but smaller than jasmine. It was fastened to a white Bible with a satin streamer that cascaded from it.

Patsy's sister Peggy was her maid of honor and Peggy's husband, Jerry, was Frank's best man. One of her bridesmaids was a cousin, Miss Sharon Conner, who lived in Portland. The altar was flanked by daffodils, acacia, and a lit candelabra. When Clarence and Patsy finished their walk down the aisle, the church's reverend began the ceremony with prayer. As Mrs. McCracken played the organ, another wedding attendant sang the song "Because." Patsy and Frank then knelt at the altar as a friend sang "The Lord's Prayer." Then they stood for the reverend's assistant to lead them in their vows.

Garlands of lacy fern and daffodil nosegays welcomed guests to the reception room afterward. Marie and Patsy had several friends who tended to guests. Marie's two best friends, Mrs. Peggy Hatfield and Mrs. Grace Scroggin, were among those who managed the guest book and gifts and who helped serve cake and drinks. Patsy then changed into a gray flannel suit. With a red wool coat on, she said her goodbyes. Frank and she had a honeymoon on the coast planned in their drive to Southern California, where they were going to live. Clarence gave his daughter a big hug. He didn't know when he'd see his baby girl again.

Although their youngest child had left home, Clarence and Marie weren't alone as 1954 unfolded. Marie's wayward son Dick had been honorably discharged from the army. He didn't return to his wife in Texas but rather moved back into his childhood bedroom. Marie expected him to pay his own way, and so he worked odd jobs, often doing yard work or chopping firewood. Her good son Bill, though, was still away. He was set in his career as a navy man.

Marie's "Needs of the Needy" column was printed five times in January, one for each Friday, starting on New Year's Day, two days before Patsy's wedding. In her third letter that month, on January 15, Polly explained to her readers—and, more importantly, to those who supported her charitable cause—how her business was conducted. It was as if this explanation was written to appease those who questioned her intentions: "Perhaps one thing I have never made clear is that the property is being bought by the Polly Potter Incorporation, not by me, and in case we should ever stop this work and end the corporation, in our by-laws, it states, 'said property shall be sold and the money given to charity and no individual shall receive this money.'"

In this same letter, Polly asked for household items for a father and his four children who had been deserted by the man's wife. She also asked for baby needs and employment for a young mother. Polly's ending words in this letter caused readers to reflect on the benefit of helping others: "Remember, the service we give to humanity is the rent we pay for occupying a place on earth."

Inside the next week, and little more than two weeks after Patsy's wedding, Marie had her golden birthday. In the week of January

20, two groups gave her quilts to help someone in need through her Polly Potter work. One group was the Rainbow Girls, who in their first meeting of the new year had a full afternoon in a sewing bee session. A women's church group made the other quilt. For Marie, they were the best birthday gifts, alleviating any uncertainty she had felt in her reflection when penning that January 15 Polly Potter letter. She was fifty years old and alive with energy.

WHEN MARIE ATTENDED the February meeting for the White Shrine of Jerusalem in Salem, her mother, Laura, went with her. Mrs. Vada Whetstone, Mrs. Peggy Patchell, and several other friends also went. It was a special night for them, as Mrs. Grace Scroggin became a member. Marie couldn't be happier for her friend Grace. This was a group in which, through its spirituality, members came together to build upon their friendships with one another and to help their community.

In other out-of-town events, Marie attended the Willamette Council of the American Legion in Springfield in April and then the 8 et 40 meeting in Harrisburg in May. Marie was especially enthused by the 8 et 40 group, the honorary group with the American Legion, as their main project was a child welfare program. Their current help was for a high school girl who suffered from tuberculosis so she could continue her studies while hospitalized.

In the first week of June, Marie's travels took her farther. Clarence and she took a vacation to Southern California to visit with all three of their daughters and grandchildren. Marie was overjoyed to see her first grandchild again. Randy was growing up fast and was a well-behaved boy who excelled in school. During their return trip home, Clarence and Marie took a scenic side trip. Virginia City, Nevada, was one of several points of interest that they toured.

Their vacations gave them a pause in their busy activities of Lebanon life to soak in their devotion to each other. Clarence's love for Marie was much different than the love she had received from her father, who had been distant when it came to matters of affection. When her father was alive, his life had been centered on how he could provide for his family, with little appreciation shown for who they were as people. Her father had provided her with a good home as a girl, like Clarence now provided a good home for her as a woman. Where Marie's father had lacked, though, Clarence more than made up for it with his support in all she did and in his caring when she faced struggles.

When Marie had been away on vacation, and then at a convention shortly after, her shop had been well cared for. Aside from many volunteers who each gave their time when they could, there was one especially helpful volunteer. In her "Needs of the Needy" column, Polly Potter often wrote about her appreciation for this person, whom she referred to by only her first name: Lily. When Marie was at her shop, Lily was at her side. When Marie was away, whether on vacation, at a convention, or on an errand, Lily managed everything, and Marie trusted her judgment. After being away, Marie was eager to hear of Lily's experiences.

Marie's column, which had first run almost every Tuesday, was now, as of this year, most often printed in the Friday issue. Sometimes her column was published on an inconsistent or infrequent basis. When it did go to print, though, readers received updates on her life, on people she had recently helped, and on others' ongoing needs. She also often opened her letters with either a biblical scripture or a well-known quote. The Polly Potter letter that was printed on June 25 didn't leave any part out—her readers were updated.

I am so grateful to all of you for helping to supply us with the many items needed to keep our shop running smoothly. With Lily there to care for the shop, I have no worries about it.

Never again will Polly Potter need to be called an untrained social worker. I am attending a class on marriage and family life at the University of Oregon. I will be able, when I have finished the course, to counsel more wisely those who are in trouble. In the past it has been rather difficult to know exactly how to handle problems brought to me by so many. Now I feel that I will be able to help many more in smoothing out their troubles.

I spent last week at Willamette University with over 200 girls who are the most outstanding girls in Oregon. I had supervision over 33 girls at Girls' State and it was without a doubt a most enjoyable week. Here these girls learn about city, county, and state government. They elect officers for all three forms of government and these officers really function for a week in the state capital. It is an awe inspiring sight to see the way in which these girls carry out the entire program. I came away with the feeling that the future of America is in good hands.

I feel it was necessary for me to be away for these three weeks so that I can be better trained to do my work, but I will be so happy to be home again to help Lily as she has a very heavy load when I am gone. But with the help of all my readers she is always able to do a good job.

On Monday evening, June 14, the Marguerite chapter of the Eastern Star had their last meeting before the summer break. They made it memorable in that they honored past and present star point officers. The five elected star point officers, who represent the biblical heroines of Adah, Ruth, Esther, Martha, and Electa, have always been regarded with high esteem. Marie had been Martha in 1944, Esther in 1945, and then Electa for two years in a row, 1949 and 1950.

Baskets of red roses decorated their chapter room, and candles were lit as their ceremony began. Worthy matrons from many different chapters in the Willamette Valley attended it. In the reception that followed, a star motif was used in the decorations. The Eastern

Star gave Marie a place to develop her spiritual strength and gain a greater understanding of her belief in a higher being, God. Through her belief, she found guidance when challenged in how best to help her fellow community members.

On the next night, Tuesday, June 15, the American Legion had its officer installation. Mrs. Gertrude Gleason became Santiam Unit 51 president. Marie and Gertrude knew each other fondly and had for many years. She was also in the Eastern Star and had been their 1945–46 worthy matron. Marie was appointed to a committee, same as many of her friends were. She became their unit's child welfare chairman. Mrs. Vada Whetstone was appointed as Junior Girls state chairman, and Marie would no doubt help her in that endeavor.

Yet another memorable ceremony was also that June. Clarence's niece, Sharon, who had been one of Patsy's bridesmaids, was in Job's Daughters and had been elected to be honored queen, the highest ranking of five officers. Job's Daughters is a fraternal organization for teenage girls, similar to the Rainbow Girls and also related to the Masonic Order. It was named after a pious man and a book in the Bible, Job, pronounced with a long-sounding *o*.

Clarence and Marie went to Portland for their niece's installation, and Marie was their pianist for it. Each girl was dressed in a plain white robe to signify piety. A purple sash was knotted in front of their robes. Sharon also wore a long purple cape. Their attire was modest and refined. As the ceremony began, the girls marched into the room while Marie played "Onward Christian Soldiers."

During their ceremonial rites, Sharon knelt at the altar, and Clarence placed her honored queen tiara on her head. He was delighted to have that privilege. Family was important to him, whether it be his own family or his extended family through his many brothers and sisters. Just as he supported Marie and their children, he also had a special place in his heart for his niece. At the ceremony's conclusion, lights were dimmed, and Marie played "Nearer, My God, to Thee."

THAT SUMMER, MARIE'S first grandchild, Randy, came to stay with his father in Lebanon. Randy was scheduled for surgery at Lebanon Memorial Hospital for a leg injury from playing. Up until the day of his operation, Marie couldn't help but worry, yet she knew it was a fine hospital with fine surgeons. She knew that the hospital she had helped to build wasn't worthy of her worries. It had been built for the worst of emergencies, and Randy's needs were but of a routine nature for doctors. He came out of surgery good as new.

On September 22, Clarence was treated to a party at *The Lebanon Express* with a cake in celebration of his fifty-ninth birthday. The cake was frosted and decorated with a big brown bear that bore the lettering of "Clarence." Several small bears were also used in the decorations. Fellow staff members explained that the big bear was him and the small bears were them as they worked like mad to get the paper finished. It probably gave Clarence belly laughs.

The week of October 10–16 was proclaimed by Mayor Elmer Fitzgerald as National Business Women's Week. When Mr. Tweed had been mayor, his proclamations had been few and far between, but Mayor Fitzgerald didn't hesitate with that week. Mr. Tweed had been mayor for nearly ten years until Mr. Fitzgerald had begun his term in January 1953, which would end at the end of this year. In January 1955, Marie's close friend Mrs. Grace Scroggin would become first lady to Lebanon. Her husband had just been elected to office.

On Wednesday evening, October 13, Marie was at the awards ceremony to hear Mrs. Lois Abrell be honored as the 1954 Woman of the Year. Aside from the many groups that Mrs. Abrell participated in, she was a past Santiam Unit 51 president of the American Legion and had helped in child welfare projects. The BPW's guest speaker was the Oregon State College dean of women, Mrs. Hugh Kirkpatrick. She urged career women to leave time for personal reflection in the midst of their busy occupations. Marie could only wonder where or how to find such time. And one could wonder how she would function in any downtime.

On Sunday, October 17, Marie's daughter Peggy had another baby. Marie now had five grandchildren: Betty's two children and three grandchildren from Peggy. As excited as Clarence was, they were soon on another vacation to California, that time to meet their second grandson.

While on vacation to visit family, Marie took a side trip to meet the director of an adult community center, Little House, that helped older needy people. The director, a charming woman who wholeheartedly believed in the success of her work, gave Marie a tour. Her center gave classes in a variety of skills and crafts and offered entertainment and outside employment opportunities.

Following Marie's visit with the director, during which they swapped stories, she was excited to detail her trip in her column, which was then printed on Tuesday, November 16. In Polly Potter's full-length letter, she expressed the interest that the director had in their "House of Mercy," as the Polly Potter work was often called. In Polly's written description, she described Little House as a place where "lonely forgotten individuals have become well integrated citizens. They have a sense of belonging, a new and gallant attitude toward life that carries civic pride." Polly had opened her letter by penning a quote by the late Swiss moral philosopher, poet, and critic H. F. Amiel: "Life is short, and we have never too much time for gladdening the hearts of those who are traveling the dark journey with us."

The year of 1954 ended with all the usual holiday parties in the groups that Clarence and Marie belonged to. Then the year 1955 began with Marie's continued membership involvement in those groups. She was also active with her Welcome Wagon business and ever so busy in her Polly Potter work. And in the midst of it all, she had her fifty-first birthday.

In January, Marie was in charge of a tea party on behalf of the American Legion for foreign students at Oregon State College in Corvallis. In February, she attended the district conference with the American Cancer Society, in which she was the Linn County commander and a vital part of their organization. Then, Mrs. Peggy Hatfield and she went to Portland for a Red Cross tea party to discuss the bloodmobile drive.

However, her travels to Salem for the monthly meeting with the White Shrine of Jerusalem took a change in March. It had been the nearest chapter to Lebanon and as such was where her membership was. On Saturday, March 12, and after much teamwork among its members, they had their first meeting for the newly formed chapter, the Cedars of Lebanon. The Odd Fellows, another fraternal organization, offered their hall to use for its meetings and events.

Many members who lived in Albany or Lebanon or in one of the smaller outlying towns transferred their membership from the Salem chapter to the new one. Their first meeting was a grand event, and Marie wore a long formal gown. She had many pretty dresses, and while she liked to look her finest on any formal occasion, she knew that some women in Lebanon didn't have such luxuries. It weighed on her heart as she helped those women who had so little in their wardrobe closets.

As Marie kept busy in all she did in the spring of 1955, she paused in June. Her son Bill was home on a short furlough. No longer serving on the *Essex*, he now served on the USS *Weeden*, which had participated in the Rose Festival in Portland right before his visit. The USS *Weeden* was also a destroyer ship, but there was nothing to destroy at that time, as the country was thankfully not currently at war. After his visit with his parents and brother, he returned to his base, stationed at Long Beach, California.

In mid-summer, *The Lebanon Express* changed their publication days from Tuesdays and Fridays to Mondays and Thursdays. When Marie penned her Polly Potter letter for the Thursday, July 14, newspaper, memories must have been fresh in her mind—some recent, such as the many spring events she had attended in which she always dressed well for those special occasions, and other memories that must have surfaced from long before.

This week I wish to pay tribute to all those wonderful women who are left, through death, desertion or any other causes to support their children. They are mother, father, breadwinner, companion, playmate and many other things to their children. And the way they take this burden and manage so well is a delight to me.

There are so many of them who do such a good job of this, and they get no credit. They are criticized because they live by unthinking neighbors and those who are watching for some flaw in others. I wish everyone knew all of these brave women that I know and that they would realize what a marvelous job these mothers are doing.

In September, several groups that Marie belonged to that had been on summer break resumed their meetings. Business Professional Women's Week was observed mid-month, and Marie was present at the annual awards banquet to congratulate fellow PTA member Mrs. Nell Reid. She was the 1955 Woman of the Year, worthy due to her volunteer work with the Crippled Children's Association.

That month, *The Lebanon Express* gave Clarence a party and a cake for his sixtieth birthday. He was unpretentious in his response for their token of appreciation. This was where he and Marie were different: She was the one who got excited when given attention. With humble spoken words, Clarence thanked his staff. They overlooked his quiet demeanor to promise him an even more elaborately decorated cake the next year. However, promises aren't always meant to come true.

JANUARY 1956 SAW Marie's birthday. It was her fifty-second one. When her "Needs of the Needy" column went to press a few days later, on January 23, Polly Potter shared about the community spirit involved in helping one another. The opening words to Polly's letter are by a Nobel Prize-winning woman scientist and author.

"Nothing in life is to be feared, it is only to be understood."
—Marie Curie

Today a person came to me and said, "I had never understood your work until recently when you helped someone near to me." Then this person went on to tell me that a very dear relative had lost everything they owned through a chain of circumstances. Expensive medical treatments and surgery had taken such a toll of their resources that they had nothing left, not even health. They heard of our desire to help, and they came to me. It was such a familiar story and just one of several brought to me that day, but to them it was a tragedy. Through the help of several wonderful people, I was able to do a great deal for this family and they now feel that they can have hope and some measure of security.

These things we never accomplish alone. This entire newspaper would not be large enough to hold all the names of those who help us in our work. The Polly Potter organization is made through the help of our entire community. It is a working together of people who care about the other fellow. It isn't just a place to come to for food, clothing, and furniture. It is a place to come to for friendship, understanding, and any sort of lift that is needed.

Another family celebration was also underway. In January, Marie's oldest daughter, Betty, remarried. Her new husband was Dale Frazier. He had two daughters and lived in San Francisco, where he worked as an architectural engineer with the telephone company. They had a small wedding on short notice, with Patsy and Frank as their only wedding attendants. Dale and Betty and their blended family made their home in Walnut Creek, California. As January 1956 unfolded, Marie helped the Lebanon PTA as they started a new calendar year. She took part in a style show given by the girls in Green Acres School and then encouraged members to attend the first meeting in a lecture series. A Portland State College professor had been retained to present the "Family Atmosphere and Child Behavior" lectures at Lebanon High School, and Marie was sure to attend the whole series.

Another important thing for schoolchildren was music. When the BPW met on Tuesday, February 7, they presented a panel of speakers to emphasize such importance. It was explained that music was for everyone in present-day schools, not just for the talented. One panel member described music as being a great equalizer. Marie was also a panel member and said, "Music transforms a person," and after several more words, added, "It is a unifying factor."

Another meeting in February was with the Red Cross, which Marie attended. It was announced that Mrs. Peggy Hatfield would lead a county disaster fund drive. Through their discussion, Marie offered to assist her friend Peggy. Oregon had seen a lot of flooding again that year. Funds needed to be raised and made available to house, feed, and clothe displaced people.

As the month drew to an end, Clarence and Marie joined several friends for a housewarming party on Saturday, February 24. The new Lebanon residents were showered with gifts, and then a late evening buffet supper was served. Clarence liked to see Marie have fun, and she had fun on that night as they played cards with other couples. She had certain friends who were her favorites when it came to choosing a card partner. But by far, Clarence was the best card partner. In the thirty years they had been playing cards together, he knew she knew that. Who could ever forget his 1,500-point double run in trump from the summer of 1939?

In March, Marie had her usual round of meetings, as well as more card games through her card clubs. On the last Saturday of the month, the Cedars of Lebanon for the White Shrine of Jerusalem had their installation service for incoming officers. The two highest-ranking officers to lead the chapter were the worthy high priestess, a woman, and the watchman of shepherds, a man. Next in their hierarchy was the officer position of noble prophetess, which Marie had been elected for. Easter lilies were used in the floral and candle decorations.

***

IN EARLY APRIL, their daughter Peggy came home to visit and brought her younger daughter with her. During their week's stay, Marie doted on her granddaughter. Although her first grandchild stayed with his father in Lebanon almost every summer, a year and a half had passed since her California trip with Clarence to see all of her grandchildren.

Aside from catching up with friends, Peggy also visited with the people she used to work with at *The Lebanon Express*. Besides, if she were to spend much time with her dad, it had to be where he worked. Except for vacations, he never skipped work. Clarence missed the days in which they had shared every day together. But he understood she had a family of her own now. When she had to leave to go back home, a tight, squeezing hug was in order, and they promised each other that they wouldn't go so long next time without seeing each other. But sometimes promises, however truthful they are when spoken, just cannot happen.

Marie's appointment book was full in mid-May with Welcome Wagon visits and several meetings, all while she kept close to her Polly Potter work. On Monday, May 7, she was with her Eastern Star chapter and then that Saturday, May 12, at her meeting with the White Shrine of Jerusalem. After her family day on Sunday, she had two American Legion events. The first one was on Monday, May 14, in which she helped host a card party, and then on Tuesday, Clarence went with her to their monthly dinner meeting.

On the next day, Clarence had another full workday. It was getting down to the wire to have the newspaper ready for its Thursday publication the next morning. His back pain had given him more trouble than usual lately, but it hadn't stopped him. His family and his work were his life. They came first before any luxury of stopping and resting out of pain. He had to be at work to make sure columns got written and their photographer had pictures ready.

Clarence managed the entire production area, and he knew his staff members well. Their shared history went back many years, with some whom he had worked with for two decades. Although he was sixty years old, an age when many men gave thought to retirement, retirement was far from Clarence's mind. Instead, everything for the next morning's paper had to be ready. All writing and editing for their news, weather, sports, court proceedings, classified advertising, social columns, announcements, and anything else that the Lebanon folk needed to know about had to be finalized. It had to be typeset, and photographs had to be laid out right, according to margins and column inches. Once that was done, the papers had to be printed and then made ready for early-morning deliveries. He had barked at his society editor, Mrs. Katherine Harris, "Where's that record copy?"

The staff understood why their supervisor had to be tough on them, and they had only kind regards for Clarence. They thought of him as their father adviser. He was always at their side while they cried, laughed, toiled together, and scrambled to meet deadlines. On that Wednesday evening, before he left work, he perched himself on the office counter and extended a happy grin to those who were still left in the office. They had done it. Readers would get their paper the next day. He said, "Goodnight."

On Thursday, when he returned to the production floor, he and his staff started the work for the Monday edition of the newspaper. His writers had to get back to their typewriters, and the photographer had to be informed of where to be on the scene next. *The Lebanon Express*'s owner, Mr. Robert Hayden, who Clarence knew as Bob, extended a thank-you to him. Thursday's paper was good, and he looked forward to what Clarence could do for their Monday paper. When all had been done that day and the last of his workers had left, Clarence closed up and locked the doors.

One of the first things Clarence did when he got home that Thursday night was to plop into his favorite chair, an easy chair in their living room. After many years of use, its plush seat sagged, and its upholstery colors had faded. Marie replaced furniture whenever needed, but she knew not to take away his chair. He liked that about Marie. In all her quirks, she never messed with what was important to him. That chair and none other was his go-to place after work. And on that evening, his bad back caused him to stop and relax, as much as he didn't want to. That day's paper was in readers' hands. He had no excuse to not sit down. Although his job hadn't been the same since Peggy and Bill had left, it was worthwhile to him. He had many endearing friends whom he worked with. His back hurt. So, too, did his chest. He was tired. He closed his eyes.

Clarence never again opened his eyes. He passed away on that late Thursday evening of May 17, 1956. He had been in his favorite chair. He had been at home where he lived with the woman he adored. His work with *The Lebanon Express* was done, not only for that day but forever. Marie understood that her life with the man she loved and who gave her happiness was over.

Chapter 17

— ❁ —

A Friend
May 1956–April 1958

"All sunshine would be boring,
and all pleasant things would make our lives too easy."
—MARIE CONNER, 1957

As I again take up my duties and responsibilities that were forgotten for a period of time when I lost my husband so suddenly, I feel a sense of obligation to so many and I know that I must go on helping others and maybe I can again know a sort of happiness.

My faith is strong, and I know that with the help of so many wonderful friends that I can continue my work for others. So many have asked if the Polly Potter work will go on and I tell them all that as long as we have the kind of help we have had in the past from our community that it will. This week our hearts were warmed when many nice young people came in with their arms laden with clothing for the shop.

That excerpt was printed in the "Needs of the Needy" column on Thursday, May 31, 1956, Betty's birthday. Marie's oldest daughter, Betty, was without the man she had come to know and love as her father. And Marie was without the man for whom her love had grown in their three decades of marriage.

Clarence had been buried on Tuesday morning, May 22. *The Lebanon Express* had closed their office for the first half of that day so the staff could pay their respects to their friend they had worked with for twenty years. Clarence's and Marie's children who lived in California had come home for his funeral. The grandchildren had stayed in California as they were too young for it. It is uncertain whether Bill came home. It was in Bill's favor that the country was not at war, so an emergency leave was probably granted. Their other son, Dick, likely had been with them. And Clarence had several brothers and sisters who had traveled far to be with them for his funeral.

The Masons had met that morning in Clarence's remembrance and then assisted Reverend White with his memorial service at Jost Funeral Home. He had been laid to rest in the IOOF Cemetery. The IOOF is the Independent Order of Odd Fellows, and their hall was the meeting place for the Cedars of Lebanon with the White Shrine of Jerusalem. The purpose of this fraternal organization is to emphasize the leaving of an old life, the start of a new one, and to help those in need.

Members of the local Elks Lodge had then assisted in his burial. Many firemen were also present and had named Clarence as an honorary member of the volunteer fire department. Marie's mother, Laura, was at her side, as was her good friend Mrs. Grace Scroggin and her husband, the Lebanon mayor. Marie had always been the strong one, the one to counsel and help those in need. The happiness that she had lost from Clarence's death, though, was a test of her strength. Could she ever be happy again?

THE MORE THAT Marie gave to her Polly Potter work, the more she thought of others and not of herself. She had always been a busy one, but now, each day that she returned home, no one greeted her. Clarence was not in his easy chair. In early July, she left her shop in Lily's hands and went to California to spend a few weeks with family. Betty was expecting her next child, to be born later that month. For now, though, Marie looked to the grandchildren she already had. To hug her first grandchild, Randy, lent a much-needed boost in her outlook on life. There could only be one first grandchild, and she had to show him that he could grow up to do great things.

Marie returned home from her trip with an active mindset to resume her community involvement. At her 8 et 40 meeting before the month's end, she accepted another yearlong term as their state musician. A guest speaker from the Oregon State Tuberculosis Hospital in Albany joined them for their formal banquet dinner and elections. He reminded members that there were many people who needed help. A film, *They Go to Live*, followed and depicted the treatment of TB patients. An ongoing philanthropic project for their American Legion honorary group was to send money and gifts to hospitals that helped those afflicted by that disease.

On the last weekend of July, Marie joined several friends from Santiam Unit 51 for the American Legion state convention in Albany, attended by over one thousand members statewide. Marie received a first-place award on behalf of her unit for the commendable service by the Child Welfare Committee under her chairmanship. In other awards, Santiam Unit 51 was recognized for its meritorious service, both at the state and national levels.

Elections were another highlight, with Mrs. Lois Abrell selected to be the state auxiliary president. Marie's unit couldn't be prouder of their fellow Lebanon member, who was also well known as a recent past Woman of the Year. Through their many business sessions and other programs, Marie served as their convention musician, whereas Mrs. Vada Whetstone was the elections chairman, and Mrs. Kee Buchanon Groves was on their Breakfast Committee.

At home, Marie could not stand to see Clarence's empty chair one more day. She hauled out all her old furniture and called a home remodeling contractor to redo her living room. If no one was going to sit in his chair, she would find someone who would. Plenty of requests had come into her Polly Potter Thrift Shop for a chair. Clarence had left her a small nest egg of money to cover the expense, and she had his Social Security benefits to fall back on. When the remodelers were done, she had a new Franklin fireplace, a front porch, a lowered ceiling in the front room, and a brick wall at her kitchen's entrance. Pleased with her new home surroundings, she had an open house party for fifty friends on Thursday morning, August 23.

That autumn, Marie let go of her Welcome Wagon business. For her, the work was enjoyable, but the commission was too low. She didn't need a middle person, the Eugene administrator, or its New York headquarters to oversee what she could do for her community. She could do it without them. Thus, she began the Good Neighbor Program to serve her local area. It worked in much the same way as the Welcome Wagon had. She garnered interest from merchants and advertised to be notified of new residents, new mothers, and newlyweds. With her social aptness, she was a natural at it, and it gave her a break from the depressing stories that came her way in the Polly Potter work.

Marie found ideas for growing the Good Neighbor Program through her meetings with the Business and Professional Women's Club. Mrs. Grace Scroggin was on a planning committee for that year's BPW awards banquet, with the 1956 Woman of the Year honor going to Mrs. Nell Reid, who was a fellow member of the hospital auxiliary board. There were many activities sponsored by the BPW, which gave Marie opportunities to expand her connections for her new business venture. Guest speakers also lent support to Marie.

With her 8 et 40 group, Marie soon entertained again in her home, that time for a late October party. Members of that American Legion honorary group who lived nearby were her guests, and she was surely pleased to show them her newly remodeled home.

A festive Halloween motif accentuated her decorations for their party. Fellow member Mrs. Vada Whetstone grabbed the prize for best costume.

As the new year of 1957 dawned, Marie participated in holiday festivities. It was her first Christmas without Clarence and one in which she had to fill the void. Her local chapter of the White Shrine of Jerusalem had a dinner party with Santa and Christmas carols. As festive as it was, it was also comforting for Marie to be present in this close-knit group of friends.

Aside from party-going, Marie's ambition to give to others was unrelentless. She joined forces with two local organizations to create the Lebanon Community Christmas Welfare Committee, which then distributed holiday baskets to needy families. In January, Marie became their secretary, following elections and other officer appointments. They coordinated with Polly Potter and other charitable organizations to ensure better coverage and less duplication.

Marie also met early 1957 with activities in the BPW that piqued her interest. At their meeting on the evening of January 16, Marie and other members of the Art and Music Committee presented an engaging program. In another committee, she helped make corsages. In their February meeting, a public social breakfast was planned with Mrs. Grace Scroggin in charge of ticket sales and Marie at her side to help. Their guest speaker that month spoke on the topic of "The Importance of Publicity in the Growth of Business and Community Life."

The BPW's March meeting welcomed their next guest speaker, Mrs. Bertha Holt. She was a Lebanon resident, famous as the author of the book, *The Seed from the East*. Mrs. Holt was involved with a project that rescued orphaned Korean children to be placed for adoption in the United States. Any event that showed how people helped children was a not-to-miss one for Marie.

In the White Shrine of Jerusalem, Marie had been elected as the worthy high priestess for her local chapter, and their installation was on Friday evening, March 22. Her reasons for welcoming this opportunity to lead the Cedars of Lebanon chapter as the highest-ranking officer were surely twofold: For one, it would give her a social outlet in Clarence's absence, and for another, it was her place to find spiritual healing from that loss.

Their installation was an elaborate affair with over two hundred guests, many of whom were in the Eastern Star. Marie wore an off-white floor-length gown, embellished with delicate embroidered flowers that glittered with silver. Other lead officers installed were Dr. Edwin Buhn as watchman of the shepherds and Mrs. Violet Olin as noble prophetess. Marie's mother, Laura, was also installed, as Bible bearer. Dr. Buhn, who was installed at Marie's side, wore a tuxedo with a starched shirt and cummerbund. All the ladies were dressed in formal dresses and the men in fine suits. Organ music was played, candles were lit, and the American flag was presented during their ceremony. Snapdragons, daisies, and violets were used in the floral decorations. A reception followed, with Mrs. Vada Whetstone in charge of its arrangements.

Marie's first meeting as worthy high priestess was on Friday evening, April 19. They celebrated their chapter's second-year anniversary and honored those who were a past district worthy high priestess or watchman of the shepherds. Mrs. Hazel McCracken, Marie's longtime neighbor and friend who had played the organ at Patsy's wedding, was among the honored attendees. A cake, cut by Mrs. Vada Whetstone, lent to the commemoration. In business matters, they discussed the upcoming national convention.

Following the weekend, they came together that next Monday evening, April 22, for a bon voyage dinner party, hosted by Mrs. Olin, for Marie and Dr. Buhn. Forty members were present to give them ideas to take to the supreme shrine meeting in Detroit, Michigan. Although their travel isn't documented, they undoubtedly flew. By 1955, passenger airplanes were a common means of long-distance travel in the United States.

Michigan apple blossoms and other decorations filled the rooms at their national convention, which convened on Sunday,

May 5, to last a week. Members from all across the country came, including a few from Oregon, one of whom was the worthy high priestess of the Salem chapter. In all, more than 5,200 members were present, and Marie basked in the social opportunity to make new friends.

Elections for officers at the national level were one highlight early in the event, with the installation at the end of the week. Marie was honored to be one of the ladies chosen to serve their national shrine as an honorary supreme page. If only she could have, she would have wanted her father to acknowledge that she had achieved great recognition in that organization. It had been twelve years ago that month since her father had been buried. Yet her tenacity, which had been formed by prominent Bend women when she was younger and still lived under his roof, never failed to leave her. That month also coincided with Clarence's funeral a year ago. He would have been happy for her.

Marie's "Needs of the Needy" column gives us glimpses of her mindset at that time. While she was proud to achieve great things, she nonetheless had faced a loss in her life. She wasn't sad, but nor was she at the peak of jubilation. Faced with those in need, she had to find her own happiness while consoling others. She knew not to dwell on her loss, and if it weren't for her closest friends, Mrs. Peggy Hatfield and Mrs. Grace Scroggin, to ever remind her of that, she wouldn't have been making the strides that she was. In her May 2 column, Polly Potter gave credit to friends.

We all know that to have a friend we must be a friend. But how many practice this? So many of the ills of the world would be cured if more would try this simple formula. Too many are worrying whether anyone is going to be friendly to them and they get so involved in that worry that they forget to be a friend.

I firmly believe this and that is why I am never unhappy for a very long time. Of course, it is more pleasant to have nice remarks made to me, but sometimes we need the unkind ones to make us stop and think.

All sunshine would be boring, and all pleasant things would make our lives too easy. I just talked with a very unhappy person, and I do hope I was able to make her see how she can be happy instead of expecting someone to make her happy. Her problem, I'll admit is a serious one, but she needs all the strength she can muster up to be able to handle it.

Her Polly Potter letter on June 27 gave more of her thoughts about friendship.

Friends are divided into two great classes, those you need and those who need you. How often this last year have I needed those whom I had the privilege of befriending in the past! When we befriend someone, little do we realize how much we need them.

Especially do we need these friends when we have lost a dearly loved one. Our hearts and prayers should be with those who have lost loved ones in our community. They really need us. Without the help from our real sincere friends, it is hard to get our feet on the ground and go on living, so please let us pause and remember those who lost so much.

MEANWHILE DURING THOSE spring months of 1957, Marie's house calls as the Good Neighbor increased, and she called on many merchants for their participation. When housewives greeted Marie, she not only shared about local businesses but also extended information about Lebanon's utility services. She met and visited with many businessmen in the downtown district to garner useful details. One such businessman was Mr. Arthur Schmidt, the office manager at the Bonneville Power Company. There were many Schmidts in Lebanon, but none related to him. It was a common name that originated from Germany as a derivative of Smith.

Marie came to know Mr. Schmidt by the name that his friends used: Art. He had a gentle nature that complemented his tall, lean stature. Dark blond hair and blue eyes added to his attractiveness. He was a little younger than her at forty-eight years old but shared the same birthday month with Marie, who was fifty-three. If there was anything that Marie overlooked, it was that he was a smoker. She didn't like the smell of cigarette smoke and considered it to be an immoral habit, but it was something that many men did. If she were to shun men for that habit, there wouldn't be many men left.

Art was new to Lebanon. Born in Whitehall, Montana, in 1909, he grew up in Washington, and much of his family lived in Vancouver. He had begun his career with Bonneville as an engineer in their Vancouver office and then later became a construction superintendent. His most recent promotion had brought him to Lebanon. He had never married, and neither had one of his sisters, Wilma. Their lives were their careers, she in court administration in Vancouver and he as an engineer, and both earned a lucrative salary.

Art was an Elks member and a Mason. He also belonged to the American Legion as a World War II veteran who had served alongside his brother in the navy. His reserved demeanor kept him from pursuing any leadership or officer position. He was, however, well aware of Marie's leadership. In Marie's forthright ways, she must have expressed that she hoped to see more of him at the American Legion. Her recent commitments often kept her from those functions, other than their monthly meetings.

During the American Legion's summer break, Art and Marie met in other places, often out to lunch or dinner. Before the end of the summer, they were in full courtship with one another. When Clarence had passed away, Marie hadn't envisioned that she could share her heart with another man, yet Art proved that notion to be wrong.

Just as her children had growing families, Marie too welcomed growth in her life with another person. She also had two more grandchildren who had been born that summer. Her oldest daughter, Betty, had another baby girl, and then her youngest daughter, Patsy, had her first child, a son. When Marie could, she would make time for another visit to California to visit her daughters and their new babies. She certainly didn't want to go long without seeing her first grandchild, Randy. Until then, she held Randy close in her thoughts, not letting go that she had to set a fine example for him. She wanted her first grandchild to grow up to be an honorable young man.

In September, Marie and other PTA members encouraged all students to participate in a poster-making contest. It was sponsored by the Lebanon office of the Oregon State Employment Service to promote National Employ the Handicapped Week of October 6–12. Mrs. Grace Scroggin was one of three judges. Neatness, originality, and aptness of thought were sought for those posters, and the first-place prize was a $25 savings bond.

At month's end, Mayor Scroggin proclaimed National Business Women's Week, and the BPW hosted the eighth annual awards banquet on Wednesday evening, September 25, in the library's civic room. When the library had moved into the building that the old hospital had occupied, the civic room became a popular space for groups to hold their functions and other events. Marie and many of her friends were in attendance. Mrs. Martha Downer, BPW president, presided over the event with the introduction of a guest speaker.

Mrs. Violet Olin was next on stage for the awards portion. Aside from being an active BPW member, Mrs. Olin was also involved in their local chapter of the White Shrine of Jerusalem as the noble prophetess. Mrs. Olin showed the audience a book she had designed. It was much larger than the average-sized book. Its title, *Woman of the Year,* was embossed in gold lettering on a pink cover. She opened it for the audience to show them that inside was a written biography of Mrs. Grace Scroggin. It was her way of showing that Lebanon's first lady, the wife of their mayor, was also the 1957 Woman of the Year. Mrs. Scroggin had been selected on the basis of her work with the Red Cross, the Rainbow Girls, the Eastern Star, the Toastmistress Club, and the hospital auxiliary board. Marie was not alone in congratulating her friend Grace.

Marie had an early afternoon party in her home a week later, on Thursday, October 3, to congratulate Grace. It was a cozy affair with only six other ladies invited, those who in years past had also been award winners for Woman of the Year. A luncheon was on their agenda, and surely Marie indulged in the opportunity to show her friends that she was happy with her lowered ceiling and the brick wall at her kitchen's entrance. Although her home wasn't large or extravagant, its recent remodeling had given it an aesthetic appeal.

They were a close-knit group of friends, with Mrs. Peggy Hatfield and Mrs. Vada Whetstone often at Marie's side in their shared civic work. Marie knew Mrs. Katherine Harris, the 1949 award winner, from her work as a writer with *The Lebanon Express.* Mrs. Mary Herron, an active PTA member; Mrs. Lois Abrell, who Marie knew well through the American Legion auxiliary; and the previous year's winner, Mrs. Nel Reid, who was in the hospital auxiliary, rounded out their circle. As sweet as October began, the month would end in a way that would test the strength of their friendship circle.

On Thursday afternoon, October 31, Marie's friend Grace returned to her apartment home after tending to some errands. Her husband, Mayor Scroggin, was at work. They had once had a spacious house that accommodated large gatherings, such as the Red Cross tea party back in November 1949, which had had an extensive guest list. Marie had given a speech in Grace's home that day to garner interest in their first Red Cross bloodmobile drive.

However, with their children grown and no longer living at home, Grace and her husband had let their house go for this apartment. It was more efficient for them.

Grace was like her good friend Marie in that she could be absent-minded at times. When Grace reached the second floor of their apartment building, she realized she had left her keys in her car. It wasn't a first for her. Not wanting to climb the stairs again, she opened the hallway's foyer window and stepped outside onto a narrow ledge, which led to her bedroom window. That wasn't a first for her either. Oftentimes she had forgotten her keys in the car and deemed it easier to get inside through her window. That day was different. The heels of her shoes caused her to slip, and she failed to navigate the ledge. She fell fifteen feet to her death, where her head met with concrete pavement.

Grace had been at Marie's side for Clarence's burial service. She couldn't be with Marie for her own funeral. In the days following Grace's death, Marie had to confront her loss. To lose their friend, and in such a tragic way, was not only devastating for Marie and other friends, but it also left a void. When Marie turned her head to see who was sitting beside her during one of her many tasks, it was no longer Grace. To work on civic projects without her good friend was a difficult feat that Marie had to surpass.

Marie was well aware of the difficult times that her father had overcome. When she was a little girl, he had served on the city council. Although young then, she had later understood that it was only out of his trip to the courthouse in the big city that the person who had served before him was made to step aside for him to take office. When she was eight years old, he had messed up with his money, which is what had brought them to Oregon. Although too young then to understand how money worked in the business world, that experience had shown her that there was always an answer when things went awry.

When Marie was thirteen years old, her father's cattle had been shot at over a grudge, yet he had fought back. Her father had always been able to turn his life around. So could she. When a young adult, not yet ever married, she had attended and participated in union meetings. There, she had met many strong women who showed her that quitting wasn't an option. Rather, one has to stay active in their actions to overcome difficult times. Although much older now, Marie had more work to do as a changemaker. She had to help others in their downtrodden times, and she had to rise above her misery to do that.

When Marie was with Art, she found that it was okay—and even good—to have fun. Distant memories of her father hid away. Memories of Grace's smile replaced her absence. Clarence had been a good husband, and she could never forget his kindness and love, but he was gone now. End-of-the-year Christmas parties were to be had and Christmas baskets for the needy made.

In Marie, Art had found a woman unlike any he had ever known before. She was strong-willed and beautiful. Together, they could make the new year anything they wanted it to be. On Friday, December 20, Marie and Art exchanged wedding vows in an informal ceremony with Reverend White at First Christian Church. They honeymooned in California during Christmas week, where they visited with Marie's daughters and their families. Her first grandchild, Randy, was twelve years old, and she made the most of her time with him. In their return to Lebanon, Art resided with Marie in her Park Street home.

MARIE PLAYED THE piano for the Masons' public installation, held on the last night of 1957. The Rainbow Girls also provided music by singing. Mr. Jim Olin was installed as worshipful master to lead their Masonic chapter. His wife, Violet, who was the noble prophetess in Marie's White Shrine of Jerusalem chapter, had the honor to present him with the officer's gavel. It was the first of several events in the first few weeks of married life for Marie and Art.

On Monday evening, January 6, of the new year, 1958, the Marguerite chapter of the Eastern Star met. They draped their altar in memory of Mrs. Grace Scroggin. Other groups also gave remembrance to Mrs. Scroggin. The hospital auxiliary board placed a special plaque in her honor in the hospital lobby. It was with the other two plaques, one for the American Legion Auxiliary and the other in dedication for war veterans.

In other shared events for Marie and Art, the Eastern Star and the Masons met every other Saturday night for a joint card party. On Friday evening, January 10, Art went with Marie, both as a guest and as a Mason member, to her White Shrine of Jerusalem chapter meeting. In the entertainment portion, Dr. Buhn's wife played a piano selection. Then, Dr. Buhn read a poem titled "A Friend." A mock wedding followed to congratulate Marie and Art, and then wedding cake was served with refreshments.

As 1958 opened up for Marie, many changes abounded. In February, she stepped down from the Good Neighbor Program and introduced Mrs. Gene Highfill as the new local greeter. She also stepped aside from her Polly Potter Thrift Shop to give her close business associate and friend, Mrs. Lily Tollett, greater management responsibilities. The Polly Potter organization, which had always been a nonprofit community service since its inception in January 1952, was operated by a board of directors, led by Mr. J. E. Estep as president.

With Marie's blessings, Lily became the primary business operator of the Polly Potter Thrift Shop that month. The Polly Potter letter in the "Needs of the Needy" column on Monday, February 24, explained her reasoning for it.

> A friend in need is a friend indeed. So often I wish that I could give more help to those in need but as money is always so limited, we are very limited in the amount of help that we can give. I was feeling especially downhearted about this when I was called by a person who desperately needed

help that had nothing to do with money. As I progress through this problem and see how much I am able to help this person without spending a penny I feel so fortunate to have this ability to help in this way.

This case involves many that will be needed to solve her problem and their reaction to the case as I approach them warms my heart because they are so willing to do whatever they can to help her. Now that Lily has agreed to run the thrift shop so that I am free to spend more time on such problems that involve contacting many people, I feel that I can do so much more for those in need.

On Friday evening, February 28, Marie hosted an American Legion party for past presidents of Santiam Unit 51. It was the last social gathering in her Park Street home. Marie's impending relocation and the effect it would have on her Polly Potter work was shared in her April 17 letter for the "Needs of the Needy" column.

To my many dear friends who have been kind enough to read this column and respond to the needs of the needy in our community, I wish to say that it will always be in my heart and mind, the Polly Potter that you have known all these years, but I will not be in such a close contact with the work as I have been in the past. Many have wondered if I will be connected with this work any longer and I felt that this week I should explain just how we will manage to keep things going even though I will be away so much.

My dear faithful Lily and her husband will continue to operate the shop as in the past and a daily record will be kept so that I can make the monthly reports from them. These reports are sent to each member of the board of directors of Polly Potter Incorporated and the yearly report required of the government will be made from the monthly reports. In this way and with the help of the members of the board, we will continue this work that has always helped so many.

I cannot give the personal help that I have given in the past, but I will write this column so that the people of our community can understand the needs of individuals who come to us for help. When I am away, Lily will send me particulars so that I will know what is needed. Even though I will live in another town I will keep a close contact with this work and remain Executive Director. This work has been so very dear to me for so long and although I have withdrawn from many of my past activities in this community, I will always be a part of our Polly Potter.

Part 4

Marie is an honored guest at the annual hospital auxiliary membership tea party, Lebanon, Oregon.

Image Credit: *The Lebanon Express*, October 11, 1967.
(Express Photo)

Chapter 18

Out of a Renewed Outlook,
Marie Embarks on Her Life's Next Chapter
1958–1967

Morning clouds parted for the city of Salem to be greeted with an afternoon of warm sunshine on Sunday, July 23, 1961. Marie opened the door to her Salem home on State Street and welcomed the first of several guests inside. Her mother, Laura, presumably sat comfortably in a chair in the formal front room. It was Laura's ninetieth birthday and a milestone that Marie could wonder if she herself would ever reach. Although her mother was frail, brought on by aging, she was mentally sharp. Like her mother, Marie also felt the effects of aging. She was in her late fifties and had left much of her civic leadership in the hands of younger women to carry the torch she had once been entrusted with.

Earlier that day, Marie had driven to Lebanon to get her mother, who still resided in the small house next door to the Park Street house, the house that had been Marie's home for many years. Now, Marie and her husband, Art, called Salem home. Her mother's house was no longer a guest house but instead its own residence with its own house number. With just three rooms, though, it was too small for a large gathering. So Marie assumed the hosting

251

duties and was more than happy to welcome her mother's friends to her home. It was less than an hour's drive, and it was a Sunday, a perfect day with perfect weather to travel by.

Marie didn't know whether she and Art would keep this house or eventually move, perhaps to a larger place or to a more thriving neighborhood. Marie was open to change. If there was anything that she had learned in the past few years alone, it was that life went on, and it was up to her to decide how to greet each new day. Her grief over the loss of Clarence and then her friend Grace had been overcome through the love from her family, which included many grandchildren. She had also reckoned with her emotional pain, felt from putting her pen down from her column, all through the trust she had in the Polly Potter Corporation, which lived on. Something else was in store for her life, even if she didn't yet know what it was.

Her Salem life was one of ease with Art. Since their relocation in the spring of 1958, they sometimes partook in local functions in Salem and at other times visited Lebanon. The American Legion, the Eastern Star, and the Masons often had events of their choosing. And they liked to gather with friends for card games.

Marie's outlook in this new beginning was one without regret. Aside from her numerous friendships and her blessings as a grandmother, she was pleased that her children were doing quite well—that is, except for her oldest son, Dick. Her daughters had hardworking husbands and were raising fine children in their California homes. Patsy, Marie's youngest daughter, was expecting her third child in October.

Of her two sons, Bill's life was well grounded in the navy. He was in his eleventh year of service, not counting the two years he had served before his January 1951 reenlistment. Stationed out of San Francisco, he was now on a different ship, as the *Essex* had retired in 1960. The American Legion had shown Marie that military service was commendable in that it helped make our country a better place for all citizens. She was proud of Bill.

As for her oldest son, though, she was darn near ready to write him off. Dick was the eyesore in her family. He wasn't a military or career man, nor a family man. He worked odd jobs and made his home through a string of rented places. The summer before, in June 1960, Marie had been given a real scare when the Lebanon sheriff had called her to say Dick was missing. He was absent from his job at the bicycle shop, and his friends didn't know of his whereabouts. The only clue was a handwritten note left in his apartment. It read that he was going to take his own life. For weeks, local police had looked for the despondent and suicidal man. He had finally been picked up by the Redmond police in central Oregon, over one hundred miles away, as he had bicycled through their town. Marie had given him a good talking-to in the hopes of encouraging him to get his life on the right track.

Marie surely set aside her thoughts of Dick on that Sunday afternoon in July when she hosted her mother's birthday party. His name wasn't worthy of mention. Rather, her mother's friends likely engaged in small talk with Marie to hear how her grandchildren were or to discuss how the Polly Potter shop fared. And Marie in turn likely asked her Lebanon guests how their children and grandchildren were, and which groups were doing what.

Salem is about forty miles northwest of Lebanon, with the interstate as one option to traverse between the two. Country roads also jut eastward out of Salem, and after a sprinkling of towns southward, Lebanon is reached. Salem was a growing city in the 1960s, with new businesses and shopping centers taking shape. It was a family-friendly place like Lebanon, but bigger. Among the most populous cities in Oregon, Salem's ever-growing population in 1958, when Marie and Art first moved there, hovered around seventy thousand. Here, Marie had several friends, and in their relocation, she made many more. Her husband, Art, whose work in the Lebanon office with the Bonneville Power Company had moved them north, was nearing his retirement.

While Lebanon was well thought of for its strawberries, Salem proudly held the title of Cherry City of the World, which it had been named in 1907. Come the early 1960s, Salem had for more than fifty years held an annual Cherry Festival. For residents and visitors alike, whether one was walking downtown where the state capital building resides or along the sidewalk in any one of its stately neighborhoods, they were greeted with cherry trees.

When Marie's father acknowledged her birth in the Oklahoma winter of 1904, he couldn't include cherries in the fruit baskets that he handed out. His cherry trees weren't in season. Here in Salem, and long after his death, there were plenty of cherries for Marie and her neighbors to enjoy. They were ready for picking each summer but first appeared in the spring as billowy pink blooms that, when caught by the breeze, fell on the shoulders of any passerby.

Salem's weather fared better than Oklahoma's, and much better than Lebanon's. It was a place with mild winters in which a few years could pass before the next snowfall. Summers brought pleasant warm days, ripe for venturing out.

In the summer of 1962, a year after her mother's birthday party, Marie had the misfortune of another car accident. Perhaps people were in a rush to make up for lost time from their business and other activities in the short work week following Memorial Day. Or maybe Marie had a social event on her mind that distracted her. Either way, in the business district of State Street, that Friday, a car driven by a young man who was in the army collided with Marie's car. The local newspaper the next day described it as a smashup.

Like with her car accident back in October 1951, this one also left her with noticeable injuries while the other driver was barely hurt. An ambulance took Marie to Salem Memorial Hospital, where she was admitted with a leg laceration and fractures to her nose and ribs. Doctors were concerned in that they feared she had internal head injuries. On Sunday, they transferred her to Providence

Hospital in Portland, where she stayed a full week. Doctors there were better equipped should brain surgery be needed.

Marie was next transferred back to the Salem hospital and then soon released to recover at home, with no need for surgery. In July, she took the army man to court, where she sued in circuit court proceedings to be compensated for her medical bills, the loss of her car, and her distress. She asked for twenty thousand dollars.

Her recovery fared well, and by the fall of that year, Marie had a new car and resumed her travels, starting with the annual installation for the 8 et 40 on Tuesday, September 25. In recent years, many new faces had been invited to join their group, the elite offshoot of the American Legion. Their officers were a new generation of young men and women. Three newly elected officers this year, though, were ladies whom Marie was well acquainted with. Two were Mrs. Blandena Wilson and Mrs. Vada Whetstone, and the other was Mrs. Alice Youman, who had been secretary when Marie had been Santiam Unit 51 president of the American Legion in 1949–50.

Marie was appointed as that year's Trophies and Awards Committee chairman when they discussed their upcoming activities and philanthropic projects. Aside from their ongoing project to help those who suffered from tuberculosis, the 8 et 40 also laid plans to help those who were afflicted with cystic fibrosis. It was a new and debilitating children's disease that caused mucus clogging in the lungs and shortness of breath. Marie assured her fellow members of her support.

On the next day, Marie attended the board meeting with the hospital auxiliary in Lebanon. Like in all years past, their election for new officers was in their September meeting. Mrs. Peggy Hatfield was chosen as vice president. They then watched a film that featured the different areas of service at the new Lebanon Community Hospital, which was now ten years old.

Six months passed before her next big event. The Cedars of Lebanon, with the White Shrine of Jerusalem, had its annual installation in early April, with several hundred guests in attendance. Marie, who had been their worthy organist for the past year, provided the music for their evening ceremony. Her close friends Mrs. Vada Whetstone and Mrs. Peggy Patchell were in charge of decorations. While they wouldn't be officers this year, Marie, Vada, and Peggy made their commitment to help committee members.

That spring, Marie and Art sold their State Street home to buy a ranch house in the northeast corner of Salem at 4137 Center Street. Same as Clarence had had his favorite chair, so too did Art. It was a blue wingback chair to which, come evening time, he'd pull a TV tray in close. Steak and potatoes were his dinner every night, except when they dined out. Marie preferred to eat a light dinner at their round oak table, situated in their kitchen nook, catty-corner to a small front-facing window. A cuckoo clock hung on the wall by the table, chiming each hour with its automated cuckoo bird that moved in tune with musical sounds.

From the kitchen, a side door led to an attached garage. It was too small for their cars, but they had plenty of parking space in their long driveway, which spanned the east side of their house from the front to the back. A hallway ran parallel and behind the front entry room and the kitchen, leading into three bedrooms and one bathroom. Although Marie and Art were affectionate, he slept in the middle bedroom while Marie preferred the bedroom on the west end of their house. Art's frequent coughing, spurned by chronic smoking, may have been a factor in their choice of separate bedrooms. Marie's bedroom window faced their side yard, abundant with trees. An older lady and widow, Hazel, lived on the other side of those trees in an old, weathered house.

Hazel was not at all like the other Hazel whom Marie had known as a neighbor when living on Park Street in Lebanon. This Hazel was more of a recluse, and Marie quickly befriended her. She'd walk a dirt path that led from their backyard to Hazel's side door to take her a cup of hot cocoa or freshly brewed iced tea and to ask if she needed anything.

A spacious lawn out front kept their house back a good distance from the busy street it was on. Flowery bushes lined the front of their home, welcoming visitors. A healthy green lawn was also out back, along with a fully grown walnut tree. Further back, and as a bonus, sat an old red barn. The previous owners had left behind many items in that barn. Marie was accustomed to weeding through piles of stuff from her days of sorting through Polly Potter donations. Thus, she didn't hesitate to clean up that old barn. Junk got hauled to the trash. Anything good was kept, mostly antiques. With a business-savvy fortitude, Marie next set up shop. She turned that old barn into a beautiful two-story antique store.

Polly's Barn Antiques opened for customers with a long wooden sign in the front yard that alerted drivers to her business presence. She had an intercom system with a doorbell installed on her store's door. Those rose in popularity during the 1960s, and Marie found her intercom system to be of great use. If Marie was in her home and hadn't noticed anyone driving up her long driveway, then when the person rang the store's doorbell, she was able to let them know over the intercom that she would be right out to greet them.

Marie often visited countryside antique stores. There were plenty of them in the Willamette Valley for her choosing. When in a social call with a fellow antiques dealer, she exuded a spirit of friendly competitiveness. She liked to score a good buy on a few items on which she might profit by reselling. Her business income, while it was fine, was not one to make her wealthy. She was okay with that. Art's salary provided an easy living for them.

As Marie embraced her newfound calling of the business of antiques, she stayed in touch with her Lebanon friends. Her life was no longer bustling with activities in the American Legion or in the PTA, the Red Cross, and other civic groups. That was in the decade prior. In this decade, her grandchildren were growing up, and through them she was on the dawn of a new beginning. They were destined to do great things. She would see to that. She expected them to be well mannered and to do as she had done. She had risen above limitations imposed on her by her father and society. She was a fine role model for them. In turn, they saw Marie as the family matriarch. She was the all-wise one.

Where Marie held her children and grandchildren responsible in all they did, her expectations of Randy were heightened. He was her first grandchild. There could only be one first grandchild. Her daughter Betty had given her great pride when he was born. Marie could never forget the summer of 1925. She had been a young woman then, damned by a broken marriage, with little Betty and another child to care for. When Marie's father had shown his disapproval in that she was the first ever in the Gosney lineage to fail at marriage, she had come back with a fervent ambition to prove that she was worthy of his love. She certainly didn't want her grandchildren to encounter the ramifications of any mistakes that could befall them. Mistakes and problems had to be avoided.

Randy graduated from high school in late May of that year, 1963. Unlike when Marie was a youth, most children in the mid-1960s finished high school. Still, he didn't let any mistake or problem keep him from his achievement. Marie was ever more pleased that he planned to attend college that coming fall with intentions set on a bachelor's degree in the medical sciences.

That fall of 1963, as Randy began college, the country went into mourning. President John F. Kennedy was assassinated on November 22. He had been president since January 1961, overcoming Richard Nixon in a tight election race, which had received enough attention to spark the first-ever televised presidential debate. When he was campaigning in 1960, people in Salem had gathered at a local shopping mall on May 17 to greet the then-Senator Kennedy. President Kennedy was a well-liked and popular president for both Republicans and Democrats. Through him, American citizens dreamed of a country free of discrimination and one that would win the space race against other countries.

With his death, life for American citizens became bleak overnight. Businesses shut down to grieve. Oregon Governor Mark Hatfield, along with his wife, went to Washington, DC, where they attended President Kennedy's funeral. Marie's friend Mrs. Peggy Hatfield was married to Governor Hatfield's brother. When President Roosevelt suddenly died back in April 1945, Marie had found solace in the American Legion. Aside from their husbands and other friends, Marie and Peggy had each other for strength and wisdom, helping them overcome the abrupt news of President Kennedy's death.

While pleasant spring weather in 1964 may have been an incentive to come out of mourning, Marie's heart was burdened by the failing health of her elderly mother, Laura. She had to be moved into a nursing home. Marie set about to sell her mother's car and disperse her furnishings and unneeded personal effects. Her mother's house had to be made ready to sell if needed. It didn't seem as if she would regain her health. And she didn't. She was too ill to notice her ninety-third birthday in July. Little more than two weeks later, on August 10, 1964, Marie's mother died.

As Marie let go of her mother, little did she know that she would soon let go of her problem son as well, although in a different way and of her own choosing. On Thursday, June 25, Dick had left home on foot from his rented apartment in Albany. He had no intention of returning home soon. When his grandmother, Laura, died in August, he was still walking. He reached Butte, Montana, in the latter days of that month. The newspaper out of Corvallis reprinted what the Butte newspaper had reported.

The tramp printer, as the Butte reporters called Dick, was on a 3,500-mile cross-country hiking trip from Albany, Oregon, to Albany, New York. He had taken an unnecessary side trip to their city in search of his father, Randall Miller, who had once moved to Montana, only to learn that he had returned to Oregon some years earlier. Dick, who used his adopted father's last name of Conner, had planned that his walking trip would take three months. Local residents informed him that more than two-thirds of his time was gone, with three-fourths of the walk still ahead of him. Dick replied, "Well, I'm not really in any hurry. I'll get there."

Two days later, the newspaper out of Albany picked up the story to report the tramp printer was now in Helena, Montana. They reported him as saying that he had only twenty-seven cents but that he sold pop bottles that he found along the highway through recycling. Dick informed them that he had walked from Missoula to Butte in twenty-two hours and from Butte to Helena in ten hours. His plans were to continue east on Highway 12 to Aberdeen, South Dakota, and from there to Minneapolis, Minnesota.

Marie was beside herself. She was beyond utterly embarrassed. If only he had turned out like her good son, Bill, and not as a tramp, collecting trash. And he had no justification to go looking for an absent father or to challenge his paternity. She had given him the best dad anyone could ever ask for, she reasoned. Clarence had been a fine father. She had given Dick plenty of talks regarding his past debacles, and she was done talking. If he were to return to Oregon, it would not be to open arms from her. If he even made it to New York, she couldn't have cared less. From then on, she deemed him a lost son, not worthy of their family.

Dick did make it to New York, although Marie likely was not aware of it. The Oregon newspapers dropped his story. The next several newspaper articles to follow his travels came in November from New York State, with one out of Buffalo and another from Poughkeepsie. When Dick was in New York, the reporters stated that the tramp printer had turned down the many rides he had been offered. Dick had responded, "I want to stick to my plan."

Marie also stuck to her plan. No matter where he was, her bad seed of a son was out of her life, she concluded. In her own words to describe him, she said, "He's a bad man." No one in Marie's family was allowed to ever mention his name again.

Under a sunny August sky, Marie strolled the downtown streets of Lebanon with her youngest daughter, Patsy, who was visiting from California with her own daughter. A year had passed since Marie's mother had died, but her memory lived on as Marie made the most of each new day. Patsy held tight to the hand of her youngest child, who was almost four years old and, in her childhood mindset, must have been excited to be on an adventure. Marie was excited too but for other reasons. She had note cards to hand out.

Marie said her hellos as they passed familiar faces. She had seen many of them in her recent past spring events. In March, the American Legion had celebrated their post's birthday, and Marie was one of several past presidents for their unit who had been honored guests. Then, in May, the American Legion Auxiliary at the state level honored Santiam Unit 51's Junior Girls group. They were recognized for their outstanding involvement in civic affairs with special acknowledgment awarded to Marie who, in March 1950 when their group began, was their auxiliary president.

The reasons for their walk through Lebanon that day were two-fold: One was for Marie to introduce her newest grandchild, and the other was to inform friends that she was starting another business. The note cards that Marie gave her friends were exquisitely crafted on pink stock paper and read that Polly's Pink Cottage was set to open on Wednesday, September 1, in Salem. Marie wanted people to drop in for a cup of tea and to look over her antiques.

Polly's Pink Cottage was a cozy shop, tiny in comparison to Polly's Barn Antiques. It was in Salem's artsy area, the West Salem urban district. West Salem had been a city of its own until it was annexed into Salem in 1949. It lies on the west side of the Willamette River, which runs through Salem and is easily accessible from the interstate. With Marie's house on the northeast end of Center Street, it was a due-west drive to the bridge. Just off the bridge and into a left-hand turn lay the newly refurbished block of older buildings, the Isle of Treasures.

Her shop was nestled in with other independently owned businesses. An art gallery with an artist supply store, a pottery shop, a flower shop, a crafts store, and a coffee shop and tearoom were well enjoyed by shoppers who walked this riverfront block. Marie might have had hired help for customers, or perhaps her antiques were on display to be paid for at a neighboring shop. Either way, her cottage of antiques kept her busy while she managed Polly's Barn Antiques from home.

As this decade progressed, her grandchildren got older, with her two oldest becoming young adults. Of her children, her son Bill made her proud when, in December 1966, he received special recognition for his role in helping his ship win an award, the Missilery "E" for Excellence. Following the *Essex*'s retirement, he served on the USS *Cogswell*, a destroyer ship, up until July 1963 when he transferred to his current one, the USS *Halsey*. It was a guided missile frigate ship designed for maneuverability and too light for war battle, but Marie couldn't help but worry for his safety. America was now in the Vietnam War.

Soon after, in early January 1967, Bill was honorably discharged after sixteen years of continuous service. That was short-lived. He reenlisted for another four years and assured his mom that she needn't worry. When Marie wasn't worried about her son, she still worried, if only for her first grandchild, Randy. His college days had been interrupted when, the summer before, he had been drafted into the army. Following boot camp, Randy had been stationed in Georgia, where, a few months earlier, in October, he had completed a communication specialist course. As Bill reenlisted, Randy was overseas in combat.

While Randy was at war, his sister Kathi faced her own battles. Kathi had pleased the family when she graduated in 1965 from Mira Loma High School in California. Then she had met a navy man who, like Bill, was stationed in San Francisco. In late 1966, they had married. She had done the right thing to marry him—she was pregnant. With her husband away on military duty, Kathi moved in with his parents, who lived in Little Rock, Arkansas.

A double-edged sword faced Marie, and like the first time around, the stakes were high. When she had been Kathi's age, her reaction to prohibition was crucial in that it influenced what was to come of her marriage to a bootlegger. Now older and wiser, she had to decide how to react to Kathi's situation. Marie did not like problems. She never had and never would, with no qualms about getting rid of problems and problem people. Marie's reaction would undoubtedly influence family dynamics. She was the family matriarch.

Marie could either be disappointed in her granddaughter's out-of-wedlock mistake, or she could overlook it in knowing that she was rectifying her mistake. The reaction that Marie had received from her father over her own failed marriage had been difficult for her. The social norms of the 1920s had surely played a part in his disappointment. Now it was no longer the 1920s, and the 1960s often showed the faces of young people who challenged conventional ways. Marie had witnessed over time that the ways in which people lived seemed to ever change.

As a changemaker herself, and while not approving of any wrongdoings, Marie chose to embrace what was to come next. In the dawn of 1967 and the advent of her sixty-third birthday, she did not hold back on her blessings or prayers for her granddaughter who was far away in Arkansas. When the winter rain in Salem subsided, promises of cherry blossoms appeared, and with that, a new growth of flowers and the promise of the next generation in Marie's lineage.

Chapter 19

Out of the Life of a New Generation, Marie Embraces Her Golden Years
1967–1979

Marie's first great-grandchild came into this world on Mother's Day in May 1967. Her arrival came late that night but with perfect timing for a Mother's Day gift to Kathi, who was living far from the family, in Arkansas. If only there was a holiday to commemorate great-grandmothers. If only Marie could hold her great-granddaughter and tell her that she was special.

If only Marie's father could have known of her milestone. Then again, he hadn't paid any real attention when her first grandchild, Randy, had been born. Her father had been near death then. Marie had disappointed her father as a young woman, but in this unparalleled event and four decades later, she had more than risen above the mistake that her father had seen in her. It was a milestone not only for Marie but also for her late father. It was like a platinum anniversary in commemoration of him, as he'd been born on May 15 in the 1860s. This life of a new generation was of special significance for Marie, and with that, she was exalted.

In all that Marie did, she shared her good news. When with customers in her antiques stores, it was a not-to-miss topic in their small talk. When at a lunch gathering or with her neighbors, she made her announcement. When with her Lebanon friends, they kept her updated in the good works being done, and Marie, in turn, shared that her first great-grandchild had been born in May. Even her distant friends, who had already heard the good news, heard it again. "Have I told you? I'm a great-grandma now."

In June, and then in October, Marie had two formal events in Lebanon that she attended, and at both, she surely spoke up with her announcement. In June, district officers with the White Shrine of Jerusalem visited the Cedars of Lebanon chapter. Marie showed her appreciation as a proud charter member when they extended honorary recognition for their chapter's outstanding membership growth. In October, the hospital auxiliary had its annual membership tea party, the Pageant of Hospitality. For that, Marie was seated at an honorary table with other past presidents. They were given special recognition, with even greater thanks going to their first-ever president, Marie. Clad in her favorite color, Marie wore a plaid blue-and-white skirt and matching jacket as she smiled and chatted among her friends and fellow members.

Those two occasions were highlights for Marie that year. Her Lebanon visits had become less frequent and her participation in Lebanon groups less involved. Yet her skirts and dresses hung in the back of her sliding closet, ready to wear at the next formal occasion, however seldom such occasions were now. Polyester slacks with a casual pullover top were her new go-to choice for daily wear, whether at home or with her customers. Her red hair had faded away, replaced by thick white strands that she swooped up on her head for a modern style. As she was now an older woman, her posture gave way to a relaxed stance that shortened her height by a couple of inches. Although her physical stature had shifted, her charismatic personality made her shine in all that she did and in all that she was proud of—the greatest of which was being a great-grandmother.

As to how Kathi and her newborn were faring, Marie relied on letters mailed to her Salem home. Long-distance phone calls in the

1960s were much too expensive and an expenditure that only the wealthiest indulged in. Each letter gave news of the baby girl, but Marie had to read between the lines to understand the intricacies that surrounded Kathi's life. It didn't appear that Kathi's marriage was good; rather, it seemed hauntingly rocky.

In late 1967, Kathi's letters brought upsetting news. Her baby girl had pneumonia. At six months old, this was her first winter. They didn't know if she would live, and she was placed in an incubator at Little Rock's university medical center. As Christmas approached, she showed signs of a viable recovery. She was a fighter, strong and resilient. For Marie, it was proof that she was a tenacious one and had it in her to grow up to be steadfast in all she set out to do. There can only be one first great-grandchild. She had to live.

In January 1968, Marie had her sixty-fourth birthday, and Art, his fifty-ninth. Marie ended her lease at the Isle of Treasures to close Polly's Pink Cottage. Without her frequent trips to West Salem, she managed Polly's Barn Antiques from home with greater ease. Art had retired from his career with the Bonneville Power Company and in his poor health, exacerbated by his smoking, preferred to sit and read in his chair. He also turned their attached garage into a woodworking shop where he'd while away an hour at a time.

Their homelife was relatively quiet and laid-back. While Art liked to read, Marie liked to watch afternoon soap operas on TV. It was a time for her to relax and be proud of her children. Her daughters had married well and had fine families. In all, Marie had eleven grandchildren, with five from her oldest daughter, Betty, whose oldest daughter was Kathi. Daughters Peggy and Patsy each had three children. And the health of her first great-grandchild was improving, with the hospital stay over.

That spring, they got word from her son Bill that he was on a new ship, a missile test ship, the USS *Norton Sound*. They also heard from her first grandchild, Randy. In April, he was discharged from the army and came to Salem to live. Although his combatting days were over, the Vietnam War raged on, with American citizens unsure as to why. Antiwar protests erupted around the country, as did riots in the struggle for civil rights. It was a confusing era for Americans, in contrast to when Marie had lived through the two world wars.

Cushioned in the northwest corner of the country, Oregon seemed far removed from the violence, protesters, and profound speeches given by civil rights leaders. Arkansas, where Marie's first great-grandchild lived, was in the thick of it. She wouldn't be for long, though. Marie got a letter from Kathi to let her know that she and her daughter were leaving to come to Salem sometime that summer. Not only was Randy's tour of duty with the army over, but so too was his sister Kathi's marriage.

Marie's birthday wishes for her first great-grandchild were sent through the mail as she waited to see them. In the meantime, she busied herself not only in her store but also with local groups, where she was often invited to speak or give a presentation on antiques. In June, it was with the Christian Women's Group of Salem for their monthly luncheon, held at an upscale hotel. Moonlight and roses was their theme, likened to the song titled "Moonlight and Roses" by Jim Reeves and his orchestra. While the country was being introduced to rock and roll music, traditional music or pop-rock ballads prevailed for some people. Orchestras were a favorite for Marie, with Lawrence Welk as an often go-to choice for her listening pleasure. She kept 8-track tapes of his music in her car.

That summer, Marie got to meet her first great-grandchild. Ending a long drive from Arkansas, Kathi pulled into her grand-mother's driveway in her little green Datsun car with her daughter bundled in blankets in the seat next to her. Marie already had the third bedroom ready for them, adorned with frilly curtains and furnished with a twin bed, a crib, and other necessities.

Marie set aside any judgmental thoughts about her granddaugh-ter's troubled situation. She knew what it was like to be young with a child in tow and struggles to face. She would be there for Kathi where her own family hadn't been for her. Marie saw this reunion with her granddaughter as an unprecedented moment, for with this reunion came this precious little girl, the life of a new generation. There could only be one first great-grandchild. She had to grow up to be a fine woman, commendable and well regarded by others. Marie would see to that. Art, too, had a smile that lit up his face in awe of the little one. Although he wasn't Marie's first husband or of any direct lineage to this little girl, it didn't change a thing. He was her great-grandfather. He would spoil her rotten with love. He would see to that.

Kathi filed for divorce, went to work in an insurance office, and began putting her life back together. Marie went to work too, but in another way. Her work was in teaching her first great-grandchild how to talk, walk, tie her shoes, and blow her nose. It would take time. She knew that. But she had all the time in the world for her. Of course, sometimes she had to dart out the door when a customer came to visit her store, but Art was on hand then. He'd come in from his woodworking shop to take over, always with a beaming smile. The little girl also lit up with happy giggles for her time with him, whom she simply called "Grandpa."

In December 1968, their Christmas tree was fat with plush green pine needles and adorned with whimsical ornaments. Underneath lay a delicate tree skirt, on top of which were many gifts wrapped in colorful paper. Marie had shopped at the finest department stores for little-girl clothes and dolls. Art had handcrafted toys in his woodworking shop to add to the gift pile. In past years, Marie had ensured that children had a good Christmas. During World War II, Marie and other American Legion ladies had boxed up food and gifts for families whose husbands and fathers were away. As Polly Potter, she had brightened the lives of many little children who were from impoverished families. This year, her attention turned to her first great-grandchild.

In January 1969, Marie had her sixty-fifth birthday, and her great-granddaughter began to grow up. Then the year melted into the 1970s. Marie's first grandchild, Randy, was well settled in Salem, and although his college days were nevermore, he found a respectable career as a mailman with the United States Postal Service. In November 1970, Marie's granddaughter Kathi remarried to an insurance salesman, and her daughter was a flower girl at their wedding. Kathi's new life brought indecision and a tug-of-war with this little girl. As a result, she never really left Marie's home, but in one way or another was always under her wing.

Christmases came and went for the little girl, with the next few after Christmas of 1968 much like that one had been. Their tree was always laden with many gifts, some too big to wrap. Art had built her a cradle and a high chair to use with her dolls. One year, she got a tricycle, and the next year, a toy tractor to pedal down the driveway out back.

Christmas 1972 was different for the little girl. For one, she had a baby brother. Kathi and her new husband had had a baby in April. For another, Art had died of a heart attack in early December on Saturday night, the 2nd. His little great-granddaughter, now five and a half years old, wandered around the house the next morning, clutching her doll in search of Grandpa.

An influx of people was in their home that morning, from friends and relatives to paramedics. Marie found a moment to step away and into her bedroom, taking her great-granddaughter with her. A blue-and-white patchwork quilt lay crumpled on her bed. She hadn't made her bed yet that day, which wasn't like her. She made her bed first thing every morning. Marie sat on her dressing room chair. It was also blue, with a plush velvet seat. There was a question to answer: "Where's Grandpa?"

Marie pulled her in close and answered, "Grandpa went to sleep last night, but he didn't wake up this morning. He went to Heaven."

It must have been a trying moment for Marie. When Clarence had passed away, her children were much older. To explain death to such a little child was difficult at best. But Marie, in her all-wise way as the family matriarch, managed their conversation well.

When Christmas passed and then the days ensued, playtime—in the childhood understanding of the word—changed. Grandpa was gone and with that, their shared time with dolls. Marie taught her songs to learn the ABCs with no need to wait until her formal schooling years, but if only she could learn to sing in tune as Marie played the piano. A puzzle of the United States helped her learn geography. And math skills came from card games, with the game of Go Fish soon replaced with rummy, double solitaire, poker, and other gambling games with nickels and quarters. Marie started a savings account for her, and some of her winnings from their card games had to be saved for college. When they made their visits to the bank, Marie always asked the bank teller, "Have you met my first great-grandchild?"

With little room in the house to play games, Marie found a way. Like when she had remodeled her Park Street home in Lebanon shortly after Clarence's death, so too did she call in the contractors after Art's passing. The back wall of his bedroom was torn down to enlarge the room. It became the game room and the place to watch TV. A wall of bookshelves was used to display her many scrapbooks. Lastly, a back patio with a sliding glass door was added on to this room. The patio door meant a quicker sprint for Marie to meet a customer at her shop out back.

Art's blue wingback chair was replaced, as well as all the other furniture in the front room, and all in white, save for an antique fainting couch in a teal shade. White draperies were hung, taking the place of tobacco-stained curtains. Glass candy dishes replaced the ashtrays, and marble statuettes adorned the room Marie used to visit with guests.

Marie's bedroom was the last room inside the house to be remodeled, where a walk-in closet and bathroom were added. The closet held her many gowns and dress shoes that she never parted with. Now that the house was larger, she had wiring installed to add two more telephones, with one put in her new bathroom and the other in the new game room while the original phone stayed on the hallway credenza.

While all that remodeling was underway, her son Bill retired from the navy following one last reenlistment. He had first joined the navy only mere months after World War II ended and then served during two wars, the Korean War and the Vietnam War. His retirement coincided with the United States military ending their involvement in the Vietnam War, which was in March that year, 1973. Bill wasn't ready to leave San Francisco yet. Marie, though, set about with one more remodeling project so that she would be ready when he was: her barn. When finished, her antique store was on one end, closest to the driveway, and a small guest house was at the far end. All was now complete.

Marie's great-granddaughter proceeded through her school years. When in the first grade, she had difficulty seeing what her teacher wrote on the chalkboard. An eye doctor informed them that she was blind in her left eye. Through that eye, she could only differentiate between light and dark or day and night. They blamed it on her time spent in the incubator as a baby. Every other year, she was seen by an optometrist at the university medical center in Portland. It was a hospital known for cutting-edge discoveries, but her prognosis never changed. There was no cure for her blindness nor any surgery that could help. All they could do was to prescribe her eyeglasses to strengthen the muscles in her left eye while protecting the vision in her right eye.

Aside from visits to the bank to add to her childhood savings account, another place Marie and her great-granddaughter frequented on a regular basis was the beauty shop. Each month, Marie took her there to get her hair permed. During each salon visit, Marie announced, "This is my first great-grandchild."

Marie was commonly met with the reply, "Yes, Mrs. Schmidt, we've already met her. Will it be Shirley Temple curls again?"

Just as her hair had to be well styled, so too did her clothes. Marie made sure of that. Her great-granddaughter's dresses were of the best quality, and some with a matching parasol. Many of her classmates, while not always well behaved, were well dressed. They came from homes whose family crest had predetermined their path. Their fathers were policemen, firemen, attorneys, politicians, doctors, and the like. Of the many neighborhood girls, Marie's great-granddaughter chose well in her friendships, with the mayor's daughter as her grade-school best friend.

Her vision impairment didn't impede her academic strengths or her creative nature. Writing came easy for her, and Marie often taped her poems and essays on the wall above the hallway credenza with pride. Most kids would be embarrassed to receive so much attention and praise, but she loved it—that is, all except for the permed hair. If she could throw a temper tantrum over the Shirley Temple look, she would have, but temper tantrums weren't allowed.

She was expected to be well behaved and well spoken. Any wrongdoings were met with a lengthy lecture from her great-grand-mother. Her ears ached as Marie, her family matriarch, said, "You are my first great-grandchild. That makes you special. You cannot act like your cousins. You are smart and bright. You have to be honest, and you have to be appreciative."

In her later grade-school years, and a little older, she was allowed to switch to a feathered hairstyle and flared jeans with embroidered flowers. Those were the '70s fashions. Participation in girl groups and school activities rounded out her girlhood days.

Meanwhile, Marie had her own activities. In early 1973, she became a regular guest at the meetings for the Sojourners, a Salem bridge club for newcomers. It offered a variety of social events, charity fundraisers, and, in May of each year, a benefit spring fashion show in which she was the pianist. This social group was a mainstay for Marie on into the 1980s.

Her presentations on antiques were given time and again for members of the Encore Club, the Daughters of the American Revolution, and the auxiliaries for the Bush Barn Art Center and the Mission Mill Museum. The Bush Barn Art Center is next to the Bush House, a historical site on a public park abundant with cherry trees and fragrant shrubbery. Marie assisted their auxiliary in many ways, sometimes as a tour guide and, for several years, as the pianist at their annual fundraising event. The Art Center offered an array of classes and other events, where Marie often gave informed presentations. These groups found Marie to be an articulate and engaging presenter, drawing attention to one of her speeches, "The State of Antiques Today."

In her talks about antiques or when with a customer, Marie made it clear that she only dealt in primitive antiques. Her pieces were furniture and household items that were made before the industrial era of mass production. When she visited other antique dealers, she wasn't shy to scold anyone who tried to pass off an item as an antique when it was only vintage.

Of her Lebanon groups, she sometimes visited the monthly meetings for the Business and Professional Women's Club to hear their speaker. Each year without fail, she attended the annual awards banquet for the Lebanon Woman of the Year. However, the award was now sponsored by a group other than the BPW and given through the Community Awards Program. Salem also recognized a woman for this award, same as many cities nationwide, but it was in Lebanon that Marie had strong ties, with some friendships going back as many as thirty years or more.

Likewise, her loyalty to the Cedars of Lebanon chapter for the White Shrine of Jerusalem was prevalent. What Marie lacked in church attendance she more than made up for in the spiritual growth that she found in that group and with the Eastern Star. She had a tightly woven social network and everlasting friendships with the ladies in both of those groups.

When visiting Lebanon, Marie was sure to stay connected with those who now helped where she once had as Polly Potter. That incorporation had since been absorbed by the Lebanon Community Council, but people still helped through their remembrance that Polly had told them to. The baby layettes that Marie had implored sewing groups to make still poured in.

Her Lebanon friends continued to support other humanitarian services as well, but after several years of their efforts being met with disappointing results, changes had to be made in how Lebanon helped its citizens. For one, the Red Cross in Linn County and its Lebanon chapter had become dependent on the United Way for partial funding. The United Way is an international and large nonprofit organization that, in the United States, affiliates itself with nonprofit agencies for fundraising efforts. The annual fundraisers of yesteryear for the Red Cross that Marie had helped spearhead for many years were, by the mid-1970s, no longer anywhere near as successful on their own. That was when they turned to the United Way for help.

Word had it, though, that the PTA continued to thrive. Where Marie had once laid the groundwork to bring Lebanon parents and teachers together in a common goal, current PTA officers were doing the same. There was always something needed for students in their path to becoming adults and upstanding citizens. In the 1975–76 school year, they brought new resources into their school libraries and updated their furniture. For projects and fundraisers, the PTA officers did what had always been done, even if their members didn't know who had first done it, with Marie as the first-ever Queen Anne School PTA president.

The year 1979 opened with Marie's birthday in January. Her great-granddaughter heard her well when she told her and others, "I'm three-quarters-of-a-century old." Marie often told people that, even well past January as the last year of the decade melted down. Her great-granddaughter could be slapping a two on an ace of spades in yet another round of double solitaire when Marie again asserted her age. "I am three-quarters-of-a-century old. You can grow up to do great things. If anything gets in your way, I know you can overcome it. Let me tell you more."

In Marie's words as the family matriarch, there was the story about when she was a little girl and her mean brothers tipped over the outhouse when she was inside. There was her moment of glory when she was not quite seventeen years old, playing "Angel Voices" on the piano for a sold-out show. There were stories about the women she had helped and how she had clothed and fed their children. She knew it was important to show up, to be active in the community, and more so, to be an active participant in her own life. There can only be one first great-grandchild. Her great-granddaughter had to make her well pleased in all she did.

In the fall of that year, 1979, Marie's great-granddaughter, who was now twelve years old, gave her a proud moment when she was initiated into the fraternal order of Job's Daughters. This was the same group that Clarence's niece Sharon, for whom they had traveled to Portland for her installation ceremony, had been in. It was a group likened to the Rainbow Girls that Marie's daughter Patsy had been an active member of as a girl. Both groups are affiliated with the Masonic Order. Job's Daughters was a fine and respectable group and one that would introduce her to more girls—and more importantly, upstanding girls—to befriend. Perhaps one day, she too would be honored queen in that group, same as Sharon had been.

As the new decade of the 1980s appeared on the horizon, Marie had a sense of fulfillment in her life. Whether in Salem making her mark or in Lebanon to show her support to the new leaders, Marie's life had come to fruition. She had made a good life for herself, for her family, and for others. It was a life that had sprung forth from her youth in Bend and away from the wilds of her birthplace, the Oklahoma Territory. Her support to many groups and her attention to her business, Polly's Barn Antiques, gave her a zestfulness in her golden years, all while she had a say in how her first great-grandchild was growing up.

Chapter 20

— ❀ —

In a Ray of Sunshine,
Marie Leaves This World

1980–1987

Marie was with several longtime friends for a reunion at a restaurant in Lebanon on Monday evening, February 4, 1980. It was a celebratory gathering in recognition of past award recipients for the Woman of the Year, with twenty past Lebanon leading ladies present. The restaurant, Darrell's Diner, was a simple place, but their place on this night had brought them together, not out of simplicity but out of the hard work and dedication that each lady had shown their community at one time or another in the thirty years past.

It was more than a reunion, with special recognition extended to Marie's good friend Mrs. Peggy Hatfield. In January, the city awarded Peggy with the honorary title of Senior First Citizen. This was the twenty-second year that Lebanon had granted this award and yet the first year in which it was given to a woman. Marie and Peggy had toiled beside each other for many years, now gone. While Peggy's volunteerism continued, Marie was remembered for leading them in the early days.

It was an event from which, if Marie had wanted to, she could have added pictures to one of her many scrapbooks that filled the bookshelves in her game room. It's unclear if she did that, as her scrapbooks were more about her days as a civic leader and less about reunions. She often picked one at random, then laid it on the table, opening it up to reveal the contents inside to her first great-grandchild. It didn't matter which scrapbook she chose. Each was filled to its capacity.

The burgeoning teenager liked to run her fingers over the edges of the newspaper clippings, now brittle from age. Marie had taken great care to tape those clippings onto the pages. There were also program brochures, some that had once been dog-eared, and ticket stubs and other memorabilia worthy of keepsake. Black-and-white photographs were sprinkled in, lending credence to this life, a life much different than any schoolgirl could envision.

Marie let her thumb through the pages. Pamphlets and brochures, some folded to fit in their scrapbook, advertised fundraising events. Those events had drawn attention to an array of needs. There were once diseases for which Marie had encouraged people to find a cure. There were families who needed her helping hand, and there had been plights felt by women for which a solution had to be found so that one day women wouldn't have to suffer.

When Marie pointed to the stories and pictures that these pages held, she did so with expectations. She wanted her first great-grandchild to see what she had done and to want to do the same—that is, to help others and to be a well-liked young woman with many friends. She wanted her to make wise decisions in her life, whether it be who to date or where to go to college or what to wear or what to say and how to say it.

Their shared moments with her scrapbooks were an opportune time for Marie to have in-depth talks with her great-granddaughter. Whether playing cards, shopping together, or revisiting her scrapbooks, Marie made it a point to talk to her about her teenage years and growing up to become a young woman. It was always an open conversation, with the girl inquisitive and, out of respect, all ears. Unbeknownst to Marie, though, her great-granddaughter would, as an adult, face troubles of her own making. She would not become the woman that Marie hoped for, at least not for a long time. Instead, she would be the one in need rather than the one lending a helping hand. Marie believed in the idea that only the best would come of her. And yet, although mistakes and problems were expected to be avoided, that would not be the case for her.

Marie also had a few scrapbooks with pictures of her children and grandchildren and their children that her great-granddaughter liked to peruse. If the girl favored any pictures, it was those of herself on Christmas morning, year after year, especially those from when Grandpa was still alive. She had many aunts, uncles, and cousins whose pictures, while not as many as those of herself, were there to choose from. The family albums didn't stay out long, though. There was always more to see in the scrapbooks that told of Marie's civic life, and so she'd pull out another for her great-granddaughter to see.

The scrapbooks showed beautiful parties where Marie was the pianist or was installed as an officer in the Eastern Star and other groups. The girl shifted her view, with the eyesight she had in but one eye, from the page to her family matriarch and then back to the page. Her great-grandma rarely wore a dress anymore, and yet there were pictures of her in long formal gowns.

She was indeed amazed by her great-grandma's work and accomplishments. But, even if she had all the time in the world, she wasn't so sure that she could make her way through every story that was found in her scrapbook collection. Besides, there were other things that she wanted to do, like play cards or be with her friends or go to the shopping mall or to the roller-skating rink. She'd look at a few pages, then set the scrapbook aside for another time.

IN THE MIDST OF the 1970s and then into the early 1980s, the lives of Marie's children and grandchildren had evolved, and each in their own way. For one, her son Bill finally left San Francisco to move into her guest house. It had been too many years of him away in the navy, with her in anticipation of his next furlough. He was her only son, she felt, and she wanted him close to her. The walnut tree in her backyard overtook the lush green lawn that was between her home and his, which offered a calming serenity and cooled the summers. Bill kept to himself, and Marie respected his privacy in her happiness to have him home.

Her oldest daughter, Betty, was well situated in her California life. Betty's marriage was troubled, but she made the best of it while she turned her attention elsewhere. She dabbled in one small business after another, with the latest being as a home decorator. Aside from her children Randy and Kathi, her other three children were also adults, with one in college living on campus in Washington.

Marie's middle daughter, Peggy, had divorced and moved to Salem with her oldest daughter, while her other two children, also adults, stayed in California. At first, Peggy and her daughter shared an apartment, but Peggy later moved in with her mom. Peggy's daughter soon got married and then had a baby boy, Marie's third great-grandchild. Peggy was a regular at a local bowling alley, where she secured a job and played in a women's bowling league. Her passion for bowling and the trophies she earned for the sport, which had begun in her Lebanon girlhood days, lived on. When a child, Peggy preferred her time with her dad over her time with her mom. As an older adult, any closeness to be had didn't appear to come naturally. Like her brother Bill, she kept to herself.

Marie's youngest daughter, Patsy, soon followed Peggy with a relocation to Salem. When Patsy's husband, Frank, retired from his engineering career, they bought a sprawling ranch house in Salem near Marie's Center Street home. As a housewife, Patsy's focus was on her children, who would soon give her grandchildren, which meant more great-grandchildren for Marie.

With Marie's children moving to Salem, their Christmases moved as well, to Marie's home. Her round oak table was now situated in her formal dining room, and they added its table leaves to make room for everyone for their holiday turkey meal and an afternoon of cards. Thirty-one was a traditional card game for them in which as many people who wanted to play, anteing up their spare change, could. They passed around family pictures to show how their children were faring. It must have been blissful for Marie to see her grandchildren grown and her great-grandchildren growing up. She had done well as their family matriarch.

Two changes in Marie's family beset her. For one, her grandson Randy moved from Salem to Portland. There, he continued his post office career and later got married. He was her first grandchild. There can only be one first grandchild. If only he'd stayed in Salem, but she understood that as an adult, he had to make his own way. She had trained him up right, and in that, she knew that he had given wise consideration to his move.

The other change was brought about by his sister Kathi, which inevitably affected Marie's first great-grandchild. In 1983, Kathi divorced and moved to the Seattle area with both her children, with her daughter rebellious in this change. She was not happy to leave her high school friends or her membership in Job's Daughters and other activities. When Kathi soon moved again, this time to a Portland suburb, her daughter gave up on a normal childhood. She left home as a teenager to move in with her adult boyfriend and began her own life through vocational schooling, and then worked in Portland while making new friends.

There can only be one first great-grandchild, and yet Marie no longer had a tight grip on her. However, Marie heard from her whenever she had a piece of good news to share. When the girl, now a young woman, although not quite eighteen years old, graduated in early 1985 with a vocational degree in clerical office skills, she called Marie. When, at age eighteen, she was hired by the Social Security Administration as a secretary, she called Marie. It was only a temporary job, but one that could lead to career advancement. Marie told her, "I'm so proud of you. You can do great things. Don't ever forget that."

She wouldn't forget it, but it would also be as if she ignored the wise words of her family matriarch. For it would be many years later, and only after enduring troubles of her own making, that she would do just that. Those days to come were in the future, all while Marie's years of life would not last to see her great-granddaughter in trouble. However, in those future days, her great-granddaughter would lean on the memory of her great-grandmother to overcome her difficulties. She would be resilient and strong, same as she had been as an infant fighting for her life from inside an incubator. It would be a fervent persistence to not only survive misfortunes but to make peace with mistakes. It would be the memory of her family matriarch's words of wisdom permeating her—and, more so, motivating her—to do so much more for the betterment of her life, and then later, the lives of others.

But in those years of the early to mid-1980s, neither Marie nor her first great-grandchild could see what was to come. In their visits, Marie's great-granddaughter opened up to her and, while not always fully revealing in what she had to say, seemed to probe Marie for answers, answers that Marie was not shy to give. Marie was the one family member she felt comfortable confiding in. Where some relatives either didn't understand or didn't approve of her choice of a boyfriend or her choice to forgo college, Marie listened to her. She remembered what it was like to be young with angst. She remembered that her father, if he could have, would have held her back from her own aspirations. They talked about that and what it meant to be true to oneself. They talked about friendships, work, fashion, and sex.

IN THE MIDST of the girl's newfound life in Portland, she didn't pay much attention to her great-grandma's health, which had been failing. It was only minor ailments, but nonetheless, Marie, who had always been fairly healthy, faced one cold after another, and the flu, and stomach aches, and age-related diabetes, and then the threat of breast cancer. It was Randy, Marie's first grandchild, who paid attention when she had fits of confusion, voicing aloud that she didn't understand why she was so often sick.

Randy, with his heart of gold, comforted Marie in her dismay. Although it could be a few years or more before he lost his grandma, he didn't hesitate to help her prepare her final wishes. She didn't want to be buried in a grave or to have a funeral for people to fuss over her death. She was emphatic that life was about living, not dying. With that in mind, he sought out the ideal resting place for when her time was to come and then began the prearrangements.

The City View Cemetery in Salem welcomes visitors with flower gardens at its gate. Its mausoleum, Mount Crest Abbey, is inside on a hilltop that is flanked by both fir and cherry trees and overlooks the cemetery and the south side of Salem. It is a private mausoleum that was dedicated to the cemetery in a Memorial Day ceremony on May 30, 1914. It was befitting for war veterans and for others who served their country and community, if not in military service then in another civic capacity. It was a befitting resting place to make ready for Marie.

Mount Crest Abbey Mausoleum is an impressive structure, built in a classic Greek-Roman style with windows made of art deco stained glass. The building itself is plain, simple, long, and made with heavy-duty concrete. Its grandeur is found in its front door entrance, built with two Doric columns. The architectural use of a Doric column is seen in city and state capital buildings and was used to build the Lincoln Memorial in Washington, DC. With a pedestal-like base at its bottom, each column features a smooth shaft that is fluted and grooved and wider at the bottom than the top. It is quite plain for being a column yet viewed by many as elegant.

This mausoleum has several hallways, each lined with niche drawers made of marble, and each drawer holds the ashes of someone worthy of remembrance. Many former Oregon governors and congressmen and other notable people are interred here. There is also an area for veterans and another for children and infants, as well as several areas for fraternal organizations. Mount Crest Abbey Mausoleum was ideal for Marie.

Marie was adamant about staying in her house up until the day the Lord took her home, but she couldn't keep up with its maintenance on her own. Although her adult daughter lived with her, and her son lived in her guest house, Marie relegated her house's upkeep to hired help. A maid came regularly, and a gardener kept her lawn mowed, her trees trimmed, and her flowers in full bloom as if beckoning visitors to her home.

Come Christmas each year, Marie hid her ailments and mental confusion while she hosted her annual family gathering. Even when her first grandchild, Randy, and then her first great-grandchild had moved to Portland, they came back for Christmas. Salem was only an hour's drive from Portland, and in their tight bond, they knew where to be at that holiday. Those two were the special ones in their matriarch's eyes.

There can only be one first grandchild and only one first great-grandchild, and they were often reminded of that, not only in words but in gifts. Marie's holiday presents to the girl had always been name-brand clothing and toys, while the other children had to make up names for their dolls. While the holiday in her home was a welcoming respite for the family, it was more than that. It was the gathering spot to be with their family matriarch.

***

MARIE WAS WITH many longtime friends for the auxiliary meeting with Lebanon Community Hospital when they met in November 1985. Mrs. Nancy Kirkpatrick, their president, welcomed Marie as she pinned a fully bloomed corsage on her white blazer's lapel. Marie was an honored guest in remembrance of her service thirty-five years earlier as their first president.

Mrs. Willa Huston, Mrs. Carrie Nichols, Mrs. Helen Gustine, Mrs. Nell Reid, and Mrs. Dorothy Page were among other charter members also in attendance. They were surely happy to see each other again. Mrs. Page's husband had been the high school football coach when Marie's son Bill had been on the team. It was their regular monthly meeting, but Mrs. Kirkpatrick had sent invitations to encourage them to come, as they often didn't. She said, "We wanted to do that so the charter members could know what they started and be proud of the lasting contribution they had made to the community through the support of this organization."

Mrs. Page gave a book review of *I Promise*, authored by a Canadian writer, Doris Neeley Haralson. Her book chronicled the early history of their hospital when it had been Lebanon General Hospital, managed by the Schuler sisters. Members also discussed current construction projects, one of which was to remodel their obstetrics wing.

That project was but one change of several for Lebanon Community Hospital, which was in its thirty-third year of service. Earlier that year, in January, a plaque—the Tree of Life—was added in tribute to recognize and thank contributors who since 1980 had given a cumulative gift of $500 or more. This plaque is quite large and made from black walnut, native to the Lebanon area, and contains a gold leaf for each contributor's engraved name. The Tree of Life plaque was put on the lobby wall in a dedication ceremony assisted by Governor Vic Atiyeh and Hospital Board President Mr. Leonard Thomas.

While it was a kind gesture to draw attention to those who gave their money, it doesn't compare on any proportionate footing to the plaques first placed in the lobby for the hospital's 1952 grand opening. In 1950, then-Hospital Board President Mr. John Nylund had made a promise. He stated that a special plaque, the only plaque to be awarded to any organization for distinctive community service, would be placed permanently in the hospital lobby.

The plaque that Mr. Nylund referred to in his promise was his gesture to thank the American Legion Auxiliary ladies who had served on the Breakfast Committee during the 1950 fundraising campaign. Marie had very much been a vital member in this recognition when she had co-led their committee. Rather than give their money, Marie and other ladies had toiled morning after morning for six weeks to ensure that the men on the fundraising campaign had breakfast and, more so, heartfelt appreciation and a spirit of encouragement.

Mr. Nylund's promise that this plaque would be forevermore in the lobby unfortunately has not held true. Other hospital directors have followed him, as have hospital auxiliary members and others of influencing power. According to the current hospital executive director, as of the time of this writing, it has been moved from the lobby wall to a centralized hallway, where it remains prominently displayed. Perhaps the move from the lobby to another place occurred when the Tree of Life plaque was dedicated and hung.

Of importance, Marie's vision of who the hospital would serve lives on. As a founding leader, Marie wanted its doors open to everyone, and her vision was fulfilled through their Memorandum of Contract and remains in full force today. If only Marie—and her late father—could have known that. She would, though, following her death, also become a financial contributor through a memorial donation gifted by the Business and Professional Women's Club.

WHILE MARIE'S LEGACY was on firm footing, the life of her first great-grandchild, in her young adulthood, was only beginning to take shape. One might wonder what her name was, but life is not about what we are called. Life is about who we are. This young woman, Marie's first great-grandchild, was making a positive path in her life, but she would encounter problems and challenges in but a few short years. Marie had shown that when troubles befall us, we can overcome them. What Marie hadn't explained to her great-granddaughter in any real words was what to do when we mess up or do something wrong. Problems simply had to be avoided.

Yet in a future not so far off from Marie's last years, her first great-granddaughter would encounter problems of her own making and then the consequences of her actions. In her emergence from these ramifications, she would next face the hardship of poverty along with discord through turbulent relationships. She would be caught in a downward spiral for many years, as if drowning in an abyss. Her journey would entail an itinerant lifestyle, but thousands of hitchhiked miles would not distance her from the crushing expectations that her great-grandma, the family matriarch, had had for her.

Only through her memory of her great-grandma's wise words would she be able to overcome her chaos and then, later, write her first book, her memoir—aptly titled *Out of Chaos*. Following the publication of her memoir, she would expand on her creativity and inquisitiveness to come to an understanding of why she had found strength out of the remembrance of her matriarch. She would no longer have access to her great-grandma's scrapbook collection other than in her memories. She would, though, turn to other resources, some in government records and some in newspaper repositories, to peel back layer after layer of a woman who, her great-granddaughter would come to find out, had lived a truly remarkable life with an uplifting spirit about her.

With her great-grandmother's legacy in her heart, and the facts laid before her, she would be the author of another book. The principles, beliefs, and visions that Marie had embodied were left to live in the hearts and memories of many people. Yet the era in which Marie lived is gone, and its people are fading away. We must not let her story fade away as people pass away. We can take the words of her story from this book to share with others. We can behold her principles, beliefs, and visions, not to savor for only a moment but instead to be a part of us as our own lives mature. Life is not about the number of years lived but about the life lived in those years.

ON FRIDAY MORNING, February 20, 1987, Marie awoke to fog and low-hanging clouds on an otherwise clear day. The forecasted weather was typical for Salem, with temperatures to linger in the forties. She did not have plans that day or any social events to make herself ready for. If anything pressed on her mind, it was how her first grandchild and great-grandchild were doing. They each were living their own lives as her life wound down. With her eyes open, she lacked any energy to get out of bed.

The fog dissipated and the sun then showed its face with a hint of winter warmth. It was far from the thunderous Oklahoma storm that she had been born in. She was eighty-three years old. One month earlier, on January 20, she had had her final birthday. As her last breaths left her, her spirit found its way to the two special people in her life before it too soon dissipated. Her first great-grandchild already knew the time of her passing had come when later that morning, she received a phone call from her uncle. In a ray of sunshine, Marie left this world.

THE END

"All sunshine would be boring,
and all pleasant things would make our lives too easy."
—Marie Conner Schmidt, née Gosney, 1904–1987

Bibliography

Books

Brogan, Phil F. *East of the Cascades*. Binford and Mort Publishers, 1977.

Deschutes County Historical Society. *Bend*. Arcadia Publishing, 2009.

Dolan, Allison. *The Family Tree Historical Maps Book*. Family Tree Books, 2014.

Erb, Bishop Allen H. "Chapter 10." In *Privileged to Serve: Memoirs of God's Grace*. Mennonite Board of Missions, 1975.

Gosney Wisda, Georgia. *Gosney Family Records, 1740-1940, and Related Families*. Hassell Street Press, 2021.

Mott, Elle. *Out of Chaos: A Memoir*. Boyle and Dalton Publishers, 2018.

Correspondence

Cox, Sheryl. Manager, Volunteer Services and Auxiliary, Lebanon Community Hospital, Lebanon, Oregon. "Auxiliary History" (email), July 25, 26, and 31, 2024.

Fisher, Julie, MMC. City Recorder, City of Lebanon, Oregon. "Submission #1389. Page 129 shows the property 471 Park Street" (email), June 30, 2025.

Ivey, Vanessa. Museum Manager, Deschutes Historical Museum, Bend, Oregon. "Website Page" (email), June 20, 2024.

O'Bannon, Brandy. Executive Director, Lebanon Community Hospital, Lebanon, Oregon. "Hospital Plaques" (email), July 26 and 29, 2024.

PERIODICALS

Brown, Sarah. "Lebanon Icon Celebrates 100th Birthday Among Family and Friends." *Lebanon Local News*, January 16, 2023. https://www.lebanonlocalnews.com/lebanon-icon-celebrates-100th-birthday-among-family-and-friends.

Brown, Sarah. "Lebanon's Longest-Lived Monarch One of Royal Line." *Lebanon Local News*, May 26, 2023. https://www.lebanonlocalnews.com/lebanons-longest-lived-monarch-one-of-royal-line.

Crooks, Mary. "Oct 29, 1929, CE: Black Tuesday." *National Geographic Society*, May 20, 2022.

Fountain, Sue. "Back to School Memories." *The Homesteader, Deschutes County Historical Society Newsletter* 46, no. 9 (September 2020): 1, 5. https://www.deschuteshistory.org/wp-content/uploads/2020/08/2020-September-Homesteader.pdf.

Hanson, Tor. "Dance the Night Away: Entertainment in the 20s and 30s." *The Homesteader, Deschutes County Historical Society Newsletter* 42, no. 4 (April 2016): 2, 6. https://www.deschuteshistory.org/wp-content/uploads/2014/07/2016-April-Homesteader-1.pdf.

MacKaye, Milton. "Does Your Town Need a Hospital?" *Saturday Evening Post*, September 13, 1952. Academic Search Premier Database: 225 (11): 24–25 and 115–118. https://research-ebsco-com.research.cincinnatilibrary.org/c/2bkdtt/viewer/pdf/h7qtl6l6mb.

Moody, Jennifer. "Remembering the Express." *Lebanon Local News*, February 16, 2023. https://www.lebanonlocalnews.com/remembering-the-express.

Polmar, Norman. "Pictorial–USS Norton Sound: The Newest Old Ship." *U.S. Naval Institute* Vol. 105/4/914, April 1979. https://www.usni.org/magazines/proceedings/1979/april/pictorial-uss-norton-sound-newest-old-ship.

Swanson, Scott. "Wells Fargo Bank Mural, Displays Stir Memories of the Past." *Lebanon Local News*, February 18, 2020. https://www.lebanonlocalnews.com/wells-fargo-bank-mural-displays-stir-memories-of-the-past.

Repositories

Ancestry Library Edition. "Family Tree, Genealogy, and Family History Records." Archived government records. https://www.ancestrylibrary.com.

Ancestry.com LLC. "Newspapers.com by Ancestry." Archived newspapers. https://www.newspapers.com.

Find A Grave, Memorial ID: 139959855. Contributed by Ann (no last name given), 47099958. https://www.findagrave.com/memorial/139959855/v-marie-schmidt.

Kansas Historical Society. "Kansas Newspaper Database." Archived newspapers. https://www.kshs.org/p/newspapers-in-kansas/11528.

Library of Congress. "Chronicling America, Historic American Newspapers." Archived newspapers. https://chroniclingamerica.loc.gov.

Oklahoma Historical Society. "The Gateway to Oklahoma History." Archived newspapers. https://www.gateway.okhistory.org.

University of Oregon Libraries. "Historic Oregon Newspapers." Archived newspapers. https://oregonnews.uoregon.edu.

Videos

The American Legion Auxiliary. "Decades of Making a Difference: American Legion Auxiliary." Produced by Highpoint Productions, November 18, 2019. Video, 8 min., 32 sec. https://www.youtube.com/watch?v=1RxmZZDXLV0.

Brownlee, John. "Lebanon Express Movie." The Lebanon Story, May 11, 2011. Video, 4 min., 8 sec. https://www.youtube.com/watch?v=-fOgjb7zBDI.

Brownlee, John. "Lebanon Story Part 1." The Lebanon Story, June 28, 2012. Video, 10 min., 34 sec. https://www.youtube.com/watch?v=e0CrJkWVV3A&t=209s.

City of Bend, Oregon, "History of Bend's Boundaries." February 9, 2021. Video, 52 min., 36 sec. https://youtu.be/WP5zTeaY4C4.

Intrigued Mind. "Portland's Dark History: Sunken City of Vanport." January 17, 2022. Video, 11 min., 1 sec. https://www.youtube.com/watch?v=Of-2Jercfkk.

Kaufmann, Steve. "Past Pandemic: A Look at Bend's Bout with the 1918 Spanish Flu." Central Oregon Daily News, April 21, 2020, updated February 9, 2024. Video, 6 min., 26 sec. https://www.centraloregondaily.com/%E2%96%B6%EF%B8%8F-past-pandemic-a-look-at-bends-bout-with-the-1918-spanish-flu.

Keller's 20th Century Documentaries. "1951 Korean War Navy Carrier Operations." November 18, 2013. Video, 12 min., 7 sec. https://www.youtube.com/watch?v=tamciWO4ITI.

Megaprojects. "Essex Class Aircraft Carriers: Revolutionizing Modern Warfare." July 19, 2021. Video, 13 min., 40 sec. https://www.youtube.com/watch?v=-3TTD6fsKmM.

Oklahoma Ghost Towns. "Jennings, Oklahoma. Land Run and Oil Boom Town." July 27, 2013. Video, 3 min., 9 sec. https://youtu.be/V93KhkfWrkU.

Oregon Public Broadcasting in partnership with Oregon Historical Society. "The Flooding of Vanport." Produced by Nadine Jelsing, November 16, 2021. Video, 59 min., 53 sec. https://www.youtube.com/watch?v=gl8dMk0Z0lc.

Points of Light Radio. "Fellowships with the Order of White Shrine." June 3, 2024. Video podcast, 31 min., 44 sec. https://youtu.be/HDbxhjdDtB4?t=145.

Recollection Road. "Peek Inside a 1940s Home." September 15, 2023. Video, 8 min. https://www.youtube.com/watch?v=Wrl233xcdt8.

Sheet Music Singer. "In the Gloaming (1877)." July 6, 2018. Musical video, 2 min., 30 sec. https://www.youtube.com/watch?v=G1RjQRHQdWs.

Websites (Business/Organizations and Personal)

Bose, Apurva. "History of Minimum Wage." Be Businessed, January 21, 2017. https://www.bebusinessed.com/history/history-of-minimum-wage.

Carey, Abigail, Army Public Affairs Fellow. "Gold Star Mother's and Family's Day." Arlington National Cemetery, September 25, 2022. https://www.arlingtoncemetery.mil/Blog/Post/12728/A-Brief-History-of-Gold-Star-Mothers-and-Family-s-Day.

Craven, Jackie. "Introduction to the Doric Column." ThoughtCo, May 9, 2019, updated May 7, 2025. https://www.thoughtco.com/what-is-a-doric-column-177508.

Great Northern Railway. "To The Scenic Northwest." St. Paul, Minnesota, 1909 (pamphlet). Kenrail, seller ID 11465, eBay. (No longer available.)

Kave-Kramer, Geneva. "The 5 Star Points." Harmony Chapter #60 Vienna Virginia Order of the Eastern Star, 2016. https://harmonychapter60. wixsite.com/harmonyoes/the-star-points.

"KGW." PDX History.com, October 24, 2016. http://www.pdxhistory.com/ html/kgw_radio.html.

"Learn Bridge." American Contract Bridge League (Horn Lake, Mississippi), n.d. https://www.acbl.org/learn.

"Learn to Play Pinochle." Bicycle Cards, 2024. https://www.bicyclecards. com/how-to-play/pinochle-2.

Longwell, Tom. Answer to "Can you describe how the card game bridge is played?" Quora, 2019. https://www.quora.com/Can-you-describe-how-the-card-game-bridge-is-played/answer/Tom-Longwell?ch=10& oid=128429594&share=5f6ffd37&srid=nyU2e&target_type=answer.

Meaghers, Deb. "Historic Cemeteries: City View, a Family Business." *Salem History Matters* (blog), May 23, 2018. https://www.salemhistorymatters. net/our-history-blog/historic-cemeteries-city-view-a-family-business.

Multiple Listing Service of Central Oregon. "77 NW McKay Ave, Bend, OR, 97703." Redfin, 2016. https://www.redfin.com/OR/Bend/77-NW-McKay-Ave-97703/home/102134985#overview.

"Order of the White Shrine of Jerusalem." Stichting Argus, n.d. https://www.stichtingargus.nl/vrijmetselarij/wsj_en.html.

"The Order of the White Shrine of Jerusalem." The Supreme Shrine, n.d. https://www.supremeshrine.org.

Porter, Paul and Susan Gibby. "Bush House." Willamette Heritage Center, August 25, 2005. https://www.willametteheritage.org/bush-house.

Reddy, Karina. "Fashion History Timeline: 1910–1919." Fashion Institute of Technology, State University of New York, May 31, 2018. https://fashionhistory.fitnyc.edu/1910-1919.

Rogers, Melanie. "1940s Makeup Fashion: Red Color Lipstick Won the Hearts of Many." *Vintage-Retro* (blog), July 28, 2022. https://www.vintage-retro.com/1940s-makeup-fashion-red-color-lipstick-won-the-hearts-of-the-many.

Smart, Sherrie. "Guide to a Stunning 1950s Makeup." *Vintage-Retro* (blog), November 8, 2022. https://www.vintage-retro.com/guide-to-a-stunning-1950s-makeup.

"Strawberry Festival Court History." Lebanon Strawberry Festival, n.d. https://www.lebanonstrawberryfest.com/court-history.html.

Tawhid (no first name given). "How Fast Did Cars Go…." Outdoor Driving, March 22, 2023. https://outdoordriving.com/how-fast-did-cars-go-in-1920.

Topinka, Lin. "Stevenson, Washington." The Columbia River, A Photographic Journey, April 2014. https://web.archive.org/web/20140422095330/http://columbiariverimages.com/Regions/Places/stevenson.html.

United States Census Bureau, cartographer. "State and County Maps of Oklahoma: 1890 Map of Indian Territory and Oklahoma." Map Geeks, September 24, 2019. https://www.mapgeeks.org/oklahoma.

"U.S. Navy–Aircraft Carrier–USS. Essex." Seaforces–Online Naval Information, n.d. https://www.seaforces.org/usnships/cv/CV-9-USS-Essex.htm.

"Welcome New Member." The Order of the Eastern Star, n.d. https://pdf4pro.com/amp/view/protected-welcome-new-member-oregon-order-2de64.html.

"What is the Forty and Eight?" La Société de Quarante Hommes et Huit Chevaux, n.d. https://www.fortyandeight.org/what-is-the-40-8.

"Who Are We?" Independent Order of Odd Fellows, The Sovereign Grand Lodge, n.d. https://www.odd-fellows.org/about.

Zornig, David. "Liberty Theater vintage postcard." Photograph, circa 1917, uploaded March 26, 2017, in contribution to Liberty Arts Collaborative (Bend, Oregon), n.d. Cinema Treasures. https://www.cinematreasures.org/theaters/27305/photos/205151.

Websites (Government)

"Atchison, Topeka, and Santa Fe Railroad Co. Land Grant Records." Kansas Historical Society, n.d. https://www.kshs.org/p/atchison-topeka-santa-fe-railroad-co-land-grant-records/19951.

"Booze and the Big House, Faces of Prohibition, 1920–1933." State of Oregon, Prohibition Exhibit, n.d. https://sos.oregon.gov/archives/exhibits/prohibition/Pages/default.aspx.

City of Lebanon. "Commission Review," "Lebanon Local Historic Registry," "Appendix A," "Appendix B." Historic Landmark Commission Meeting Agenda, May 18, 2022 (pdf file). (No longer electronically retrievable.) https://www.ci.lebanon.or.us.

Fugate, Tally D. "Broom Factories." The Encyclopedia of Oklahoma History and Culture, January 15, 2010. https://www.okhistory.org/publications/enc/entry.php?entry=BR024.

Gibby, Susan and Paul Porter. "Bush House." Willamette Heritage Center, 2006. https://www.willametteheritage.org/bush-house.

Great Northern Railway. "Brochure, Opening Up Central Oregon." Oregon History Project, Oregon Historical Society (Catalog No. Mss 6000), n.d. https://www.oregonhistoryproject.org/articles/historical-records/brochure-opening-up-central-oregon.

Green, Virginia. "Salem in 1960." *Shine on Salem* (blog), 2019. Salem Heritage Network. https://www.shineonsalem.org/salem-in-1960.

"Kansas Memory." Kansas Historical Society, n.d. https://www.kansasmemory.org/locate.php?categories=264-1349-1407-3962.

McGregor, Michael N. "The Vanport Flood." Oregon History Project, Oregon Historical Society, 2003. https://www.oregonhistoryproject.org/articles/essays/the-vanport-flood.

"Oklahoma." OKGenWeb: Sooner State Genealogy, n.d. https://www.okgenweb.net.

"On Her Own Wings, Oregon Women and the Struggle for Suffrage." State of Oregon, Woman Suffrage Exhibit, n.d. https://sos.oregon.gov/archives/exhibits/suffrage/Pages/default.aspx.

Robbins, William G. "This Land, Oregon: Oregon in Depression and War, 1925–1945." Oregon History Project, Oregon Historical Society, 2002, updated and revised by editors in 2014. https://www.oregonhistoryproject.org/narratives/this-land-oregon/oregon-in-depression-and-war-1925-1945/hard-times.

"Stars and Stripes Collection: A World at War, Timeline 1914–1921." Library of Congress, n.d. https://www.loc.gov/collections/stars-and-stripes/articles-and-essays/a-world-at-war/timeline-1914-1921.

State Historic Preservation Office, Oregon State Parks. "471-Park-Street-PDF." State of Oregon Inventory of Historic Properties, 1984." (No longer available.)

Tonsfeldt, Ward and Paul G. Claeyssens. "Railroads into Central Oregon." Oregon History Project, Oregon Historical Society, 2004, updated and revised 2014. https://www.oregonhistoryproject.org/narratives/central-oregon-adaptation-and-compromise-in-an-arid-landscape/industrial-period-1910-1970/railroads-into-central-oregon.

Wilson, Linda D. "The Encyclopedia of Oklahoma History and Culture: Cleveland." Oklahoma Historical Society, n.d. https://www.okhistory.org/publications/enc/entry?entry=CL012.

Women's Business Ownership Act of 1988, Public Law 100-533. United States Congress, October 25, 1988. https://www.congress.gov/100/statute/STATUTE-102/STATUTE-102-Pg2689.pdf.

Ziedrich, Linda. "Lebanon (city)." Oregon Encyclopedia, a project of Oregon Historical Society, Portland State University, March 23, 2022. https://www.oregonencyclopedia.org/articles/lebanon-town.

Websites (Universities)

Building Oregon, University of Oregon. "Mount Crest Abbey Mausoleum (Salem, Oregon)." Oregon Digital. https://www.oregondigital.org/concern/documents/df67rc46k.

Gregory, James and Jessie Kindig. "A Concise History of the Great Depression in Washington State." The Great Depression in Washington State Project, Civil Rights and Labor History Consortium, University of Washington, n.d. https://www.depts.washington.edu/depress/history.shtml.

James, Amanda. "The Historic Bend Liberty Theater." Oregon Theater Project, University of Oregon, June 7, 2022. https://oregontheaterproject.uoregon.edu/articles/historic-bend-liberty-theater.

Lewis, David. "City of Salem." Oregon Encyclopedia, a project of Oregon Historical Society, Portland State University, December 30, 2022. https://www.oregonencyclopedia.org/articles/salem_city_of.

Peterson, Elizabeth and Michael Aronson. "Liberty Theater." Oregon Theater Project, University of Oregon, c. 2020. https://oregontheaterproject.uoregon.edu/theaters/liberty-theater-0.

Rolston, Ryan. "The Vanport Flood of 1948." Archives Capstone Project (PDX file), Portland State University, June 7, 2005. https://web.pdx.edu/~schechp/ARC%20Final/vanportfinal.htm.

PUBLIC DOMAIN

Franklin D. Roosevelt Presidential Library and Museum. *FDR Library's Digital Collections: Eleanor Roosevelt Selected Correspondence, 1933– 1945 and 1945–1947.* University of Illinois at Urbana-Champaign. http://www.fdrlibrary.marist.edu/archives/collections/franklin.

The National Federation of Business and Professional Women's Clubs, Inc. *Handbook of Federation Procedures.* New York City, New York, 1936.
Physical book for public use is available only at the University of Illinois at Urbana-Champaign.
Electronic copy retrieved from the digitized repository with HathiTrust, an academic and research library collaborative. https://babel.hathitrust.org/cgi/t?id=uiug.30112088199846&seq=3 7&q1=%22National+Business+Women%E2%80%99s+Week%22.

The Portland Chamber of Commerce. *Oregon: The Land of Opportunity.* Portland, Oregon, 1911.

Acknowledgments

Having an idea and turning it into a book is as hard as it sounds. It was no light task to write Marie's story, given the sheer volume of research materials available to me and the many rabbit holes I went down. Most importantly, I must thank my late great-grandmother, who was a great muse for me.

Two people made this book markedly more readable: Janet Martin-Rush and Brad Hudepohl, both two very patient beta readers. This book is divided into four parts. After reading each part, my beta readers gave me their questions, inputs, and suggestions to use in my rewrite. Then we continued on into the next part.

Like me, dear Janet is a morning person. I especially loved our regular get-togethers. As the sun was only beginning to rise, we'd settle comfortably in my living room with coffee and pastries to talk freely about my muse and how best to share her story with you.

Brad was also instrumental in that he made cold calls on my behalf to garner more details to add to my research pile. He spoke with the director at the hospital in Lebanon, Oregon, and exchanged emails with her and others who had information up their sleeves, or otherwise at their disposal, to kindly share. I am so grateful to these women who so freely gave their time to pass information along.

In the beginning, my research was rudimentary. It began with searching in genealogy repositories, accessed for free from the Cincinnati & Hamilton County Public Library. That was a baby step. A big shout-out and thank-you goes to the library workers in the genealogy department and the virtual information center. Their guidance through the library's databases, and in helping me find gold mines in the digitized repositories held by academic and research libraries, was of great use.

Additionally, my appreciation goes to my friends and to those I've met in my social media hangouts and author support groups. Their kindliness and expertise moved me onward as I got closer to the finish line. And my friend Mickey Preston deserves a thank-you for her undying anticipation.

As I think of friends and others who extended their support, a certain reader comes to mind: Andrew Lutes. From the birth of my first book to my blogging days to seeing this book come into fruition, he has never wavered when it comes to following my writing journey. I ask readers to leave a review of my book wherever they hang out. Andrew has done this more times than one can count, and without a doubt, he will do the same with this book. When he attends an event or meets someone for a drink, he is sure to ask his companion, "Have you read Elle's book yet?"

About the Author

Photo Credit: Scott Seipp (ScottieMidnight Photography)

Elle Mott writes creative nonfiction. This is her third book. She is the author of *Out of Chaos: A Memoir* and *People Helping People*. Her other writing pieces have been featured in literary journals, news magazines, and anthologies. She has a background working in libraries, both at the college level and, for more than ten years, at the public library in downtown Cincinnati, Ohio. While library work is her livelihood, writing is her passion. Free time finds her volunteering. She was humbled to be awarded "Community Service Leader of the Year, 2017" by an activist organization local to her area. She makes her home in northern Kentucky with two cats and several pet birds. Connect with Elle through her website at https://ellemottauthor.com.